Being and Becoming a Speaker of Japanese

SECOND LANGUAGE ACQUISITION
Series Editor: Professor David Singleton, *Trinity College, Dublin, Ireland*

This series brings together titles dealing with a variety of aspects of language acquisition and processing in situations where a language or languages other than the native language is involved. Second language is thus interpreted in its broadest possible sense. The volumes included in the series all offer in their different ways, on the one hand, exposition and discussion of empirical findings and, on the other, some degree of theoretical reflection. In this latter connection, no particular theoretical stance is privileged in the series; nor is any relevant perspective – sociolinguistic, psycholinguistic, neurolinguistic, etc. – deemed out of place. The intended readership of the series includes final-year undergraduates working on second language acquisition projects, postgraduate students involved in second language acquisition research, and researchers and teachers in general whose interests include a second language acquisition component.

Full details of all the books in this series and of all our other publications can be found on http://www.multilingual-matters.com, or by writing to Multilingual Matters, St Nicholas House, 31–34 High Street, Bristol BS1 2AW, UK.

SECOND LANGUAGE ACQUISITION
Series Editor: David Singleton

Being and Becoming a Speaker of Japanese
An Autoethnographic Account

Andrea Simon-Maeda

MULTILINGUAL MATTERS
Bristol • Buffalo • Toronto

Library of Congress Cataloging in Publication Data
A catalog record for this book is available from the Library of Congress.
Simon-Maeda, Andrea, 1951-
Being and Becoming a Speaker of Japanese: An Auto-Ethnographic Account/
Andrea Simon-Maeda.
Second Language Acquisition
Includes bibliographical references and index.
1. Japanese language--Study and teaching. 2. Second language acquisition--Study and teaching. I. Title. PL519.S57 2011
495.6'8071–dc22
2011000608

British Library Cataloguing in Publication Data
A catalogue entry for this book is available from the British Library.

ISBN-13: 978-1-84769-361-7 (hbk)
ISBN-13: 978-1-84769-360-0 (pbk)

Multilingual Matters
UK: St Nicholas House, 31–34 High Street, Bristol, BS1 2AW, UK.
USA: UTP, 2250 Military Road, Tonawanda, NY 14150, USA.
Canada: UTP, 5201 Dufferin Street, North York, Ontario, M3H 5T8, Canada.

Copyright © 2011 Andrea Simon-Maeda.

All rights reserved. No part of this work may be reproduced in any form or by any means without permission in writing from the publisher.

The policy of Multilingual Matters/Channel View Publications is to use papers that are natural, renewable and recyclable products, made from wood grown in sustainable forests. In the manufacturing process of our books, and to further support our policy, preference is given to printers that have FSC and PEFC Chain of Custody certification. The FSC and/or PEFC logos will appear on those books where full certification has been granted to the printer concerned.

Typeset by Techset Composition Ltd, Salisbury, UK.
Printed and bound in Great Britain by Short Run Press Ltd.

Contents

Acknowledgements vii

Part 1

   Introduction 3
      Conceptual Framework... 3
      Locating Autoethnography in SLA and Applied Linguistics..... 6
      Researcher Positionality 8
      Organization of the Book 8

1   The Postmodern Basis of Autoethnography 12
      Language, Subjectivity, Reflexivity.......................... 12
      What Autoethnography Does and How It Does It 16

2   Narrative Inquiry in SLA and Applied Linguistics 21
      Postmodernist Interpretations of the Interconnectedness
         of SLA and Identity 23
      Summary.. 25

Part 2

3   In the Beginning: Situating the Story 31
      A Precarious Position 32
      'Even if You Can Speak Japanese?' 33
      Getting by as Functional, Semiliterate and Privileged 38
      'Are You Sure There's No Mistake?' 41
      A Sea of Languages... 45
      Summary.. 49

4   In the Middle: Love, Marriage, Family......................... 54
      Love at First Sight and Sound 55
      The Language of Love....................................... 60
      Marriage 63
      Neighbors 64
      Family Life and Language at Home 67

    L2 Parenting 77
    The Regime of *Obentoo* 79

5 Career Discourse(s) 88
    Language at Work 89
    Workplace Discourse(s). 92
    Walk the Walk and Talk the Talk 96
    Meetings 98
    Students as Cultural and Linguistic Informants 104
    Texting. 106
    Summary. 111

6 Where I Am Now: Two Days in the Life of an Expatriate 115
    Next Day, December 30. 129
    Epilogue 131

    Closing Discussion 134
        Theoretical Starting Point. 135
        Implications for SLA and Applied Linguistics Research. 140

Appendix 1 Foreign population. 148

Appendix 2 Newspaper article 149

Appendix 3 Typical examples of Mayor Kawamura's
               'Nagoya dialect' 150

Appendix 4 Examples of Japanese emoticons 151

Appendix 5 Manual for high school visits. 152

References 153
Index 163

Acknowledgements

First, I would like to thank Multilingual Matters for their support and open-minded decision to publish a book that adopted an alternative approach to exploring second language acquisition. The theoretical stance and writing style I used for my autoethnographic account are, as one reviewer commented, different from the 'conventional teleological process in traditional academic texts', hence readers have the opportunity to think about second language learning from a unique vantage point. I am especially grateful to Anna Roderick who made my first attempt at writing a book a pleasant experience.

Mentors and colleagues in my doctoral cohort at Temple University Japan line the road of my academic career and have contributed in various ways to this book project. In particular, Steve Cornwell has remained my good buddy telling me to 'shut up' when necessary and 'way to go' when I needed the encouragement. Dwight Atkinson must also be acknowledged for suggesting the idea of writing an autoethnography.

My husband *Junji* is the main reason I decided to spend the rest of my life in Japan, and my son *Yuji* is affirmation that I made the right decision. I thank these two wonderful people for their patience. My parents were bilingual speakers; father was a first-generation immigrant from Lebanon and mother was of French-Canadian descent. It was only much later in life that I realized how fortunate I had been to be surrounded by a polyphony of foreign languages during my childhood and teenage years. Early L2 and additional language experiences in the United States no doubt had a lasting influence on my subsequent life and career paths in Japan.

This book is dedicated in loving memory to my sister Janet, our family's historian who helped me excavate old photos and memories of my past life in the United States.

Note

The following people and organizations have granted permission to use their material in this book: Arudou Debito for allowing use of the pub sign photo in Chapter 3; the Association of Foreign Wives of Japan for quotes from the *AFWF Journal* and online discussion postings; and the *Asahi*, *Mainichi* and *Japan Times* newspapers for the use of articles.

Part 1

Introduction

Conceptual Framework

Figure 1 First day in Japan

> The Photograph does not necessarily say *what is no longer*, but only and for certain *what has been*. This distinction is decisive. In front of a photograph, our consciousness does not necessarily take the nostalgic path of memory ... but for every photograph existing in the world, the path of certainty: the Photograph's essence is to ratify what it represents. (Barthes, 1981: 85, italics in original)

The statement above by Roland Barthes, the French social theorist, is a poststructuralist, philosophical response to positivism's reliance on hard scientific facts when describing the human condition. For Barthes, the representational force of a photograph is not amenable to scientific analysis; hence, an alternative disciplinary approach is necessary to understand the complex ways in which photographs and other types of visual imagery help us make meanings about our world. Objectivist, scientific analyses of social phenomena take a particular theoretical stance toward the nature of reality and tailor their positivistic methodologies accordingly. Poststructuralist and postmodernist paradigms,[1] on the other hand, embrace subjectivity and life's multiple realities that qualitative researchers weave into their investigative 'bricolage – a pieced-together set of representations that is fitted to the specifics of a complex situation' (Denzin & Lincoln, 2000: 4). Whereas a methodological goal of positivistic studies is to erase the subjectivity of the researcher, in qualitative approaches such as autoethnography, 'the subject and object of research collapse into the body/thoughts/feelings of the (auto)ethnographer located in his or her particular space and time' (Gannon, 2006: 475). Photographs, therefore, used as qualitative data in autoethnography are not merely flat reflections of the narrator's private life but rather are multidimensional 'commentaries on cultural histories and the texts that shaped and formed us' (Finley, 2005: 686).

Autoethnography, as one genre of qualitative research, differs from classic ethnographic (e.g. Malinowski, 1967) depictions of culture as something apart from the researcher, and instead 'shifts the gaze inward toward a self as a site for interpreting cultural experience' (Neumann, 1996: 183). This methodological strategy is carried out through 'highly personalized accounts where authors draw on their own experiences to extend understanding of a particular discipline or culture' (Holt, 2003: 2). Arthur Bochner provides a succinct explanation:

> The narrative turn moves away from a singular, monolithic conception of social science toward a pluralism that promotes multiple forms of representation and research; away from facts and toward meanings; away from master narratives and toward local stories; away from idolizing categorical thought and abstracted theory and toward embracing the values of irony, emotionality, and activism; away from assuming the stance of the disinterested spectator and toward assuming the posture of a feeling, embodied, and vulnerable observer; away from writing essays and toward telling stories. (Bochner, 2001: 134–135)

In autoethnographic reports, visual and textual materials are presented as interactive referents to ongoing constructions of the narrator's social, cultural and linguistic worlds. Hence, personal photos that document my ever-evolving existence as a second language learner of Japanese are interspersed throughout this book together with fieldnotes, documents and transcripts of recorded interactions to provide the reader with an in-depth account of my Japanese as a second language (JSL) history.

The photo above (see Figure 1), taken together with my former English-as-a-second-language (ESL) students in the United States on the first day of my arrival in Japan in April 1975, is a visual artifact of where and who I was at the beginning of my JSL learning trajectory. Looking at this photo 35 years later, I reflect on Barthes' remark that the effect of viewing a past image of oneself 'is not to restore what has been abolished (by time, by distance) but to attest that what I see has indeed existed' (Barthes, 1981: 82). Someone else looking at this photo would only see a group of people, one of whom appears to be of a different racial background, having their picture taken at a famous landmark, much like a scene in photo albums of tourists worldwide. From a postmodernist viewpoint, however, travel scenes are blurred images, since notions of geographical locality, nationality and culture have become unhinged from their traditional representations as bounded, unifying entities. Socio-political upheavals and global diasporas have led to a keen awareness of how these phenomena impact on peoples' ways of describing themselves as 'foreigner', 'expatriate', 'tourist', 'native/nonnative' and of how these self-identifications fluctuate according to life circumstances. Drawing on Gloria Anzaldúa's (1987) concept of 'border crossings' to depict the fluidity in Mexican women's identity constructions, Akhil Gupta and James Ferguson comment that

> [t]he fiction of cultures as discrete, objectlike phenomena occupying discrete spaces becomes implausible for those who inhabit the borderlands. Related to border inhabitants are those who live a life of border crossings – migrant workers, nomads, and members of the transnational business and professional elite. What is 'the culture' of farm workers who spend half a year in Mexico and half in the United States? Finally, there are those who cross borders more or less permanently – immigrants, refugees, exiles, and expatriates. In their case, the disjuncture of place and culture is especially clear. (Gupta & Ferguson, 2001: 34)

In subsequent chapters, the story of my own transnational disjuncture will be presented in all of its textual, visual and ideological manifestations. Similar to numerous reports from transplanted individuals who come to grips (or not) with ambivalent feelings of displacement and loss [see Pavlenko (2006) for a collection of up-to-date, comprehensive analyses of the languages and lives of bi/multilingual speakers], my autoethnography highlights how my disconnection from a life left behind in the United States is neither complete nor has it followed a preordained path. My lives before and after relocating to Japan are depicted in my narrative as being interrelated experiences that together propelled my trajectory to where and who I am now. Although my JSL language behavior is inherently embedded in local, concrete social interactions and larger ideological discourses[2] in Japan, my being and becoming a Japanese speaker is, at the same time, an idiosyncratic assemblage of my past, present and imagined language experiences and identities.[3] This line of theorizing is based on a cultural anthropological model that, as Holland *et al.* explain, aims

> to respect humans as social and cultural creatures and therefore bounded, yet to recognize the processes whereby human collectives

and individuals often move themselves – led by hope, desperation, or even playfulness, but certainly by no rational plan – from one set of socially and culturally formed subjectivities to another. (Holland *et al.*, 1998: 6–7)

Locating Autoethnography in SLA and Applied Linguistics

Previous diary studies (Bailey, 1983; Schmidt & Frota, 1986; Schumann & Schumann, 1977), autobiographical reports of L2 educators and scholars (Belcher & Connor, 2001) and stories of bi/multilingual speakers (Kanno, 2003; Pavlenko, 2001; Pavlenko & Blackledge, 2004) have made significant contributions to the fields of SLA and applied linguistics by giving emic[4] (insider) perspectives on second language learning and use. Meryl Siegal's (1996) ethnographic study of white western women studying Japanese in Japan and Karen Ogulnick's (1998) diary study of her own JSL learning processes were earnest attempts to capture the sociolinguistic complexities in resolving the dissonance between newly acquired linguistic and cultural experiences and one's previous ways of speaking and behaving. In her review of narrative analysis in language studies, Deborah Schiffrin remarks that 'stories are resources not just for the development and presentation of a self as a psychological entity but as someone located within a social and cultural world' (Schiffrin, 1996: 169). Similarly, through the telling of my story I describe my JSL development not as a psycholinguistically based, mastery learning model of language acquisition. Rather, my focus is on the important role of sociocultural contexts and interactions between myself and both Japanese and non-Japanese individuals with whom I have come into contact over the course of my personal and professional life in Japan.

While not dismissing the important contributions of conventional structural analyses of bilingualism (see relevant chapters in Bhatia & Ritchie, 2006), current conceptualizations of SLA processes take into more serious consideration the crucial role of socialization factors (see e.g. Bayley & Schecter, 2003) that defy quantification of isolated variables. Relatedly, the following quote from Steven Thorne stresses the importance of not overlooking the interconnectedness of speech and social contexts:

> Style, intonation, prosody, and talk-in-interaction and its organizational structure are all implicated in this larger understanding of the organization of communicative practices, their historical and situated qualities, and the dialectical process whereby talk-in-interaction and grammaticized features of a language are the sociocultural qualities which co-constitute the context within which communicative practices occur, and reciprocally, the cultural-historical-discursive qualities of social context tend to (re)inculcate communicative practices in their social, ideological, and culturally specific forms. (Thorne, 2000: 235)

Investigative importance is also increasingly being placed on the sociopolitical implications of L2 minority speakers' attempts to gain access to mainstream society (see e.g. Heller, 2007 and also Menard-Warwick, 2009). My situation in Japan is different from that of L2 populations worldwide who 'are placed at a disadvantage in situations where their linguistic performance is judged by members of classes other than their own ... [who] have to do what they can with what they have, given the structural relations of inequality in which they find themselves' (Heller, 2007: 14). However, as I explain in subsequent chapters, my privileged sociolinguistic position is highly subject to the vagaries of Japan's ideological discourses concerning *gaikokujin* (literally, a person outside of the country).

My conceptual framework drew on reflexive research practices in the social sciences (Clandinin & Connelly, 2000; Richardson, 2000) and recent SLA and applied linguistics theoretical alternatives (e.g. Atkinson, 2011; Block, 2003) to positivistic paradigms that continue to 'seek the Grail of objective and factual reporting of objective reality' (Clough, 2002: xii). Ethnographic case studies of bi/multilingual speakers' lives (e.g. Simon-Maeda, 2009) can uncover the unquantifiable, personal and socially interactive aspects of language experiences hidden in statistical results that often serve simply as fodder for sweeping generalizations about L2 processes.

In sum, this book is not merely a nostalgic tale of my social and linguistic encounters in Japan. As Ogulnick concludes in her collection of various authors' language-learning stories, 'there is a dialectic between language learning and identity that is inextricably linked to our historical experiences and the sociopolitical contexts in which we find ourselves' (Ogulnick, 2000: 170). Introspective analyses of the interconnectedness of language learning, identity and larger socio-historical contexts have increased in visibility and consequently academic legitimacy, due noticeably to the voluminous work of Aneta Pavlenko (see section References) over the past decade. Bi/multilingual speakers' subjective analyses of their language histories are no longer considered to be solely a source of interesting anecdotal data used to complement experimental studies. In the fields of SLA and applied linguistics, narrative research is now recognized as a research paradigm in its own right (see *TESOL Quarterly* 2011 special topic issue, also see Aneta Pavlenko's 2007 review of autobiographic narratives in applied linguistics) with an array of methodological strategies that can lead to more holistic interpretations of L2 and additional language experiences.

The autoethnographic research and writing style chosen for this book features detailed descriptions and analyses of the local exigencies of my daily life in Japan that have significantly influenced my JSL trajectory. As part of the postmodernist shift in qualitative research traditions (see Denzin & Lincoln, 2000; see also Ellis & Bochner, 1996) autoethnography can provide SLA and applied linguistics theorists with a unique insight into the multifaceted, socially mediated nature of language acquisition. As such, this volume's overall postmodernist stance is in line with recent views of 'language learning as an emergent process [that] focuses on doing, knowing, and becoming rather than on the attainment of a steady state understood as a well-defined set of rules, principles, parameters, and so on.' (Lantolf & Thorne, 2006: 138).

Researcher Positionality

Western academics always run the risk of exoticizing non-western cultures and their respective languages (see Kubota, 2005; Mohanty, 1988), and I do not profess to be endowed with the ability to wipe my researcher lens clean of essentializing perspectives on the situations I observed and analyzed.[5] Furthermore, as Ladson-Billings comments, 'there is no magic in employing participant observation, narrative inquiry, or interviews ... the qualitative researcher must guard against the connotation that qualitative work represents some more "authentic" form of research' (Ladson-Billings, 2000: 272).[6] Nevertheless, despite the challenge of accurately portraying my own and others' situations, this book confronts the 'crisis of representation' (see Denzin & Lincoln, 2005: 18–20) by adhering to a comprehensive rendering of 'the personal, concrete, and mundane details of experience as a window to understanding the relationships between self and other or between individual and community' (Holman Jones, 2005: 766).

Along with the practice of forefronting researcher positionality in qualitative studies, mention must also be made of the methodological criterion of 'transferability' (see comprehensive explanation in Denzin & Lincoln, 2000). Contrary to positivistic analyses' dependency on the generalizability of statistical results, transferability is qualitative research's gold standard for judging the robustness of 'the contextual similarity between the described situation and the situation to which the theory is to be transferred' (Davis, 1995: 441). In other words, the trustworthiness of my interpretive commentary depends on how well readers across different strands of L2 research are able to recognize in my study comparable trends and issues in their own disciplines, leading to theoretical cross-fertilization and ultimately new insights on language learning and use.

Organization of the Book

Although for organizational coherence this book is separated into chapters focusing on particular themes in my past and present lives, as in most narrative accounts temporality is not neatly delineated, as Ochs and Capps explain:

> [T]he domains of past, present, and yet-to-be-realized time are not neatly segmented in narratives of personal experience.... Rather, narratives ebb back and forth across different time zones, as narrators mine the significance of life events. Such temporal elasticity lies

at the very heart of personal narrative, in that narrative time is human time, and human time flows back and forth from moments remembered, to the unfolding present, to moments imagined. (Ochs & Capps, 2001: 200)

Therefore, while narrating a certain segment of my JSL trajectory, events from different time periods will be interwoven throughout the storyline. The incorporation of previous events, thoughts and the actual words of my own or others into my account is a literary device that Mikhail Bakhtin has described as a dialogical process wherein 'any utterance is a link in a very complexly organized chain of other utterances' (Bakhtin, 1986: 69). As such, my authorial voice becomes decentered through the telling of my story that is essentially a collaboratively constructed (re)presentation of my JSL life.

The book is divided into two parts. Part I contains an introductory chapter and two subsequent chapters that explain the conceptual framework of the volume. In Chapter 1, I elaborate on how autoethnography is a postmodernist methodological approach to examining the link between language and identity. Key concepts in the opening sections serve as a guidepost for readers in understanding postmodernist thought and how it constitutes the basis of autoethnographic research. Chapter 2 outlines the academic research history of narrative inquiry in SLA and applied linguistics with numerous citations from the relevant literature. Later sections focus on recent postmodernist interpretations of the interconnectedness of second language acquisition and identity. I adopt a more narrative style in Part II that opens with Chapter 3 featuring the origins of my language-learning history with photographs and verbatim transcripts interspersed throughout the narrative storyline and interpretive commentary. In order to probe my JSL narrative in all of its dialectically complex dimensions I have included transcribed verbatim data segments of interactions between myself and participants in my two-year ethnographic study of bi/multilingual speakers in Japan (Simon-Maeda, 2009). For me and my bi/multilingual participants, our shared 'multilingual habitus' (House, 2003) evolved through diverse speech activities analyzed from both micro (discourse analytical) and macro (ethnographic) perspectives. This analytical plan brought to the fore the mutually constitutive nature of discourse behavior and sociocultural contexts and the resultant effect on our L2 identities shaped on the periphery of Japanese society that does not always welcome foreigners. Throughout this and subsequent chapters I critically reflect in postmodernist terms on my position as an expatriate in Japan and the place of language in the formation of my outsider identity. More intimate ethnographic details of my life in Japan are presented in Chapter 4. I relate how my evolving identities as a wife and mother have profoundly impacted on my JSL development. Special note is made of the gendered nature of partner and family relationships and of how Japanese societal norms concerning the role of women have affected my (re)construction of self and language. Chapter 5 is set in my university workplace where my professional identity is constantly being (re)negotiated through interactions with colleagues and students. Chapter 6 further depicts the complexities of being and becoming a Japanese speaker. Mundane interactions, past and present, are recreated in a composite account obtained from multiple sources (photographs, journal entries, verbatim data segments) that illustrate the interactional strategies I deploy in particular circumstances to pass in, out and around mainstream Japanese society. This chapter also includes an epilogue in which I present two vignettes that exemplify the unpredictable nature and significance of bi/multilingualism in contemporary global communities. In the closing discussion, I pull together the theoretical framework of the introductory and opening chapters in an attempt to reemphasize the contribution that autoethnography can make to the field. While not dismissing the importance of traditional analyses of second and additional language acquisition I contend that an autoethnographic approach can provide a more complete picture of language practices. Specifically, in light of a growing appreciation of the socio-interactional features of bi/multilingual speech I propose that SLA researchers need to widen their investigative lens through the use of alternative methodologies, such as autoethnography, in order to capture the multilayered nature of language learning and use.

Readers are invited to become active participants in my L2 learning experience by reflecting on their own second and additional language situations, and ultimately the verisimilitude of my interpretations will depend on how well my account 'evokes in readers a feeling that the experience described is lifelike, believable, and possible' (Bochner & Ellis, 2000: 751).

Notes

1. The terms 'poststructuralism' and 'postmodernism' are often used interchangeably in academic research literature, but there are differences in their origins and interpretations. Patti Lather uses *'postmodern* to mean the larger cultural shifts of a post-industrial, post-colonial era and *poststructural* to mean the working out of those shifts within the arenas of academic theory' (Lather, 1991: 4, italics in original). For purposes of consistency, I will only use the term 'postmodernism' in subsequent sections in relation to my narrative's theoretical standpoint.
2. Throughout this book, the words 'discourse' and 'discourses' appear regularly and often in tandem, thus a preliminary explanation is needed to clarify how they operate both singly and jointly to generate meaning. The first use is generally taken to coincide with the concern of traditional discourse analyses focusing primarily on the linguistic details of language in use, typically in textual forms (e.g. transcribed conversations, stories, documents). The second use can be best explained in the words of James Paul Gee, who states that discourses 'are ways of behaving, interacting, valuing, thinking, believing,

speaking, and often reading and writing that are accepted as instantiations of particular roles (or 'types of people') by specific *groups of people*.... Discourses are ways of being 'people like us'. They are 'ways of being in the world'; they are 'forms of life'. They are, thus, always and everywhere *social* and products of social histories' (Gee, 1996: viii, italics in original). This latter definition has important ramifications for how my JSL identity was shaped by Japanese societal discourses surrounding the notion of 'foreigner'. Also see notes 1 and 4 in Chapter 1 for a Foucauldian interpretation of discourse(s) that can never be seen as purely linguistic since they work in powerful ways to regulate our ways of thinking and acting in the world.

3. David Block's explication of social scientists' views of 'identity/identities' is highly relevant to the main thesis of my book: '[I]dentities [are]socially constructed, self-conscious, ongoing narratives that individuals perform, interpret and project in dress, bodily movements, actions and language.... Identities are about negotiating new subject positions at the crossroads of the past, present and future. Individuals are shaped by their sociohistories but they also shape their sociohistories as life goes on ... identities are related to different traditionally demographic categories such as ethnicity, race, nationality, migration, gender, social class and language' (Block, 2007a: 27).

4. The term 'emic' is usually contrasted with its quantitative counterpart 'etic' in descriptions of the methodological differences between qualitative and quantitative research. An etic approach typically involves controlled experimentation to isolate variables that the researcher hypothesizes are the causes of certain phenomena. Qualitative researchers primarily rely on emic procedures to interpret experiences from their informants' perspectives. Clifford Geertz explains the differences in these two approaches by emphasizing the 'actor-oriented' (Geertz, 1973: 14) component of emic analysis as opposed to etic analyses' focus on empirical evidence obtained from a supposedly detached researcher perspective.

5. Michelle Fine's seminal postmodernist treatise on how qualitative researchers are not immune from ethical infractions deserves mention here:

> '[Q]ualitative researchers need to recognize that our work stands in some relation to Othering.... When we look, get involved, demur, analyze, interpret, probe, speak, remain silent, walk away, organize for outrage, or sanitize our stories, and when we construct our texts in or on their words, we decide how to nuance our relations with/for/despite those who have been deemed Others. When we write essays about subjugated Others as if *they* were a homogeneous mass (of vice or virtue) free-floating and severed from contexts of oppression, and as if we were neutral transmitters of voices and stories, we tilt toward a narrative strategy that reproduces Othering on, despite, or even "for"'. (Fine, 1994: 74, italics in original)

6. Lee and Simon-Maeda explain that even in emancipatory studies of marginalized individuals in one's own racial or ethnic group, a bias-free researcher perspective is not automatically guaranteed. The authors propose the following antidote to essentializing research practices: 'In both same and cross-group studies carried out by researchers in privileged positions, it is crucial to first acknowledge our own potential implicatedness in the exclusion of participants' points of view through our methodologies and reporting styles' (Lee & Simon-Maeda, 2006: 589). This reflective awareness of researcher positionality constitutes the starting point in many types of qualitative investigations.

Chapter 1
The Postmodern Basis of Autoethnography

In this chapter, I explain how autoethnography is a postmodernist methodological approach to examining the link between language and identity; however, to accomplish this task it is necessary to introduce some key concepts in the sections below. Postmodernism encompasses a vast area of intellectual inquiry across multiple disciplines, and hence the following is not meant to be a comprehensive listing but merely a guidepost for understanding postmodernist thought and how it serves as the basis for autoethnographic research.

Language, Subjectivity, Reflexivity

As my autoethnographic inquiry deals primarily with language acquisition, I first present postmodernist perspectives on *language*, which is not considered to be an innate, fixed set of sound–meaning associations that simply reflect reality, as described in pre-Saussurean linguistics. Postmodernists view 'language as a system always existing in historically specific discourses ... the place where our sense of ourselves, our subjectivity, is *constructed*' (Weedon, 1997: 21–23, italics in original). This emphasis on the social constructionist aspect of language is a radical departure from traditional linguistic theories that focus on individual utterances (see St Pierre, 2000: 480–484 for a postmodern critique of structural linguistics). In contrast, according to Michel Foucault, discourse is conceptualized as 'practices that systematically form the objects of which they speak' (Foucault, 1972: 54). It then follows that analytical attention shifts from decontextualized strings of speech or text to the ways in which certain groups of people and institutions come to regulate the (social, political, religious, medical, etc.) rules of discourse that normalize our ways of thinking and acting in the world.[1] Whereas structural linguists are concerned primarily with describing the mechanics of discourse (see Mills, 2004 for a review of traditional discourse analysis), Foucault's theory takes a more philosophical view of 'how language gathers itself together according to socially constructed rules and regularities that allow certain statements to be made and not others' (St Pierre, 2000: 485). As such, language and its effects are not constituted in a free-floating vacuum but are always specific to particular historical and cultural circumstances. Patti Lather's definition of postmodernism is germane to the discussion being developed here:

> [T]he essence of the postmodern argument is that the dualisms which continue to dominate Western thought are inadequate for understanding a world of multiple causes and effects interacting in complex and non-linear ways, all of which are rooted in a limitless array of historical and cultural specificities. (Lather, 1991: 21)

The historical and cultural specificity of social life and language has important implications for how speakers acquire first and additional languages. Because I am a female learner of Japanese in a predominantly male-dominant society [see Fujimura-Fanselow & Kameda (1995) and also see Gelb (2003) for a comprehensive description of sexism in Japan], the analysis of my JSL life has necessarily been undertaken from a feminist standpoint. Unlike traditional discourse approaches that eschew ideological interpretations of linguistic behavior, I recognize the importance of going beyond a myopic interpretation of my immediate sociolinguistic circumstances to a broader analysis that takes into account 'the way in which dominant cultural understandings of identity categories are maintained, reproduced and normalised in everyday text and practices of interactions' (Benwell & Stokoe, 2006: 46–47). Seen from this analytical approach, my Japanese self has been fashioned within and oftentimes against prevalent gendered norms of mainstream Japanese social life and language behavior. Autoethnography proved to be a highly effective tool for making visible the socio-political situatedness of my microlevel JSL experiences embedded within broader contexts for women in Japan.

A postmodernist focus on the situated nature of language and its fundamental role in identity construction can also be found in Etienne Wenger's (1998) community of practice (CoP) notion which gained a popular foothold in the SLA world in the 1990s (see Norton & Toohey, 2001). In CoP theory, a person is not regarded as an autonomous entity but rather as a social being whose subjectivity is produced through everyday interactions. An understanding of language learning and use from a postmodern standpoint entails recognition that as members of communities of practice our L2 linguistic identities both depend on and influence broader societal discourses – a bidirectional process missing from traditional explanations of speech behavior. This perspective has important ramifications in analyses of how languages are acquired, and Chapter 2 will explicate this point in more detail. In line with the postmodernist view of language as a social practice, through my JSL autoethnography I am, in effect, illuminating how language and life experiences are interrelated processes that lie beneath the surface of cognitivist explanations of SLA phenomena.

In short, postmodern inquiries into the nature of language start with a different set of questions than investigations concerned primarily with psychometric, reductivist descriptions of language. Also missing from these latter research paradigms is the notion of *subjectivity*[2] and its integral relation to language development. In a postmodern world, subjectivity is understood to be 'precarious, contradictory and in process, constantly being reconstituted in discourse each time we think or speak' (Weedon, 1997: 32). That is, an individual does not exist as the stable, rational self of humanist[3] discourses, but rather is constituted as an ongoing assemblage of identity formations. A parallel postmodernist insight from performativity theory (Butler, 1993) can also expand our understanding of the mutually constitutive roles of language behavior and subjectivity. Don Kulick explains that a 'performative approach to linguistic phenomena does not start or end with identity ... conventionally presented as a more or less conscious claim-staking of a particular sociological position' (Kulick, 2006: 293). Kulick suggests that the term 'identification' better represents the performative nature of the processes through which an individual's sense of self develops. That is to say, the categories into which we are positioned linguistically and socially both by others and by ourselves are not fixed or predetermined but rather emerge and shift through recurring interactions mediated through language embedded in larger competing discourses of gender, class, ableism, race and so on.[4] It is this relational, provisional self-in-the-making notion of postmodernism that distinguishes it from humanist (see note 3) theories of the individual and that makes autoethnography a particularly suitable methodology for highlighting the intersubjective dynamic of identity formations.

The defining feature of autoethnographic research is *reflexivity*, a concept that has also been claimed by postmodernist theorists to be one of their central epistemological[5] oppositions to objective, detached observations and descriptions of social phenomena. Reflexive research practices involve, 'an ongoing self-awareness during the research process which aids in making visible the practice and construction of knowledge within research in order to produce more accurate analyses of our research' (Pillow, 2003: 178). This approach is a direct challenge to positivist research agendas that disavow the legitimacy of looking inward to our own subjective experiences in order to fully understand the situation being examined. Charlotte Linde (1993) comments on this paradoxical nature of reflexivity as follows:

> Reflexivity in narrative is created by the separation of the narrator from the protagonist of the narrative. It permits the narrator to observe, reflect, and correct the self that is being created. The act of narration itself requires self-regard and editing, since, a distance in time and standpoint necessarily separates the actions being narrated from the act of narration. (Linde, 1993: 122)

Thus, while my autoethnography is an introspective rendering of my JSL trajectory it is also a form of distancing that enables me to reflect on events from an outside observer position. Moreover, as Jerome Bruner notes, the construction of self through narrative is never a solo performance but rather an intersubjective undertaking highly dependent on 'the interpretations others offer of your version' (Bruner, 2001: 34). This reciprocal relationship is the basis for how an autobiographical identity emerges in line with prevalent cultural templates concerning, as in the case of this book, the social and linguistic life of an expatriate in Japan.

Researchers who adhere to reflexive principles address the logicopositivist critique of indulging in narcissistic navel gazing by incorporating throughout their investigations a rigorous 'reflexivity that accounts for multiplicity without making it singular and that acknowledges the unknowable without making it familiar' (Pillow, 2003: 181). Likewise, James Clifford's response to positivism's illusory quest for a universal truth is that:

> Ethnographic truths are thus inherently *partial* – committed and incomplete. This point is now widely asserted – and resisted at strategic points by those who fear the collapse of clear standards of verification. But once accepted and built into ethnographic art, a rigorous sense of partiality can be a source of representational tact. (Clifford, 1986: 7, italics in original)

The theme of partial truths runs throughout postmodernist thought concerning representations of reality and the subject, as expressed in Donna Haraway's influential treatise:

> Subjectivity is multidimensional; so therefore is vision. The knowing self is partial in all its guises, never finished, whole, simply there and original; it is always constructed and stitched together imperfectly, and *therefore* able to join with another, to see together without claiming to be another. (Haraway, 1988: 586, italics in original)

Positivist methodologies that assume an unreflective, all-knowing 'view from above' (Haraway, 1988: 589) can at best provide only a very narrow perspective of social life as deducted from single-cause analyses and universalizing theories. Reflexive methodologies, on the other hand, are grounded in an inductive, interpretive approach that perceives reality to be socially and continually co-constructed and not merely the end product of intervening variables (see articles in the special 2006 issue of the *International Journal of Qualitative Studies in Education* on paradigm debates following US government mandates concerning educational research).

Reflexivity has been a cornerstone of postmodern feminist theory for decades. As a stellar example, Michelle Fine's treatise, 'Working the Hyphens', is an important model for researchers with critical feminist goals who have been admonished to continually take into consideration how 'Self and Other are knottily entangled' (Fine, 1994: 92). In other words, for a researcher to deny her implication in the very situation she claims to be concerned about (see Lee & Simon-Maeda, 2006) or to maintain an objective, authoritative stance is to revert to 'positivist standards that measure acceptability of knowledge in terms of some ideal, unchanging body of knowledge' (Oleson, 2000: 236). Reflexivity's role in our coming to terms with how language constitutes (and not merely reflects) reality is foregrounded in Lather's comments on the strategic integration of feminist and postmodern theories:

> Postmodernism offers feminists ways to work within and yet challenge dominant discourses. Within postmodernist feminism, language moves from representational to constitutive; binary logic implodes, and debates about 'the real' shift from a radical constructivism to a discursively reflexive position which recognizes how our knowledge is mediated by the concepts and categories of our understanding. (Lather, 1991: 39)

As noted previously, my location as a female learner and speaker of Japanese profoundly influences and depends on larger gendered societal discourses – a bidirectional process elaborated on throughout subsequent chapters. In short, the postmodernist concepts described above – language as social practice, subjectivity, reflexivity – are integral components of autoethnographic research without which we are left with a uni-dimensional picture of language learning and use.

What Autoethnography Does and How It Does It

In practical terms, the methodological task for those engaged in reflexive interpretive qualitative research such as autoethnography involves prolonged (re)interpretation of multiple texts (written and visual) in relation to one's own self, yet simultaneously in ways that engage and challenge readers to reflect on their own meaning-making processes. The (re)presentation of the autoethnographer's individualized self, although unique and different, is fashioned by referring to other individuals and contexts (real or imagined) for an interactively constructed depiction of a particular situation. How an autoethnography brings to the fore the multilayered aspects of a person's life is explained by Michael Bamberg as follows:

> [N]arratives, irrespective of whether they deal with one's life or an episode or event in the life of someone else, always reveal the speaker's identity. The narrative point-of-view from where the characters are ordered in the story world gives away – and most often is meant to give away – the point-of-view from where the speaker represents

him-/herself. By offering and telling a narrative the speaker lodges a claim for him/herself in terms of who he/she is. (Bamberg, 2005: 223)

Bamberg continues to elaborate on how a display of self through narrative hinges on a self-reflective stance concerning how a subject is simultaneously 'being positioned' and 'positioning itself' (Bamberg, 2005: 224) with, through, and sometimes against prevailing discourses. That is to say, the self is not a static, preexisting entity but rather evolves through a dialectal relationship between different ways of interacting and speaking in the world. This interpretation of the mutually constitutive nature of discursive behavior and identity constructions is the epistemological cornerstone of my JSL account.

When delienating the fundamental concepts and practical applications of autoethnography it must be noted that the oppositional tension between positivist and postmodern paradigms as I have explained above does not mean that autoethnography along with its qualitative research counterparts have emerged as the uncontested champions in the 'paradigm wars' [Kuhn, 1962; see also Lather's (2006) mapping of paradigm shifts in the social sciences]. To accord autoethnography privileged status as the one true mode of knowledge production would be to replace one 'regime of truth' (Foucault, 1980: 133) with another. Instead of resorting to debilitating epistemological and methodological one-upmanship, current postmodernist commentaries caution against a neat categorization or valorization of a particular research paradigm. Lather, in reference to the current proliferation of research paradigms in educational research, puts it this way:

> In our particular context of educational research where grand narratives and one-best-way of thinking are being reasserted under the banner of SRE [Scientific Research in Education] my major claim is that such efforts need to be situated in a context of a historical time marked by multiplicity and competing discourses that do not map tidily onto one another, a time of unevenly legitimized and resourced incommensurabilities regarding the politics of knowing and being known.... But this 'how to be of use' concern, framed within a necessary complicity, is key in framing issues away from the binary of either qualitative or quantitative, with its fostering of 'my paradigm is bigger or better than yours' or 'real science' versus that which does not meet scientific demarcation criteria. The move is, rather, toward a recognition that we all do our work within a crisis of authority and legitimization, proliferation and fragmentation of centers, and blurred genres. (Lather, 2006: 47)

Lather's comments speak to the ontological (ways of defining reality) futility of dwelling on exclusionary taxonomies when in fact theories with overlapping historical roots run across different research strands that are all shaped by prevalent sociopolitical circumstances.[6] Hence, my choice of autoethnography for this project was not based on the mistaken notion that a life history method provides the definitive explanation for how subjective experiences affect language acquisition processes and vice versa. My aim is to show how the narrative process can explicate in ways that conventional methods cannot the dynamic coexistence of personal and socially mediated properties of L2 learning and use.

Additionally, it is important to mention that the positivistic criteria of reliability and validity do not apply when describing what autoethnography does and how it does it, as explained by Donald Polkinghorne:

> The results of narrative research cannot claim to correspond exactly with what has actually occurred – that is, they are not 'true' if 'truth' is taken to mean exact correspondence or conformity to actuality. Research investigating the realm of meaning aims rather for verisimilitude, or results that have the appearance of truth or reality.... Narrative research, then, uses the ideal of a scholarly consensus as the test of verisimilitude rather than the test of logical or mathematical validity. (Polkinghorne, 1988: 176)

The above quote represents autoethnographers' response to the oft-made criticism that qualitative research standards of logic and truth inevitably slip away into anything goes relativism. The validity of narrative truth is based on the precept that conferring 'new meanings onto the past is not necessarily to falsify it, but only to situate it within a broader interpretive scheme, one that may have been unavailable at the time of experience' (Freeman, 2001: 291). In the SLA field, Lantolf and Pavlenko soundly addressed the marginalization of first-person narratives as a legitimate data source by explaining that language researchers have traditionally 'subscribed uncritically to the rationalist epistemology and experimental methodology of the hard sciences' (Lantolf & Pavlenko, 2000: 157). The authors provide a compelling counter-argument to the 'hegemony currently enjoyed by experimental/observational methodologies' (Lantolf & Pavlenko, 2000: 159) and emphasize that the dependability of narrative research is based on the concept of 'ecological validity' (Lantolf & Thorne, 2006: 139) that is not dependent on third-person, detached, statistical measurements but rather on in-depth, first-person renderings of real-world experiences.

In summary, as part of the postmodernist shift in the field of SLA, narrative inquiry can fill the gaps in studies operating under the modernist myth that discourse and language are closed systems internalized by autonomous, ahistoric agents. On the basis of the perspective that 'discourse can never be just linguistic since it organizes a way of thinking into a way of acting in the world' (St Pierre, 2000: 484) my JSL development is presented in subsequent chapters as a series of discourses that have been constructed and continue to be constructed by the everyday circumstances of my life in Japan.

Notes

1. Foucault's analyses of language moved far beyond the word and sentence level. His primary concern, using the evolution of discourses surrounding sexuality as an example, was 'to account for the fact that it [sex] is spoken about, to discover who does the speaking, the positions and viewpoints from which they speak, the institutions which prompt people to speak about it and which store and distribute the things that are said. What is at issue, briefly, is the over-all "discursive fact", the way in which sex is "put into discourse"' (Foucault, 1978: 11). Foucault's theses on the origins and effects of sexuality discourses have been widely used by recent gender and language scholars (e.g. Cameron & Kulick, 2003) to explain how heteronormative discourses marginalize lesbian, gay, bisexual and transgendered (LGBT) individuals whose sexual identities are categorized as 'abnormal' within a heterosexist society.
2. The choice to use either 'identity' or 'subjectivity' is usually based on one's theoretical (e.g. modernist, postmodernist, behaviorist, etc.) orientation to analyses of individual and social behavior. While identity is most often found in conventional (e.g. Erikson, 1968) theories concerning the human psyche, postmodern scholars prefer to use subjectivity along with 'subject position(s)' to denote the more fluid, emergent properties of a self-in-the-making. While recognizing this important difference in theoretical terminology, for the sake of consistency 'identity' will be used in most cases throughout this book.
3. It is worth quoting at length Judith Baxter's explanation of the difference between humanist and poststructuralist conceptions of human identities:

    [H]umanist discourses presuppose an *essence* at the core of the individual, which is unique, fixed and coherent, and which makes a person recognizably possess a character of personality. Conversely, poststructuralist theory argues that individuals are never outside cultural forces or discursive practices but always 'subject' to them. Their identities are determined by a range of 'subject positions' ('ways of being'), approved by their culture, and made available to them by means of the particular discourses operating within a given discourse context. (Baxter, 2003: 25, italics in original)

4. Baxter gives an example of how 'competing discourses' (Baxter, 2003: 9) serve to construct social realities. In mixed gender business meetings, men may be in more powerful positions due to general societal norms concerning male/female leadership roles. 'However, according to an FPDA [feminist poststructural discourse analysis] perspective, individuals are rarely consistently positioned as powerful across *all* the discourses at work within a given context – they are often located simultaneously as both powerful and powerless. In other words, it is possible for a speaker to be positioned as relatively powerful within one discourse but as relatively powerless within another, perhaps competing discourse' (Baxter, 2003: 9, italics in original).
5. A researcher's epistemological perspective (i.e. a set of beliefs concerning the nature of truth and reality) will determine her choice of investigative methodologies (see Denzin & Lincoln, 1994: 108–109 for examples of different paradigms' (e.g. positivism, postpositivism, critical theory, constructivism) epistemological criteria and methodologies).

6. In addition to arguing that undue emphasis should not be placed on the demarcation of different research paradigms, Patti Lather also states, 'Paradigm shifts occur as reaction formations to the perceived inadequate explanatory power of existing paradigms. Therefore, someone who works in emancipatory paradigms, for example, is often aware of the theoretical assumptions as well as the critiques of positivism and interpretivism. Note also that some theories that start out in one paradigm change considerably when they are taken up in another; e.g. poststructural feminism is considerably different from liberal, emancipatory feminism. Conventional science is positivist but when science's assumptions are rethought in interpretive or post paradigms, it is not the same; *i.e. science is not the same in all paradigms in terms of ontology, epistemology and methodology*' (Lather, 2006: 37, italics in original).

Chapter 2
Narrative Inquiry in SLA and Applied Linguistics

In the fields of SLA and applied linguistics, narrative inquiry and its various genres of autoethnography, life history, case study, autobiography, diary study and so on highlight the personal and socially constructed aspects of language acquisition and how languages are considered 'not only as constitutive of meaning, but also as contexts within which individuals position themselves and are positioned' (Burck, 2005: 13). From this perspective, positivistic analyses that depend largely on experiments in controlled settings are considered to be inadequate indices of how an individual like me became a fluent Japanese speaker. This is not to say, however, that psychometric studies of bi/multilingual speakers' cognitive processes have no place in the field (see Altarriba, 2006 and also see Harris *et al.*, 2006), but rather that there are alternative approaches that yield equally valid insights on language learning and use.

The interpenetration of the postmodern concepts of situatedness and identity formations and a focus on the centrality of activity in learning have been extensively explored in the fields of general education (Kirshner & Whitson, 1997; Lave & Wenger, 1991; Rogoff & Lave, 1999) and developmental psychology (Thelen & Smith, 1994). It is only recently, however, that SLA studies building on the work of Sociocultural Theory (Lantolf, 2000), Activity Theory (Leontiev, 1978; Wertsch, 1998) and discourse analyses that stress the importance of context and social interaction in language use/acquisition (e.g. Duranti & Goodwin, 1992) have helped create an environment conducive to a 'social turn in SLA' (Block, 2003) promising to be a viable counterpoint to 'the more orthodox psycholinguistic bias of the field' (Block, 2003: 1).

Lantolf and Thorne are proponents of a social-interactionist view of SLA that places analytical emphasis on speakers' (inter)personal trajectories and interactions, and the authors state that 'language learning as an emergent process focuses on doing, knowing, and becoming rather than on the attainment of a steady state understood as a well-defined set of rules, principles, parameters, etc.' (Lantolf & Thorne, 2006: 138). Lantolf and Pavlenko emphasize the need to 'discuss learner language in all its complexity' (Lantolf & Pavlenko, 2001: 155) and proffer that first-person narratives of L2 speakers are an important counter-balance to '[l]inguistic theories, including those prevalent in SLA research, [which] have traditionally assumed monolingualism to be the unmarked case' (Lantolf & Pavlenko, 2001: 157). Likewise, Norton's (2000) interpretive analyses of the language practices and identity formations of L2 individuals in Canada indicate that SLA phenomena cannot be examined as isolated variables unconnected to sociocultural contexts, especially those in which power inequities exist between mainstream and language minority speakers. Through her book-length ethnographic account of immigrant women's language socialization experiences as recorded in their diaries, Norton puts forth a convincing case for the explanatory power of interpretive qualitative analyses of SLA phenomena.

The key studies mentioned above concerning the interrelatedness of social identities and language processes have provided a solid theoretical foundation for narrative inquiry in the SLA field aimed at uncovering the unquantifiable, personal and socially interactive aspects of language experiences. In the same vein, stories of bi/multilingual speakers in London were used in Block's study of 'transnational communities' (Block, 2006: 18) to explain the sociopolitical and linguistic circumstances of individuals who either by choice or necessity have moved to a foreign country for short or long periods of time. Yasuko Kanno (2003) analyzed first-person narratives of bilingual students to understand the complex construction of their linguistic and cross-cultural identities. In an edited collection (Belcher & Connor, 2001) of the language learning stories of L2 educators and scholars, and also in Pavlenko and Blackledge's (2004) volume, the interrelatedness of language and identity was brought to the fore through the voices of a diverse group of bi/multilingual speakers. The authors proposed that power and sociopolitical circumstances inevitably shaped L2 speakers' identity and language practices bound together in a bidirectional relationship that constituted an appropriation or contestation of L1 majority norms. A recent contribution to theories concerned with the inherent connection between identity and language learning is Menard-Warwick's critical ethnography of immigrant ESL learners in the United States. Through extensive field work and in-depth analysis of her participants' life stories, the author suggests that the metaphor of a 'trajectory' (Menard-Warwick, 2009: 46) aptly depicts how L2 identities and their discursive enactments evolved over time through different social interactions. The theoretical understanding of identity 'as multiple, fluid, dynamic, and constituted in discourse' (Menard-Warwick, 2009: 45) is congruent with postmodernist interpretations of the interconnectedness of SLA and identity.

Postmodernist Interpretations of the Interconnectedness of SLA and Identity

Postmodern commentators have long been well attuned to the way that identities evolve and shift (Anzaldúa, 1987; Butler, 1993; Pillow, 2003; St Pierre, 2000; Weedon, 1997, 1999) within and sometimes against prevailing sociocultural contexts, and insights from this field informed the narrativization of my experiences as a JSL speaker. Concepts such as 'cultural hybridity' (Bhaba, 1985), 'new mestiza' and 'border crossings' (Anzaldúa, 1987), and in the SLA field Kramsch's (1993) applications of the notions of 'third space' and 'border experiences' in L2 learning/teaching best capture the messy, caught-in-the-middle aspects of my JSL learning trajectory. That is to say, my JSL persona[1] has not simply emerged as an offshoot of my L1 self within a static sociolinguistic vacuum but rather is the product of multiple 'cross-overs' (Pavlenko & Lantolf, 2000) into the social and linguistics worlds of native Japanese speakers who in turn go through their own discombobulating mind shift when communicating with a red-haired, fair-skinned, definitely non-Japanese individual who speaks *Nagoyaben*[2] (Nagoya dialect).

Koven comments on the mutually constitutive nature of language, social contexts and identity in his report of French-Portuguese bilinguals' narratives of their L2 experiences:

> [H]ow French and Portuguese mediate these speakers' different expressions and experiences of the self is not merely a question of what can be said in both but, rather, depends on the kinds of socioculturally recognized personas speakers can perform in each. The self is not so much labeled or described as it is enacted. Second, different language forms have the power to transform self-expression and experience because of their capacity to index, to bring into being, other contexts and identities.... Different ways of speaking, within and across languages, create socially and psychologically real effects for people, producing for the same speaker multiple expressions and experiences of socially recognizable selves. (Koven, 1998: 437)

Koven's description above resonates with Kulick's (2006) postmodernist application of Butler's (1993) performative theory used to expand our understanding of the roles of speech, social contexts and bi/multicultural cultural identities. Thus, when I speak Japanese I am evoking my Japanese persona, which does not obliterate my English-speaking self but rather becomes incorporated into who I am (or who I think I am) and the social activities I am engaged in at the time. It should be noted that this process is not to be conflated with a 'switch on-off' theory (see Myers-Scotton, 1993) but is more in line with the dynamic theory approach of Herdina and

Jessner (2002). In short, my social and linguistic crossovers as a Japanese speaker are the cumulative result of continuous re-enactments of my L2 self vis-à-vis other Japanese speakers in particular situations.

The theme of identity construction in a new language as a kind of performance also runs throughout Burck's collection of stories from bi/multilingual individuals who moved to a new country as adults. Different from the experiences of those who learned additional languages at an early age, adult learners are more 'aware of processes of constructing themselves through their interactions with others, processes that were invisible and had become naturalised in their first languages' (Burck, 2005: 81). My JSL life began at the age of 25, and from the start I was continually aware of how my Japanese-speaking identity was an ongoing performance of doing being Japanese. In this sense, the postmodernist concept of a de-centered subject's multiple and shifting identities coincides with the experiences of bi/multilingual individuals who use their 'doubleness' (Burck, 2005: 90–91) as a strategic resource to cope with the sociolinguistic exigencies of their everyday lives (see Simon-Maeda, 2009).

Relatedly, the notion of a 'working self-concept' as developed by Markus and Nurius (1986) may be instructive here as it more accurately captures the dynamic aspects of identity construction that traditional psychological theorists (e.g. Erikson, 1968; Maslow, 1968) had squelched into 'a fairly uniform, monolithic structure, consistent over time, comprising some number of physical features or psychological structures that abstract the essential traits from the individual's past behavior' (Markus & Nurius, 1986: 957). Instead, in line with postmodernist interpretations of the relationship between identities and linguistic practices, a working self-concept is defined as follows:

> It can be viewed as a continually active, shifting array of available self-knowledge. The array changes as individuals experience variation in internal states and social circumstances. The content of the working self-concept depends on what self-conceptions have been active just before, on what has been elicited or made dominant by the particular social environment, and on what has been more purposefully invoked by the individual in response to a given experience, event, or situation. (Markus & Nurius, 1986: 957)

The above view of a malleable identity adapting to changing situations, while also serving to buttress a relatively stable projection of what may be considered to be an 'authentic self' (Markus & Nurius, 1986: 965), allows for a more realistic understanding of life and language behavior.

Jay Lemke (2002) also puts forth a similar interpretation in his discussion on how language use is best understood as being situated within and constitutive of ongoing social interactions rather than being a fixed, decontextualized phenomenon:

> Language is a formal sign system that arises for most (but not all) of us within the context of speaking-within-vocalizing-within-action. What linguistics calls 'language' is not, taken in isolation, an appropriate unit for analysis for developmental research; such units need to be defined more functionally, out of the flow and patternings of communicative-interactive-motor behavior.... You cannot, neither materially nor physiologically nor culturally, make meaning *only* with the formal linguistic sign system; other modes of meaning-making are always functionally coupled with language use in real activity .... Speaking is not possible without the constitution and construal of what we believe, what we value, and where we find ourselves in the systems of social classification. (Lemke, 2002: 72, italics in original)

Summary

In the opening chapters of this volume I presented the overall conceptual framework and theoretical underpinnings of my autoethnographic investigation that is part of a recent surge in alternative SLA and applied linguistics approaches to capturing the complexities of language learning and use. Beginning in Chapter 1 with an overview of some key points of postmodernist thought, I explained that the humanist conception of an individual as an autonomous, stable being no longer fits with current understandings of how our social identities are constantly being (re)constructed through a range of experiences articulated through language. Included in the postmodernist perspective on language is an important distinction that has been made between what James Paul Gee has labeled 'language-in-use ... "discourse" with a "little d"' (Gee, 1999: 7) and

> 'Discourses' with a capital 'D', that is, different ways in which we humans integrate language with non-language 'stuff', such as different ways of thinking, acting, interacting, valuing, feeling, believing, and using symbols, tools, and objects in the right places and at the right times so as to enact and recognize different identities and activities. (Gee, 1999: 13)

It is the 'stuff' in Gee's quote above that has recently moved to front and center stage in SLA and applied linguistics circles due to the important work being done by researchers many of whom, as bi/multilingual speakers themselves, intuitively know that 'language is not the expression of unique individuality; it constructs the individual's subjectivity in ways which are socially specific' (Weedon, 1997: 21). Therefore, as social contexts change, so does one's subjectivity, or more precisely one's multiple subjectivities that both constitute and are constituted by our location in unpredictable life situations. This bidirectional process wherein subjectivities are built up through social interactions, and vice versa, provides a variety of sites for the (re)construction of L2 speaker identities. Clearly, this postmodernist interpretation of language behavior entails methodological strategies capable of unraveling the interwoven relationship of language learning and use, identity formations and social contexts. Chapter 2 made note of qualitative research reports in the fields of SLA and applied linguistics that have taken up the slack left by positivistic studies by providing alternative analyses that are, as Pavlenko and Blackledge explain, 'well equipped to capture the complexity of identities in postmodern societies, where languages may not only be "markers of identity" but also sites of resistance, empowerment, solidarity, or discrimination' (Pavlenko & Blackledge, 2004: 3–4).

The notion of reflexivity was also introduced as a fundamental concept that researchers working from a postmodernist standpoint adhere to throughout their investigations. Charlotte Davies explains that 'reflexivity expresses researchers' awareness of their necessary connection to the research situation and hence their effects upon it' (Davies, 2008: 7). In the case of an autoethnography, the author 'sets out to interrogate his [sic] own experiences, acting as both ethnographer and principal informant' (Davies, 2008: 224), while always keeping in mind that he/she does not have a privileged, bias-free outlook on the situation. Additionally, Davies states that ethnographers who use an autobiographical component in their reports 'commonly find their ethnographic self engaged in a process of othering their social self ... [h]owever, it is precisely in this process of interaction between ethnographer-as-self and ethnographer-as-other that social knowledge of general interest and significance is produced' (Davies, 2008: 228). This last point has important implications for the contribution that autoethnographies of language acquisition can make to the field of SLA/applied linguistics and will be taken up in the concluding chapter.

In closing, a recurring theme throughout the opening chapters has been the entwined nature of language and social identities along with the crucial role of contexts. Not simply construed as isolated variables (gender, age, race, class, etc.) that unidirectionally influence speakers' discursive behavior, contexts, as Teun van Dijk says, are '(inter)subjective constructs designed and ongoingly updated in interaction by participants as members of groups and communities' (2008: x). As such, language is 'simultaneously individual and collective in nature' (Block, 2006: 37) in that our multiple speaker identities (wife, mother, professional educator, etc.) and surrounding circumstances are linked together in a dynamic relationship that defines how we position ourselves and are positioned by others.

Having said the above, it then follows that although my book is a personal account of my being and becoming a speaker of Japanese, I do not hold exclusive rights to the story. My narrative is essentially a joint production between me, the people I have interacted with before and after coming to Japan and the readers of this text. I am the principal character and author, yet my narrative has been informed, as Susanne Gannon explains, by 'memory, the body, photographs, other texts, and, most importantly, other people' (Gannon, 2006: 491). This postmodernist interpretation of how subjective experiences are constructed and understood through interactions with others is a basic tenet of autoethnography that, if well crafted, has the ability to engage readers in dialogue and reflection on their own life experiences. Through elaboration on diverse episodes in my life I offer to readers 'multiple places to stand in the story, multiple levels of emotionality and experience to which they can connect through their own experiences in the world' (Berger, 2001: 508). To this end, I adopt a more narrative style in the following chapters to depict the ebb and flow of social interactions with a variety of people, past and present, who play a significant role in the story of my being and becoming a speaker of Japanese.

Notes

1. My use of the term 'persona' here and elsewhere in the book, in lieu of identity, is meant to coincide with the notion often expressed by bi/multilingual speakers in reference to the enactment of their L2 speaking selves 'as a mask, performance, social role, or simply acting' (Pavlenko, 2006: 18).
2. For ease of readability the romanization used in this book generally follows the Hepburn style, but long vowels are marked by doubling the vowel rather than by a macron. All Japanese words, people and place names, phrases and longer segments are italicized, were translated by the author, and checked by a native speaker of Japanese. Unless otherwise noted, the real names of persons and places are used in subsequent chapters and dysfluencies in both the English and Japanese data excerpts have not been edited.

Part 2

Chapter 3
In the Beginning: Situating the Story

My Japanese as a second language autoethnography begins at a local supermarket in Japan, a place where my professional life as an English as a Foreign Language (EFL) university teacher and academic researcher, and my domestic life as a wife and mother have changed gears for the past 35 years. Against a backdrop of fruits, vegetables, fish and meat products I map out the development of my JSL abilities with occasional references to my past L2 lives in the United States before coming to Japan in 1975 at the age of 24. I was inspired to begin my story in this mundane site after recalling a segment from Dorinne Kondo's ethnography of a working-class Japanese community. Kondo gives the following emotive account of her reaction to seeing her self-reflection at the supermarket:

> Promptly at four p.m., the hour when most Japanese housewives do their shopping for the evening meal, I lifted the baby in her stroller and pushed her along ahead of me as I inspected the fish, selected the freshest looking vegetables, and mentally planned the meal for the evening. As I glanced into the shiny metal surface of the butcher's display case, I noticed someone who looked terribly familiar: a typical young housewife, clad in slip-on sandals and the loose, cotton shift called 'home wear' (*hōmu wea*), a woman walking with a characteristically Japanese bend to the knees and a sliding of the feet. Suddenly I clutched the handle of the stroller to steady myself as a wave of dizziness washed over me, for I realized I had caught a glimpse of nothing less than my own reflection. Fear that perhaps I would never emerge from this world into which I was immersed, inserted itself into my mind and stubbornly refused to leave, until I resolved to move into a new apartment, to distance myself from my Japanese home and my Japanese existence. (Kondo, 1990: 16–17)

Kondo's identity crisis speaks to the sometimes frightening aspects of living in a foreign culture where one's sense of self and the linguistic accoutrements used to maintain a stable self are constantly in a state of readjusting to the immediate environment.

Reconstructing oneself in a new language is fraught with identity discordance often described as a 'sense of doubleness' (Burck, 2005: 85) for individuals who shuttle between different ways of being and becoming bi/multilingual speakers. As explained in the previous chapter, examining the interconnectedness of identity and language of L2 populations has become a preoccupation of SLA research over the past decade, notably represented in the scholarly work of Bonny Norton (2000), Aneta Pavlenko (2007), Pavlenko *et al.* (2001) and David Block (2006). In the same vein, Leo van Lier comments that, 'We can only speak the second language when thoughts, identities and self are aligned. In the new culture and language that means the development of compatible identities that do not negate existing ones, nor erode the self' (van Lier, 2004: 128). This alignment procedure is a formidable task as the multiple identities within a single individual are a myriad assemblage of gendered, classed, racialized experiences accumulated before and after relocating to a new culture.

Mary Bucholtz's (1995) report on minority language members' attempts at passing into the dominant L1 community and how language was used to accommodate or challenge mainstream assumptions resonates with my own experiences in Japan. I arrived as a young, college-educated, upper-middle-class, white female from the United States who had lived predominantly in urban environments for 24 years. After marriage to a Japanese national, I found myself attempting to manage an identity as a suburban housewife whose position as a college instructor was deemed of lesser value than my ability to make *miso* (red bean paste) soup and *onigiri* (rice ball), raise children, participate in local neighborhood festivities and tend a vegetable garden. My language facilities hence had to switch on a daily basis from those deployed by professional women in a higher educational work setting in Japan to speech styles used among stay-at-home moms whose lives are devoted primarily to running a tidy household and managing their children's education. The different sociolinguistic roles I take up during the course of two days (Chapter 6) constitute a set of ongoing performances [cf. Judith Butler's (1993) thesis on gender as a performance] enacted to meet the particular exigencies at hand. This is not to say, however, that these enactments always achieve the desired results. More often than not I feel as if my L2 dysfluencies, although understandable, have ultimately prevented my becoming a legitimate member of mainstream Japanese society and that I will forever remain a *henna gaijin* (literally, strange foreigner, a convoluted descriptor for non-Japanese who speak Japanese very well and are quite knowledgeable of Japanese culture).

A Precarious Position

What sets my autoethnography apart from most immigrants' stories of alienation is that simply by virtue of my white, western,[1] English-speaking background I have enjoyed a relatively advantageous social position in

Japan. The word 'relatively' in the previous sentence signals a postmodernist slant on identity formations. That is to say, my social position is not a static entity but rather is constantly evolving in relation to surrounding circumstances – a situation wherein I juggle a long-term insider's perspective on certain aspects of Japanese life with my location as an outsider. An acute understanding of this precarious insider/outsider position has evolved vis-à-vis my awareness of the visibly disadvantaged position of people from countries (e.g. the Philippines, Korea, China, Southeast Asia, South America) who constitute a major portion of the foreign worker (*gaijin roodoosha*)[2] population in Japan (see Appendix 1). I am usually categorized as either *gaijin* or the more politically correct form, *gaikokujin* (foreigner), even though I officially hold permanent resident status. My legal surname is Simon since I am not a Japanese citizen, but I am usually referred to both professionally and privately as *Maeda-san* (my husband's surname). My students call me *Andy-sensei* (*Andy teacher*) or simply *Andy*, a naming practice that sets me apart from their Japanese teachers who instruct students to always address them with the title of 'teacher' attached to their last names, for example *Suzuki-sensei*. This formal naming practice is intended to prepare students for interviews and practice teaching experiences where deference to superiors is mandatory. Inevitably, however, when the stricter teachers are out of earshot, students refer to their teachers with cleverly invented nicknames.

While the term 'expatriate' may connote a chic cosmopolitanism, 'foreign worker', as in most countries, is not considered to be a prestigious social position, especially when the work involved is unskilled manual labor or jobs in the sex industry. In most cases, foreign workers do not intermarry with Japanese citizens[3] and live mainly in communities of the same cultural background. These marginalized groups need only acquire a survival level of Japanese to fit in at their workplaces, use public transportation or go shopping. This state of affairs has serious ramifications for those seeking long-term, more stable employment opportunities in light of the recent recession wherein foreign laborers are the first to be dismissed from part-time positions due to their lack of Japanese fluency. Since minority populations' L1s (e.g. Tagalog, Portuguese, Thai) are not considered to be prestigious foreign languages in Japan these individuals are expected to achieve a high level of Japanese proficiency if they intend to become full participating members of Japanese society.

'Even if You Can Speak Japanese?'

The disparate level in the amount of prestige accorded to one's native language and cultural background plays a significant role in how one is positioned and positions oneself in the host country [cf. Menard-Warwick's (2009) critical ethnography of immigrant ESL learners in the United States].

This last point is dramatically illustrated in the following conversational data segments from my ethnographic study (Simon-Maeda, 2009) of a group of international students at my university, focusing on how they construct their 'foreigner' status within Japanese society. In the first excerpt, Mahe, a Sri Lankan national who had been in Japan for approximately five years at the time and spoke fluent Japanese, is the main protagonist in an account of how he was treated rudely at a local train station. Mahe and some other students in my office were in the midst of talking about their feelings of sometimes feeling ostracized from mainstream society because of their cultural backgrounds, and when I directed the conversation to Mahe he proceeded to share his story. The transcript symbols are based on those developed by Gail Jefferson (Sacks *et al.*, 1974), and English translations are provided in double quotes below lines spoken in Japanese.

Excerpt 1 (10/27/04)

1	Andy:	And how about Mahe?
2	Mahe:	Yes.
3	Andy:	In Japan you feel [sometimes,]
4	Mahe:	[Yes,] sometime.
5	Andy:	Yeah, like when?
6	Mahe:	Like uh:, sometime uh, if I if we ask something, from the station
7		or something, they don't care,
8	Andy:	°E:!°
		"What!"
9	Mahe:	about us, because we are, foreigners.
10	Andy:	°*Un un.*° Even if you can speak Japanese?
		"Huh uh."
11	Mahe:	<u>Yes</u>. That I had a bad experience at that *Kariya* station before 2 months
		ago.
12		I asked in Japanese, uh: to *Nagoya*, uh:, *Nagoya no, un:,*
13		*Nagoya eki no: densya wa nan ji desuka to ittara, itte mittete.* ((pointing
		over his left shoulder with index finger of right hand in imitation
		of the train station employee))
		"When I asked what time is the train to *Nagoya* station he said go and
		look."
14	Andy:	E!
		"What!"
15	Mahe:	*Un. Asoko ni aru kara itte mitette.*
		"Yeah. It's over there so go and look."
16	Andy:	°E::°
		"Hmm."
17	Mahe:	*Sore dattara watashi wa <u>honto</u> ni okorutte.*
		"If that's the case then I would really get mad."

In the Beginning: Situating the Story 35

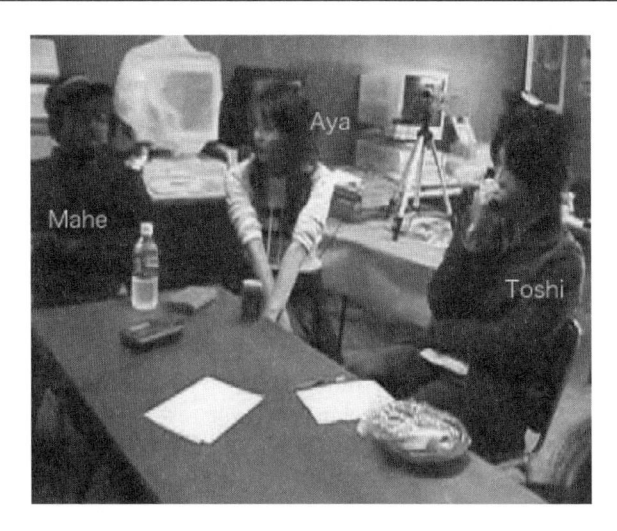

Figure 3.1 Mahe pointing to timetable

18	**Andy:**	O:::
		"Oh."
19	**Mahe:**	Maybe again I I I want to ex uh::, explain about that to him
20		but uh, that time I gave up.
21	**Andy:**	Yeah I know that feeling.
22	**Mahe:**	Yes.
23	**Andy:**	°E:: °That's really ba:d.
		"Hmm."
24	**Mahe:**	Yes.

Although in line 21 Andy (the author) supplied the empathetic, 'Yeah I know that feeling', my own irritation at sometimes being treated rudely is minimal compared to the experiences of Mahe whose marked visibility as a man of color is a constant source of his being racially discriminated against.[4] My interpretation of this incident is based on interviews and numerous informal conversations with Mahe over the two-year period of my study through which I learned of his many encounters with racist attitudes; a radically different situation from my life in Japan where my 'whiteness' usually acts as the prime catalyst of preferential treatment, irrespective of whether my Japanese is understandable or not. On the other hand, Mahe's 'blackness' overrode his Japanese fluency in the eyes and mind of the train station employee who had no reservation about making a rude remark, or at least what Mahe perceived to be rude, since he had asked in perfectly understandable Japanese about the train schedule and the employee could have easily enough told him the time of the next train.

The following excerpt was recorded on a different occasion, and the topic of donating blood at the Red Cross booth set up at our school festival a few days earlier had come up. Shu was a Chinese student at our university who often joined other international students in my office for informal discussions about their lives in Japan. Leading up to this segment was Mahe's explanation of how he had not been allowed to donate blood. Beginning at line 29, Shu gives his take on what happened to Mahe.

Excerpt 2 (11/10/04)

29	**Shu:**	It's a (chuckle), it's a *jinshu sabetsu* (chuckle).
		"racial discrimination"
30	**Andy:**	Yeah, that's what I was thinking too
31		it's a kind of discrimination.
31	**Mahe:**	I don't know, why. I didn't ask.
32	**Andy:**	It must be just for foreigners. So you're a foreigner,
		(while pointing to the non-Japanese members in the group)
		you're a foreigner
33		[I'm a foreigner,]
34	**Shu:**	[You had better,] you had better,
35	**Mahe:**	Why why do I ask.
36	**Shu:**	You had better not *kikanai hoo ga ii* (chuckle).
		"It's better not to ask."
37	**Mahe:**	Why?
38	**Risa:**	Un?
		"What?"
39	**Shu:**	Because you, (0.2) because (chuckle), (0.2) uh::
40	**Mahe:**	Black, >black black?< (pointing to back of right hand)
41	**Shu:**	>No no no no.<
42	**Andy:**	Yeah I know what he, I think I know what he wants to say.
43	**Shu:**	(chuckle) It's very difficult to to=

Figure 3.2 Mahe pointing to hand

44	**Mahe:**	=Explain?
45	**Shu:**	to say in public.
46	**Mahe:**	Why? What is the reason?
47	**Shu:**	>No no no no.<

I was concerned about Mahe's being refused at the blood donation center and phoned the *Nagoya* Red Cross headquarters to get the details of their vetting procedure for foreigners, since I had donated blood on a few occasions in the past without any problem. The explanation I received was that because Mahe was from Sri Lanka, a country with a high rate of infectious diseases and had not been in Japan for the required amount of time, he was refused. I relayed this information to Mahe to relieve his frustration, but what is significant about this segment is that Mahe had immediately pointed to the back of his hand and repeated 'black' three times, a gesture that exhibited his self-identification as a man of color and as someone who had been marginalized in the past on the basis of his outward appearance. An awareness of how other JSL speakers are positioned in Japan has been critical in helping me to reach an understanding, however partial, of how my own precarious position and L2 interactions are subject to prevalent attitudes toward foreigners.

As part of the same ethnographic study above, I visited the workplace of one of my Chinese international student participants, Haku, who was working part-time in a massage parlor with other Chinese students enrolled at different universities in *Nagoya*. Haku's Japanese ability at the time was good enough for her to talk to her Japanese clientele, some of whom I suspected were getting more than just a massage:

> I drive Haku into town to get a massage at her workplace. Jeez, a narrow staircase leads up to a sleezy lookin' massage parlor. The other girls are slender and good-looking Chinese girls (mostly students according to Haku) who greet me with smiles. Haku's wish to lose weight now makes sense in light of what she said before about becoming more attractive in order to get more customers. While I'm getting the massage and there's a silence I overhear conversations from the other stalls that border on sexual bantering with soft giggles from the girls. The floors are dirty and the lighting darker than would be normal for a regular massage place. Haku mentions that her plan now is to stay in Japan forever and that she may even marry a Japanese guy. The price for 30 mins. (¥4.000 when the girl is designated) is also suspiciously high, i.e. the customers may get more than just a massage if they like! despite Haku's comment in response to my asking her if there's no danger of a *henna hito* [strange person] coming in, especially because there's no male boss around, *'Koko wa majime na massaaji dakara'* [Because this place is a serious massage]. Uhm, I wonder about that. (fieldnotes, June 2005)

I often worried about Haku's safety and was relieved when she secured a company job in Tokyo after graduating from our university. During the two-year span of my ethnographic study of the international students I came to realize that having one's L2 abilities and worth as a human being acknowledged entails more than just being a fluent Japanese speaker. Issues of race and national background significantly impact on an individual's opportunities to interact with people in the local community that in turn affects the development of one's L2 proficiency. The exasperation felt by individuals like Mahe and Haku who exert an inordinate amount of energy in learning the language of their host country and behaving in what they perceive to be a socially acceptable mode only to be excluded from mainstream society has been discussed by David Block in reference to immigrant communities, that 'there is the grating experience of presenting an acceptable multimodal package (accent, cultural capital, dress, movement, etc.) but still being positioned as "foreign" by those who conform to the default assumed racial phenotype and overall physical appearance of the host community' (Block, 2000a: 42).

Before returning to my opening story, mention should be made of how in ethnographic studies, a comprehensive description of the research setting is a methodological strategy (see explanation of 'thick description' in Geertz, 1973) intended to provide as clear a picture as possible of the context under investigation from an emic perspective. The lengthy exposition above of the situation for foreign workers and other marginalized groups was intended to make the dissimilar contexts of their lives and mine stand out in stark relief. As such, although my autoethnography is a story of my personal JSL history, it is at the same time an interpersonal account infused with the stories and experiences of other JSL speakers. Herein lies one of the values of autoethnography; it 'allow[s] another person's world of experience to inspire critical reflection on your own' (Ellis & Bochner, 1996: 22). The postmodern concept of reflexivity as described in Chapter 1 has played an important role in helping me to maintain a critically balanced awareness of the intersubjectively constructed nature of my JSL life and how I have chosen to interpret it in relation to other JSL speakers' lives. Doing otherwise would have been tantamount to ignoring the fact that my story is not only about me but that it is primarily 'a means – in fact, the only means – of coming to know, however imperfectly, other aspects of social reality' (Davies, 2008: 254).

Getting by as Functional, Semiliterate and Privileged

My sociolinguistic situation is quite different from that of foreign workers and international students from non-western countries. During my early years in Japan I was not expected nor did I expect to become a highly fluent Japanese speaker, and I was constantly admonished to not use any

Japanese when teaching in my EFL classroom.[5] My cultural capital (Bourdieu, 1991), or rather my cultural 'currency, which indicates a liquidity of flow and an embodied dynamism' (Phipps, 2007: 60) was contingent primarily on my existence as a white, western, English-speaking person, and being an inarticulate Japanese speaker was an acceptable state of affairs. Needless to say, this English-as-a-prestige-language situation is especially beneficial for those individuals who local language school employers consider to be speakers of standard English from countries such as the United States, the United Kingdom and Australia. Although lacking EFL teacher credentials, these so-called native English speakers can often find teaching jobs while qualified EFL instructors from non-Center countries continue to face numerous obstacles in gaining a foothold in the EFL profession in Japan (see Simon-Maeda, 2004).

My Japanese husband, *Junji*, in the beginning handled many domestic chores that entail Japanese proficiency such as banking, making household purchases, managing our son's education, and so on. However, as years passed by and moving back permanently to the United States was no longer considered a life option, it became necessary for me to take on more responsibilities both in my private and professional lives with the appropriate language skills. As a consequence, my L2 facilities evolved in a particular way such that I now tend to define myself as a functional, semiliterate Japanese speaker.[6] My spoken Japanese and reading abilities are sufficient for everyday social activities and for the majority of my professional duties at my university workplace. Nevertheless, writing coherently in Japanese is an ongoing challenge made less daunting by software programs that provide the appropriate *kanji* (Chinese characters) when composing work-related reports or sending email messages to Japanese friends, students and colleagues. I can read and understand the general meaning of newspaper articles, official documents and literary pieces even though I might not always be able to retrieve the correct pronunciation of the *kanji*. For example, during a recent school break I decided to read a modern Japanese bestseller, *1Q84: Book 1* (Murakami, 2009), to see how I would manage, and I found that parts of the novel containing conversations between the characters were not problematic, for example:

青豆 (character's name):	ここで降ります。(*Koko de orimasu.*)
	I'll get off here.
運転手 (taxi driver):	領収書は？(*Ryooshuusho wa?*)
	Do you need a receipt?
青豆:	けっこうです。(*Kekkoo desu.*)
	That's okay.
運転手:	それはどうも (*Sore wa doomo.*)
	Thank you.

運転手: 風が強そうですから、気をつけて下さい。足を滑らせた
りしないように. (*Kaze ga tsuyosoo desu kara, ki o tsukete kudasai. Ashi o suberasetari sinai yoo ni.*)
Seems like there's a strong wind so be careful not to slip.
青豆: 気をつけます。 (*Ki o tsukemasu.*)
I'll be careful. (2009: 22)

In addition to the use of elementary *kanji* and the simple conversational style used in this particular segment, the situation of using a taxi in Japan is one I am very familiar with. On the other hand, passages containing more difficult *kanji* used for more esoteric or technical language, or in descriptions of historical events in Japan required a dictionary and/or kanji reference book, although I sometimes skipped the use of these 'affordances' (see Lantolf, 2000 and also van Lier, 2004) because I felt I got the general meaning. For example, in the following passage, one character explains something to another character about a man called 深田 (*Fukada*):

時が径過するにつれ、中間的な存在が受けれられる余地はどんどん狭くなっていった。やがて深田も、どちらの立場を選ばなくてはならないところに最終てきに追い込まれた。その頃にはかれも、1970年代の日本には革命を起こす余地も気運もないことをおおむね悟っていた。
(Murakami, 2009: 228)

Toki ga keika suru ni tsure, chukanteki na sonzai ga ukererareru yochi wa dondon semakunatte itta. Yagate, Fukada mo, dochira no tachiba o erabanakute wa naranai tokoro ni saishuuteki ni oikomirareta. Sono goro ni wa kare mo, 1970 nen dai no Nihon ni wa kakumei o okosu yoochi mo kiun mo nai koto o oomune o satotteita.

As time went by, it became increasingly difficult for him to maintain a half-way existence. *Fukada* also was finally forced to choose a position. Around that time, he was also generally aware that in Japan in the 1970s there was no way or possibility for a revolution to take place.

Typing in the above sentences of the original *kanji* from the book passages followed by the *hiragana* that I supplied here for pronunciation purposes took approximately 45 minutes, including interruptions to go to the kitchen to wash the rice for dinner, put it in the *suihanki* (rice cooker), give the dog a snack, wash some dishes left over from lunch, briefly chat with my husband and dig out the *kanji* reference book from under the rubble on my desk. While writing this section, *Junji* happened to come into my study/bedroom and I asked him to read two *kanji* that I could not recognize. He then sarcastically commented, '*Ee, sonna muzukashii hon o yondeiru no?*' (Huhh, you're reading such a difficult book?) Although I usually try to avoid asking either *Junji* or my son *Yuji*, whose level of friendly cooperation depends on their mood at the moment, there are times when their help is indispensable for reading important documents (tax returns, salary and tenure conditions, physical exam results and so on) that contain a certain amount of difficult *kanji*.

'Are You Sure There's No Mistake?'

While intimate friends and relatives who are well aware of how long I have lived in Japan occasionally make sarcastic remarks about my dysfluency, I more often than not receive unwarranted praise from casual acquaintances or people I meet for the first time when I display even a modicum of Japanese spoken or written proficiency. In addition to stereotypical physical features (tall, blonde, blue-eyed), the image of the westerner, as popularized in the media, is someone incapable of mastering Japanese beyond simple greetings and who flagrantly violates Japanese customs. Since Japanese is popularly perceived by Japanese and non-Japanese alike to be a difficult (read: exotic) language, individuals like me attempting to make socialization inroads often find themselves in a state of sociolinguistic exasperation. One memorable incident (fieldnotes, July 13, 2004) that exemplifies this situation occurred at a local bookstore that supplies the test-taking practice materials for the *ikkyuu* (top level) Japanese proficiency test. When I brought the materials up to the cash register the clerk said, '*Machigai ga nai desuka? Nihonjin demo gougaku dekinai yo*' (Are you sure there's no mistake? Even Japanese cannot pass this level). Invoking a *nihonjinron*[7] discourse, the clerk thus positioned me on the periphery of Japanese society. After a few months of vigorous studying, I passed the test and was tempted to bring my diploma to the store to show the clerk but later decided this would be a waste of my time. My fieldnotes made during the time I was going through practice booklets (as I had heard that learning 'how' to take the test was crucial for passing) in preparation for taking the test describe my meta-awareness of certain literacy practices that I invoked in order to approach this difficult task and also my reflections on the implications of passing the test:

> For test items involving recognition of *kanji* imbedded in sentences, I find myself concentrating on getting the whole sense of the sentence in order to figure out the individual *kanji*. In many cases, I recognize where I've seen the *kanji* before, for example, official school documents, newspapers, etc., and that these *kanji* were learned through repeated 'contextualization' and not 'memorization'. This is different from what outsiders often criticize the Japanese foreign language educational system for; rote, de-contextualized learning. I recall that when I first arrived in 1975 my predecessors, other gaijin who were already here and who spoke Japanese, inspired me to take Japanese lessons and

study independently. After marriage, however, the books were put away and there no longer seemed to be any real motive to becoming proficient since I was managing to get by on my dysfluent Japanese. Deciding to take the exam after almost 30 years in Japan involved no clear motive other than academic curiosity to see how I would do. For an older 'established' person like me it's no big deal if I pass or not, but for immigrants whose livelihood in Japan depends on proficiency it's another set of issues. (fieldnotes composite, August–December 2004)

Although my score was just barely over the passing line, I am able to list this accomplishment on my CV since the test is recognized to be quite difficult. I consider the *ikkyuu* level certificate I received from the testing organization to be a textual reification of my being and becoming a Japanese speaker. At the same time, however, the 'real' test of my Japanese proficiency is how well I manage everyday interactions in different spheres of social activity. Difficult literary pieces, newspaper articles or official documents continue to be challenging, and yet I nevertheless feel linguistically confident in my daily round of routines, such as trips to the supermarket where I feel most like a Japanese *okusan* (housewife) with all the sociolinguistic components involved in being a 'good' Japanese housewife. I can read most of the food labels written in either *kanji, romaji or katakana* (three types of Japanese scripts), politely greet or chit chat with Japanese acquaintances from my *kinjo* (neighborhood) who I might happen to meet, dutifully use my *ecobaggu* (ecologically correct, nonplastic shopping bag), silently count out Japanese money after hearing the *reji no obasan* (middle-aged female cashier) tell me how much to pay and taking a quick look at the amount on the digital screen above the register to make sure what I heard was correct, think about the *miso nikomi udon* (noodles, chicken and vegetables in a red bean paste broth) meal I will prepare for dinner, after which I will watch Japanese TV programs with my son, briefly chat with my Japanese husband in Japanese, fill the *ofuro* (bath), lay out the *futon* (bedding) on the *tatami* (straw mat) and fall asleep, but not without thinking about what I will put in my son's *bentoo* (lunchbox) the next morning. In this short description of my daily life, I inserted Japanese vocabulary not merely as linguistic encoding devices but because, as numerous testimonies from bilingual speakers attest to, the English translations do not quite fit into my L2 sociocultural repertoire and cannot adequately impart the depth of meaning embedded in the Japanese items. Anna Wierzbicka puts it this way:

> Shifting from one language to another is not like shifting from one code to another to express a meaning expressible equally well in both these codes. Often, the very reason why a bilingual speaker shifts

from one language to another is that the meaning they want to express 'belongs' to the other language. (Wierzbicka, 2004: 102)

The above notion concerning the difficulty for bi/multilingual speakers to explain a particular cultural phenomenon in a different language was recently brought to my attention at a get-together with a group of foreign wives and their Japanese husbands at a local restaurant. In the midst of an American wife's explanation in English concerning her traditional Japanese neighborhood to one of the Japanese husbands, a fluent English speaker, the woman suddenly switched to Japanese because, as she said, '*Eigo de setsumei dekinai*' (I can't explain in English) (fieldnotes, March 6, 2010). In discussions among foreign wives who have spent a significant amount of time in Japan, there are numerous instances of switching from one language to another, especially when talking about matters concerned with L2 parenting, a topic I will elaborate on in Chapter 4.

After 35 years of living in Japan, I increasingly find myself worrying when I go to the supermarket in my hometown in Massachusetts during summer vacations that figuratively speaking my Japanese *kappoogi* (Japanese style apron) fringe is showing and that I may not be doing things the right way or interacting with the cashier in a sociopragmatically appropriate American English-speaking style. I have even caught myself back-channeling with *hai* (yes) or *soo da ne* (right), and gesturing in a Japanese fashion during conversations with people in the United States. This unsettling metacognitive awareness of my Japanese/English codeswitching[8] proclivities is exacerbated by comments from old friends and relatives who I meet during trips back home who say, 'You speak English with a Japanese accent, short and abrupt' or 'Why are you continually nodding your head while I'm talking to you?' On these occasions, I feel like a stranger in my own country not completely comfortable with admitting to myself and others that I am an expatriate whose family loyalties, community obligations and professional associations no longer exist exclusively within the sociospatial domain of the United States which I, and some of my expatriate American friends in Japan, jokingly refer to as 'the old country' – a bittersweet joke wrought with feelings of having lost a part of how we once defined ourselves as human beings. This sense of displacement also permeates the stories of Charlotte Burck's immigrant participants who describe how 'bits' (Burck, 2005: 90) were missing from their new lives due to constraining sociolinguistic situations. This is particularly true for those who do not immigrate freely but rather are forced to relocate in order to secure a sustainable income not possible in one's home country.

On a day in the summer of 2004 when I decided to officially start documenting my JSL autobiography, which evolved as an offshoot of my larger ethnography of bi/multilingual speakers in Japan, trying to locate a point in my life in Japan from which to start, I happened to be waiting in the supermarket checkout line and noticed two Eurasian-looking young men animatedly speaking Portuguese and receiving curious glances from other customers. I can easily identify people of mixed ethnic backgrounds, not only when I am close enough to be able to hear them speaking their native language, but also from a distance because they often resemble my son, *Yuji*, who is also of a mixed racial background (Japanese/Anglo-American). With physical features and linguistic/nonlinguistic mannerisms different from their Japanese counterparts, young men and women from South American countries, mainly Chile, Peru and Brazil, have either just arrived or are the sons and daughters of settled immigrants in Japan working at the many small factories in the area where I live on the outskirts of *Nagoya*. These children and their families, like many immigrants worldwide, are often subjected to both overt and covert racist treatment in their host country, and I am always reminded of how my JSL life has evolved in ways different from those individuals who, because of their racial/ethnic background, are denied the same privileges I receive simply by virtue of my skin color, nationality and native language. It should be noted, however, that while it would be a gross overstatement to depict Japan as a racist nation it would be equally fallacious to present Japan as a country that wholeheartedly welcomes foreigners (see Notes 2, 3, 4 and also see Arudou Debito's collection of 'Japanese only' signs, see Figure 3.3 below, that overtly discriminate against foreigners from certain countries <http://www.debito.org>

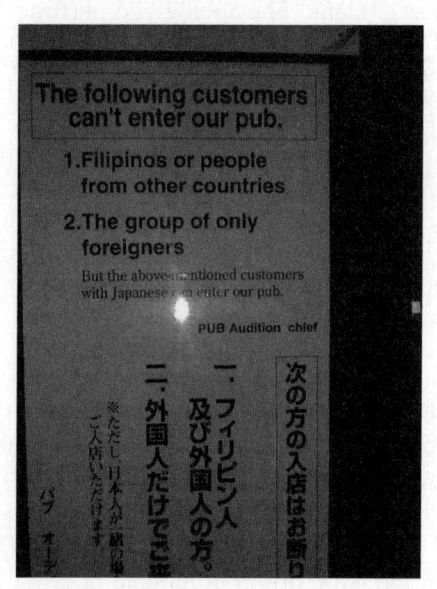

Figure 3.3 Pub sign

In the Beginning: Situating the Story

To this day, I am not completely comfortable with my self/other description as an expatriate mainly because this term smacks of elitism, excludes those who are labeled 'foreign workers', and is a rather flat descriptor of the multilayered sociolinguistic life I lead. This awareness of my positionality vis-à-vis Japanese sociocultural norms concerning foreigners has not been left unexamined or reassessed. A postmodernist interpretation of life and language situations entails recognition of the vagaries of human existence and our modes of resistance or accommodation to everyday circumstances. Consider the following incident (fieldnotes, January 13, 2005) at the local immigration office. When my turn came to receive the necessary documents for a reentry permit, a necessary document for non-Japanese when leaving Japan, the official who was handling the paperwork checked with another nearby official to see if I was the one who needed the form by asking, '*Kono hito ni shorui o wataseba ii?*' (Should I give the documents to this person?). She then proceeded to plop the form on the counter in front of me with a disgruntled look on her face. Usually, in a Japanese bank, post office and other public or official places a certain level of formality pervades interactions with customers; however, the immigration officer's use of the less polite '*kono hito*' in lieu of '*kono kata*' coupled with the way she plopped the form down on the counter immediately positioned me in a subordinate position. After I finished the paperwork, I decided to let her know that I thought it was rude to substitute '*hito*' for '*kata*' and added that non-Japanese residents deserve the same respect accorded to Japanese citizens.[9] She apologized perfunctorily, and I left the scene fearing that my deportation papers would be in the mail the next day. I asked my husband later if he thought I over-reacted, but he concurred with my opinion and said that indeed I had been addressed in a rude manner. My husband has witnessed on numerous occasions the ways in which I am treated as an outsider, particularly in situations involving my noncitizen status in Japan for example at airport immigration control, the local ward office, and so on. These incidents are always an awakening to how privilege is context dependent and intimately connected with linguistic practices on both the producing and receiving end of social exchanges.

A Sea of Languages

I will now continue my narrative moving back and forth in time in order to illustrate how I have managed to deftly surf across a sea of languages using the sociocultural and linguistic tools at hand to fashion my second language speaker identity. My father was also a transplanted person (see Figure 3.4), and although he was 14 years old when he emigrated from Lebanon to the United States, his English remained heavily accented throughout his life.

Figure 3.4 Immigration photo

I recall being ashamed to have friends meet my father not only because of his dysfluent English but also because of his socially inappropriate profession as a bookie. This piece of my family background may have contributed to my always connecting poor English ability with a lower stratum of US society. I have often wondered how my son feels about having a nonnative Japanese-speaking parent and how our family interactions both influence and are influenced by my L2 speech behavior; points I will take up in detail in Chapter 4. Most of the runners (people who take horse bets) in my father's gambling operation were Lebanese acquaintances of my father, and I associated the sound of them speaking Arabic with criminality, the main theme of my recurring nightmare of our house being raided by the police, as it once was when I was a small child. The negative appraisal of my father's linguistic and social character changed somewhat when our immigrating Lebanese cousins spent time at our house before moving on to their new lives in the States. I was a teenager by then, and my cousins, unlike my father who arrived at a young age and never had the opportunity to attend secondary school in Lebanon, also spoke French, the language of Lebanon's one-time colonizer. My cousins were handsome, possessed a certain European charm and sophistication, and helped me with my high school French homework. The heady smell of their Gaulois cigarettes and expensive cologne added to the Middle Eastern allure that I had come to appreciate belatedly through my father's ethnic cooking. The words kibbee, humus, tabuli and arak remain fixed in my mind, and I take Mikhail Bakhtin's (1986) exhortation literally to heart (and stomach) when he says, 'Each word tastes of the context and contexts in which it has lived its socially charged life' (Bakhtin, 1981: 293). Antoine, Éli and Georges taught me Arabic swearwords and other phrases useful for shock-value, and to meet the remaining members of my father's family I travelled to Lebanon after graduation from high school only to become violently ill with a nasty stomach ailment and totally dismayed at the sexist attitudes of Middle Eastern men. Although I enrolled in an Arabic course in college, I found the learning experience dry and bereft of the luscious Lebanese experience I had had at home, and to my regret I never became a fluent Arabic speaker.

In my neighborhood in New Bedford (a middle-size city located in the southeastern part of Massachusetts) where I grew up there was a symbolic line of societal demarcation drawn between established Anglo families, many of whom were descendants of prosperous whaling sea captains who worked in the government and professional buildings downtown, and Portuguese immigrants from the Azore Islands who were the mainstay of the local fishing industry. Because of my present 'outsider' status in Japan, whenever I visit my hometown I become increasingly aware of the social stratification processes that operate according to race or national origin. During the course of my study of bi/multilingual speakers (Simon-Maeda, 2009), I wrote the following reflective fieldnotes after attending two separate events in my hometown during my summer vacation:

> August 7, 2005, Yacht Club, New Bedford At the annual yacht club event in the suburbs, most of the attendees were upper-class white people and the servers were people of color (most likely Cape Verdean or African-American). The white crowd speaks that 'preppy' variety while the servers speak the downtown variety, just a few miles apart geographically but light years away socially. This scene is quite different from last week's Portuguese Festival attended by mostly dark-skinned types talking with that 'special' New Bedford accent that I always associated with the tough crowd when I was in high school. I noticed that the mayor (white, upper class) in his opening speech for the

festival made a token remark, 'the Portuguese community has made a significant contribution to our city!' Yeah, right, after generations of discrimination they have finally managed to move up a few notches into a higher socioeconomic stratum. Whenever I'm in U.S. cities with a large immigrant population I now notice more than I did before a cacophony of different languages and accents, e.g. taxi drivers in New York, maids in hotels, porters at the airport, workers at WalMart, but the language of power is still a white, privileged English variety.

As mentioned above, my family's wealth was accrued through nefarious means, and even though I was formally presented as a debutante in our local Franco-American community, my 'cultural capital' (Bourdieu, 1991) remained on shaky ground in contrast to our city's established Anglo society. At the time, I did not consider my French language ability to be a prestigious part of my social self and only something that guaranteed a problem-free passage through the foreign language requirements in high school and college. Moreover, my winning top honors in Latin did not procure the desired in-group membership reserved for the more attractive girls in my high school. My success with Latin was no doubt due to my French background that later served me well when I majored in Spanish and French as part of the requirements for my Romance Languages bachelors degree in college. My mother was the descendant of French-Canadian immigrants to the United States, and I have fond memories of being taken care of by my Franco-American grandparents, eating savory French meat pies, listening incredulously to stories of how there was some Saskatchewan Indian blood in our veins, being the butt of Canuck jokes, and excelling academically at my Franco-American grammar school despite the torture inflicted by Catholic nuns whose class management tactics involved rapping 'naughty' students' knuckles with wooden yardsticks. In the summer of my junior year of high school, I participated in a six-week French course in Lausanne, Switzerland where I discovered that my Canuck dialect was lower on the language hierarchy scale than classical French. However, this did not prevent my skipping classes with other 'naughty' students to socialize with local French boys who were not at all concerned with our French proficiency level.

Choosing Spanish in college as a second language elective course was also the result of my brief fling with 1970s anti-establishment student movements. My radical boyfriend had convinced me that being able to speak Spanish would be an inroad to organizing Puerto Rican immigrants in our fight against social discrimination in Boston. A summer language program and homestay experience in Mexico enhanced my Spanish fluency; another addition to the sea of languages I had been swimming in since birth. During a college semester I tutored ESL students, the majority of whom were Spanish-speaking immigrants living in Boston's low-income housing projects, and I became increasingly attuned to the sociopolitical nature of language learning and teaching. This experience subsequently influenced my decision to pursue a master's degree in TESOL (Teaching English to Speakers of Other Languages) at the University of Arizona in Tucson. To fulfill my graduate school practice-teaching requirements, I taught ESL on a volunteer basis to Mexican immigrants at a local adult education center. Although the sociohistorical backgrounds of Puerto Ricans in Boston and Hispanics in Arizona differ in many aspects, I learned that both groups share the exasperating dilemma of being denied access to mainstream society due to their lack of English proficiency [see Menard-Warwick (2009) for a fine-grained analysis of the similarities and differences between and within immigrant communities and how a conflation of racial/ethnic L2 identities into a monolithic category of 'immigrant' leads to ineffectual educational policies]. It was my developing awareness of what it means to be marginalized due to one's sociocultural and linguistic background that would later bring to the fore my privileged status in Japan that stands out in stark contrast to the situation of other minority groups.

After completing my Master's degree, I returned to Boston and taught ESL at a language school for a short period. During this time, I kept in contact (by air mail letters predating email by a quarter of a century) with some international students from Japan who I had befriended at the University of Arizona, and the idea of going to Japan to teach EFL started to brew in my brain. I became acquainted with the language school's Japanese instructor, a native of *Nagoya*, who kindly offered to help me find a college-level EFL teaching job. These contacts constituted the starting point of a series of major life-changing events, as I will describe in the next chapter.

Summary

As I read over and reflect on what I have written above concerning my early encounters with foreign languages (French, Portuguese, Spanish, Arabic), it appears that my L2 and additional language experiences were influenced by particular sociolinguistic events that significantly impacted on my subsequent Japanese language-learning proclivities as much as, or even more than, an intrinsic motivation to master a second language through any kind of formal learning arrangement. Although I diligently studied Japanese in a formal classroom situation and independently on my own for several years after my arrival, my informal learning contexts are ultimately what I consider to be the crucial factors in my JSL development. In the beginning, Japanese seemed like a mystery to me and I was at first not expected by others to become a fluent speaker; however, I never felt that Japanese would be impossible to learn. I attribute my linguistic confidence primarily to my having been immersed in a sea of languages for many years prior to my arrival in Japan and because I knew intuitively that a foreign language is not necessarily something acquired incrementally in a formal learning situation but is rather one of the many social interactionist tools deployed on the fly in naturalistic settings for joking, seducing, expressing one's anger and so on (see Pavlenko, 2006). This is not to say, however, that foreign language instruction is a total waste of time and money, but rather that traditional pedagogical practices often do not take into full account the emergent[10] properties of language acquisition. Formal foreign language classrooms can at best only provide a simulated context of L2 interactions because, as ZhaoHong Han reports, 'the classroom provides limited and restrictive practice opportunities' (Han, 2004: 161). Citing numerous SLA researchers' studies of the effects of foreign language pedagogy, Han concludes that formal instruction 'occurring at the right time, may serve to prevent fossilization. Nevertheless, it is also important to keep in mind that the influence of instruction is mitigated by a variety of linguistic and psycholinguistic variables' (Han, 2004: 162). Among these variables, a learner's 'personal agenda' (Han, 2004: 162) is a formidable entity that a prepackaged pedagogical setting cannot easily accommodate. For an 'advanced' learner like me who is immersed daily in an L2 environment and who plans to remain permanently in Japan, a decontextualized language classroom is not the best place to further develop my JSL abilities. The appropriate learning situation is more complex, as Alene Moyer explains:

> If issues of community and belonging are central to late language development, we must appreciate what it means to learn another language at a point in life when linguistic and cultural identities are already well developed. This has profound implications for the extent to which immigrant language acquirers may desire native-level status in L2. If so, ultimate attainment research should explore individual adaptations to the new language and culture from the viewpoint of social, economic, political and educational realities. (Moyer, 2004: 146–147)

As developed in this and previous chapters, a postmodernist approach to analyzing the interconnectedness of identity formations and language learning includes a reflective accounting of how I am located as a *gaikokujin*, to name only one (albeit a crucial one) of the many realities impacting on my JSL development. My Japanese-speaking abilities were and continue to be fashioned to fit my immediate social contexts that in turn have become redefined in new and unique ways. Teun van Dijk describes this process as a dynamic one in which

> [contexts] are constructed for each new communicative situation and then ongoingly *updated* and *adapted* to (the subjective interpretation of)

the current constraints of the situation, including the immediately preceding discourse and interaction. In other words, contexts develop 'ongoingly' and 'on line,' that is in parallel with interaction and (other) thoughts. (van Dijk, 2008: 18, italics in original)

This chapter also highlighted the influence of diverse interactions with immigrants (my Lebanese and French-Canadian relatives, Portuguese nationals in my hometown, Puerto Ricans in Boston, Mexicans in Arizona, foreign laborers and international students in Japan) and how I now find myself in a similar yet in some respects very different situation than people who refashion their social and linguistic selves in a new country. The reports of L2 scholars (Kellman, 2000; Kinginger, 2003; Koven, 1998, 2001; Lantolf & Pavlenko, 2001; Mori, 1997; Ogulnick, 1998, 2000; Siegal, 1996) and testimonies of bi/multilingual literary figures (Conrad, 1912/1996; Hoffman, 1989) attest to how

> patterns of social and cultural behaviors (such as domination, control, and the impact of silence) are revealed in the process of language learning; how people negotiate their life experiences through different languages; how language relates to the ways people define their identities and maintain subcultures; and how the process of language learning interacts with psychological, emotional, sociocultural, and political realities. (Ogulnick, 2000: 3)

The next chapter highlights the emotional realities of my JSL life and how romance, marriage and parenting experiences have provided the underlying impetus for developing new ways of articulating my affective states in Japanese and a renewed sense of how my linguistic selves, while being a personal construction, are at the same time highly dependent on cultural models of intimacy and family affiliations.

Notes

1. Throughout the book I use 'white', 'western', 'Asian', and so on, to designate racial/ethnic groups. However, I acknowledge that these terms are not fixed categories and that there is immeasurable variation within different racial/ethnic communities. David Block discusses the distinctions that have been made by researchers between 'race' and 'ethnicity' that are 'sometimes conflated with nationality and quite often conflated with skin colour' (Block, 2007: 28). Recognizing the problematic nature of making distinctions (or not) I have nevertheless chosen to use 'race' most often in my book. Also, the use of 'culture' in different chapters is based on what Atkinson (1999) refers to as 'postmodernist-influenced concepts ... [that] indicate the shard perspective that cultures are anything but homogeneous, all-encompassing entities' (Atkinson, 1999: 626–627).
2. Yoshio Sugimoto reports that the huge influx of foreign workers over the last two decades served to fill jobs in Japan that were described as 'the three undesirable Ks (or Ds in English): *kitanai* (dirty), *kitsui* (difficult), and *kiken*

(dangerous)' (Sugimoto, 2003: 204). Sugimoto adds that the 'media tend to play up crimes committed by foreigners, fueling xenophobic apprehensions in the community. Considerable evidence suggests that crime statistics on foreigners in Japan are distorted and inflated' (Sugimoto, 2008: 205).

3. The tendency to either eschew or desire a particular interracial marriage partner exists on both sides of racial divisions around the globe. Even within intra-racial marriages, there is a range of factors (e.g. socioeconomic status, educational background, physical attraction) that influence one's preferences. However, Japan's particularly negative view of interracial marriage has been noted by Japan scholars such as Takeyuki Tsuda who summarizes the attitudes of Japanese informants in his ethnographic study of *nikkeijin* as follows:

> [E]ven my Japanese interviewees who expressed the most tolerant attitudes and were willing to accept a permanent immigrant population in Japan as an unavoidable necessity were notably less tolerant about the prospect of racial intermixture between Japanese and foreigners, especially among *miuchi* (family and relatives). In other words, contamination of Japanese culture on a national level is begrudgingly tolerated, but not the contamination of one's own 'pure' bloodline. (Tsuda, 2003: 129, italics in original)

4. This newspaper article exemplifies the racialized treatment of people of color often experienced in Japan: 'The Saitama District Court has ordered a real estate agency and an employee to pay 500,000 yen in compensation to an Indian man for asking him the color of his skin when he phoned to rent a home, court officials said on Wednesday. An employee of Nikken Juhan persistently asked the man, 'What color is your skin?' and 'Is your skin an ordinary color?' When the plaintiff asked what 'an ordinary color' means, the woman responded, 'It is a color like Japanese', according to the ruling' ('Racist question', *Asahi Shimbum*, 2003: 20).

5. In my narrative study of the professional identity construction of female educators in Japan, one of the participants included the following remark in an account of her college job interview:

> Julia: 'Well, we expect you to be 100% American when you come here'. [Laughter]. And what does it mean to be 100% American? ... In fact, what they did, something they liked [Julia's Japanese fluency], but they didn't want to face that up front, that, yes, they knew that my Japanese would be a real advantage, but they didn't want that up front at all, like, 'On the surface we want you to be 100% American'. (Simon-Maeda, 2004: 420–421)

6. There are numerous and often conflicting definitions and assessments of bilingualism and multilingualism depending on the language components (receptive/productive skills) under examination. Traditionally, two broad distinctions have been made for research purposes between 'individual bilingualism and societal bilingualism' (Baker, 1996: 4–5) operating at different levels of ability and use; however, this dichotomization cannot fully address the multilayered complexities of bi/multilingual speakers' experiences. Recent studies of linguistic practices in bi/multilingual communities [see e.g. Bayley & Schecter's 2003 edited volume and the forerunner seminal articles by Ochs, (1986) and Ochs & Schieffelin (1995)] have adopted a language socialization perspective that 'shifts our gaze from bilingual children's internalization of a set of abstract grammatical rules and sociolinguistic norms, to how they *use*

their languages in a diversity of interactions and negotiations with interlocutors whose own language socialization is also ongoing' (Luykx, 2003: 41, italics in original). Likewise, my own Japanese/English bilingualism does not fit into any neat categorization scheme (balanced, coordinate, additive, etc.) and rather, as I describe in the main text, is in a constant state of becoming in order to deal with the diverse sociolinguistic exigencies of my life in Japan. Thus, I have coined the term 'functional, semi-literate', which I feel best describes my current state of (dys)fluency.

7. *Nihonjinron* is a popular stereotyping of Japanese culture defined by its 'uniqueness in terms of qualities such as harmony, cooperation, vertical social structure, and an emphasis on intuition and non-verbal communication; all characteristics which, supposedly, are found only in Japan' (Fawcett, 2001: 75).

8. Although conversation and discourse analyses of bilingual speech traditionally differentiate between codemixing and codeswitching, for purposes of consistency throughout the book I use codeswitching to broadly describe speakers' syntactical alternation between different language systems including the insertion and combination in either the L1 or L2 items such as words, affixes and clauses within a single utterance.

9. The following newspaper article shows how antiforeigner sentiment can also spill over onto discriminatory actions against Japanese citizens as well:

> Kawaguchi, Saitama
>
> Red-faced police released a woman they had arrested for not carrying her passport after she proved to be Japanese, police officials said. The officials said local police had deemed that she was non-Japanese because she looked like a foreigner and did not say anything in response to questions in Japanese. The local police were apologetic about the mistake. 'We caused great trouble to the woman. We'll take measures to prevent a recurrence', the head of Kawaguchi Police Station said. At around 7:40 p.m. on Saturday, three officers spoke to a 28-year-old woman walking on a street in Kawaguchi, and asked her name and nationality because she looked like a woman from Southeast Asia, according to the officials. After saying, 'I'm Japanese', she refused to talk to the officers, who took her to the police station. After she refused to respond to the questions officers asked her in Japanese, police seemed that she was a foreigner. The officers confirmed that she was not carrying her passport, and arrested her for violating the Immigration Control and Refugee Recognition Law. She subsequently wrote down the name of one of her family members on a sheet of paper. One of the officers contacted her family and found out she is a Japanese national. Police quoted the woman's mother as telling them, 'My daughter wouldn't talk to anybody she doesn't know'. ('Red-faced police', *Mainichi Shimbun*, February 28, 2006: 2)

10. Leo van Lier explains that the emergent nature of language comprises the ways that: 'languages shift and change, either through internal processes, or through external pressures and social processes.... Like culture, it is contested, open to processes of inclusion and exclusion, prescribed and proscribed patterns of use, permeated by value judgments, markers of identity, and signs of success' (van Lier, 2004: 85).

Chapter 4
In the Middle: Love, Marriage, Family

Although references to daily interactions that have influenced my L2 development were made throughout previous chapters, this chapter will present more intimate details of my JSL life. Personal experiences are packed with emotional ups and downs, and Pavlenko's (2006) edited volume of studies concerning the relationship between bi/multilingual speakers' affective states and language use attests to the nontrivial role of humor, passion, fear and so on in second language development. Using one language or another for a particular emotional moment is not only a personal choice but is also a sociocultural phenomenon. My romantic relationship and subsequent marriage to my husband along with the addition of our son to our family represent emotionally laden slices of life that have significantly influenced the development of my Japanese repertoire. Inevitably, the emotional impact of these events is 'lost in translation' [see Hoffman's (1989) memoir, *Lost in Translation*], and I find it difficult to satisfactorily describe in English what my private life in Japan has been like for the past three decades. As Besemeres explains, '[F]eelings are shaped by concepts specific to a particular language .... Outside of that language, it becomes harder to talk about these feelings, to have them recognized' (Besemeres, 2006: 36). The difficulty of conveying in my L1 the emotional impact of events in my JSL life resonates with current treatises concerning the interrelatedness of emotions and language. That is to say, 'language has an effect on memory retrieval, with memories preferentially retrieved in the language in which they were encoded' (Schrauf & Durazo-Arvizu, 2006: 306). Thus, the emotional intensity of the events described below and the language in which they were experienced (Japanese) are permanently linked together in my autobiographical memory.

As outlined in the opening chapters of this volume, it is theoretically and methodologically unsound to analyze my JSL development in a vacuum without referring to social interactions I have had within different 'communities of practice' (CoP) (Wenger, 1998). There are sociohistorical reasons for why I have managed to become a competent Japanese speaker while the two *nikkeijin* (second-generation Japanese) at the supermarket in

Chapter 3 are not always provided with the sociolinguistic means to gain more access to mainstream Japanese society.[1] Marginalized on the basis of cultural background or racial origin, *nikkeijin* and other minority groups in Japan are in a double bind wherein they need to attain a high level of Japanese proficiency in order to fit in but yet are denied the opportunity to interact more fully with Japanese people. Contrary to the L2 development of disadvantaged groups in Japan, my Japanese fluency is significantly interrelated with my situatedness[2] as a permanent resident in a relatively prestigious social position, which is both affected by and contributes to my level of participation in different, overlapping communities of practice. The following sections delineate major life events in my 'constellation of CoPs' (Wenger, 1998: 126) that have impacted on the discursive enactment of my Japanese-speaking persona.

Love at First Sight and Sound

A key factor in the development of my JSL trajectory was my romantic relationship and subsequent marriage to a Japanese man, *Junji*, who I met soon after my arrival in Japan. As mentioned in the previous chapter, the Japanese instructor at the language school in Boston helped me search for college-level EFL teaching positions, and after I secured a job at a women's college in *Nagoya* she handed me the *meishi* (calling card) of her friend, *Taeko*, who would help me get around. *Taeko* introduced me to *Junji*, who I met in the spring of 1975 and eventually married in 1981.

Before relocating to Japan, I had previously taught ESL to Japanese men in the United States and considered them on the whole to be quite amiable, but 'hot' was certainly not a descriptor I would have ascribed at the time to this particular group. Moreover, interracial dating was not part of my personal history, and I never imagined that I would be sexually attracted to an Asian man.[3] Because my hometown, New Bedford, was an international fishing port, many ships from Asian countries arrived at the docks and their crew could often be seen strolling the downtown streets. Needless to say, an Anglo woman accompanied by an Asian sailor was not held in high esteem, and I often felt, what I would later learn is described in Japanese as *seken*[4] (literally, the world), the ever-watching, scrutinizing gaze of society upon *Junji* and I when we returned together to New Bedford and walked around the city. The announcement of our *kokusai kekkon* (international marriage) after a five-year dating period ruffled a few feathers on both sides of the Pacific Ocean, and I distinctly remember my father's comment when I showed him photos of our *Shinto* wedding ceremony in Japan that he was unable to attend, 'Are you really married?' As a church-going individual, the *Shinto* rituals were far beyond his cultural frame of reference, and although he never outwardly disapproved of our marriage he remained forever skeptical of its legality.

My father and I never talked at any great length about my marriage to a 'foreigner', but I always assumed that due to his own personal history of immigration, naturalization and marriage to my mother he implicitly knew that the workings of the heart do not follow any rules based on nationality or cultural background. In Figure 4.1 below of our marriage ceremony, my mother can be seen between the two women dressed in ritual *Shinto* costumes looking a bit anxious. Indeed, throughout the remainder of her life, although she loved and respected *Junji*, my mother continuously worried about my physical and mental well-being, especially during the years (described below) when living with my mother-in-law became difficult.

As for the legality of our marriage in Japan, there are three official documents that continue to be a thorn in the side of foreign nationals married to Japanese citizens: *koseki toohon* (family register), *jyuuminhyo* (resident registration) and *gaikokujin toorokusho* (alien registration card).[5] These documents are part of the labyrinth of paperwork for buying a car, taking out a loan or starting a business in Japan, made even more difficult when one's legal name is not Japanese. *Junji* and I are officially married in both the United States and Japan; however, my surname is not *Maeda* and I am always required to carry my alien registration card. Of special note is how non-Japanese citizens' names are oftentimes configured to accommodate

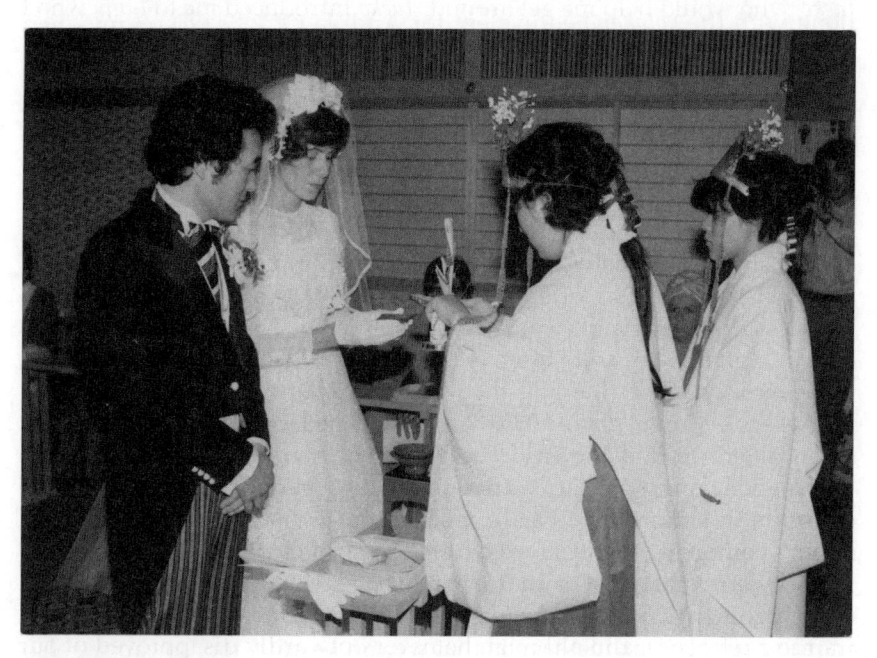

Figure 4.1 Wedding

In the Middle: Love, Marriage, Family 57

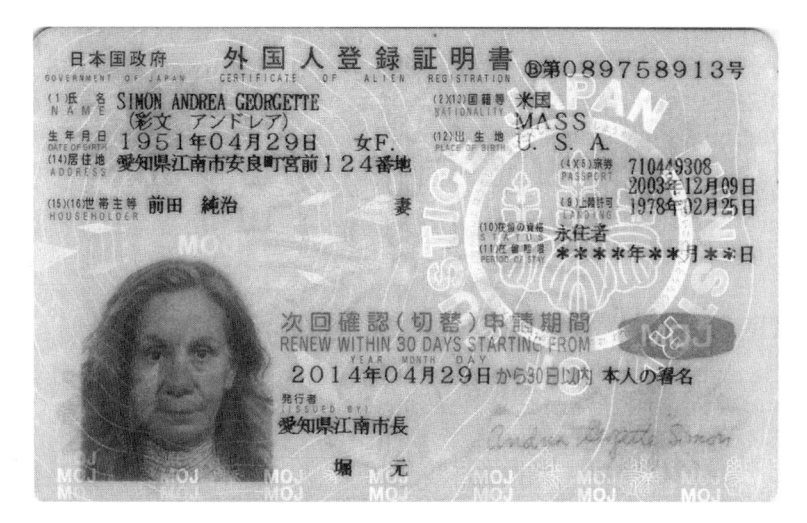

Figure 4.2 Alien registration card

the Japanese legal system. Because I am not legally part of the *Maeda* household, official documents such as my alien registration card, license, health insurance card and so on must retain my American maiden name (Andrea Georgette Simon). However, the *kanji* characters 彩文 (*Saimon*) along with the *katakana* equivalent for Andrea (アンドレア) on my alien registration card (see Figure 4.2) serve to Japanize my name, and my personhood as well, to fit the system.

Many non-Japanese spouses of Japanese nationals are unhappy with how their names are listed separately in parentheses on the family register in the 'remarks' section and are concerned about the discriminatory overtone of these documents. Although many districts in Japan are now revising resident and family registration forms to be more inclusive of foreign spouses, the online exchanges below are still not uncommon among foreigners in Japan. As a sort of publicity stunt, the city of *Yokohama*'s *Nishi* ward had granted (unofficial) residency to a seal (nicknamed *Tama-chan*) that had strayed into the harbor causing a group of social activists to hold a demonstration in protest:

> YOKOHAMA – About 20 foreign residents in Japan staged a rally Saturday calling on authorities to provide registry certificates for non-Japanese nationals after the popular seal 'Tama-chan', apparently from the Bering Sea, recently was issued a 'residency certificate' from the city of Yokohama. The participants called themselves 'the friends of Tama-chan', saying that as foreigners they feel a certain solidarity with the animal. 'Our message is that we can be cute, too, so can we also have a residency certificate'.

> 'I thought Nishi Ward's action was interesting because a usually inflexible local government took such a step', one of the protesters said. 'But then I had mixed emotions, given that I am not eligible for the ID even though I have been here for longer than he (Tama-chan) has.'
>
> A Korean born in Japan can't get residency, but a worthless fucking seal can ...
>
> Anyone up for some 'clubbing'?
>
> (Tama-chan: Japanese resident!?, posted February 23, 2003)

The first entries are said in a sarcastically joking style, but the last posting indicates the unfairness of the situation for Japan-born Koreans (*zainichi kankokujin*), who continue to be overtly discriminated against in many areas (educational, political, employment) of Japanese society [see Fukuoka (2000) for a comprehensive description of the history and current status of *zainichi*]. I always try to temper my personal feelings of frustration in consideration of the hardships of Koreans and other marginalized groups in Japan, and I occasionally even make light of my not being properly listed in *Junji*'s family register by saying that it makes it that much easier for us to get a divorce, if this ever became necessary. My lighthearted stance on divorce, however, is a dangerously unrealistic view since it has been reported that Japanese '[l]egal authorities have limited the enforcement of any judgments of the family court, and it is a statistical reality that an overwhelming majority of divorcees raise their children without the financial support of their former husband' (Sugimoto, 2003: 172).

When I first applied for my alien registration card 35 years ago it was mandatory to have our fingerprints taken; however, due to the efforts of human rights activists this procedure has been abolished. Crimes committed by non-Japanese have escalated over the past decade (see statistics in the 2005 Japan Almanac) and so one must always have her alien registration card ready to show the police, if asked to do so, and it must also be shown to immigration authorities when leaving or entering Japan, along with the mandatory fingerprinting for all foreigners entering Japan. This last procedure is another source of aggravation for those of us with permanent residency, and various discussion group members vent their anger in imaginative ways:

> Are you permanent residents feeling a little unloved, unwanted, ... not 'special'? cheer up, think of the extra time and attention immigration wants to spend on you! They want to take your picture to keep as a wonderful memory of your 'visit'! fingerprinting – just an excuse to touch your hand! Still moody? Why not start a protest organization, how about Permanent Residents Against Wankers in National Security

(PRAWNS)? (online discussion, Association of Foreign Wives, September 2007)

Whereas during my first few years in Japan I could sometimes wiggle my way out of traffic violations (not stopping at a stop sign, going down a one-way street, making an illegal U-turn) with a smile and a 'Sorry' said in English, after a careful look at the initial processing date (1978) of my alien registration card police officers now show me no mercy. The last time I tried pretending that I could not speak Japanese was when I was stopped several years ago for going a bit over the speed limit. The officer, aggravated at my charade, made me sit in the back seat of his patrol car and his first remark to me was, *'Nihongo shabereru deshoo'* (You can speak Japanese, right?). At this point I gave up and replied with a meek, *'Hai, soo desu'* (Yes, that's right) and was promptly handed a ticket for ¥15,000 (approximately $125.00 at the time).

But now back to the history of my relationship with *Junji*. My new acquaintance *Taeko* had arranged a trip for me and some of her friends to a local sightseeing spot and made a point of inviting *Junji*, her husband's friend, with the express purpose of introducing him to the *gaijin* woman. After graduating from college, *Junji* had spent two years as a hippie traveling throughout Europe and India where he acquired a hybridized English used on the road for communicating with people from various countries. *Taeko* had correctly assumed that *Junji* and I would immediately hit it off, as we were of a similar 'exotic' ilk. I was fascinated by *Junji's* long hair, pierced ear and unique English repertoire that consisted of 1960s slang words such as 'hey man', 'far out' and 'bummer'. We dated continually for six years during which time *Junji* became my main cultural and linguistic interpreter. As mentioned above, before moving to Japan I had never considered a sexual relationship with an Asian man; however, I was instantly attracted to *Junji* who I thought resembled *Seiji Ozawa*, a former conductor of the Boston Symphony orchestra. In addition to *Junji's* English-speaking panache, he often dressed in an interesting style that consisted of, for example, an Indian shirt over tight bell-bottom pants, a leather head band and an assortment of ethnic jewelry acquired during his hippie sojourn abroad (see Figure 4.3). In contrast to the conservative suit and tie and stereotypically humorless *'sararii man'* (literally, salary man, businessman), *Junji's* unique flair for fashion, his upbeat personality and his artsy profession as a graphic designer were irresistible features, and after only a month or so in Japan my life plans took off in a direction that I could never have imagined.

Dating an American woman certainly did not follow the usual mating patterns of *Junji's* male peers, not to mention the dismay it caused his parents and the buzz in the neighborhood whenever I visited his home and thereafter when I became a new member of our neighborhood CoP as the

Figure 4.3 *Junji*

gaijin no yomesan (foreign bride). The newspaper article in Appendix 2 was written in 1995 when our family was one of the increasing number of international families in Japan but still one of the very few in our neighborhood and surrounding area. Hence, the *Maeda* family became a 'hot' newsworthy item for local newspapers. However, as I read the article now I notice (in addition to the disgruntled look on my son's face) that while *Junji*'s career was described in much detail there was no mention of my educational background and professional career other than my being an English teacher and a conference planner for the Japan Association for Language Teaching (JALT). In light of societal emphasis on a strong patriarchal figure in Japanese families it follows that my career would be downplayed in the article, and later sections will describe in detail the negative stereotyping of foreign wives married to Japanese men.

The Language of Love

In any sexual relationship language plays a crucial erotic role, and learning the L2 equivalents for erogenous body parts and sensuous behavior only added to the pleasure of dating a man who dispelled, in my mind (and body), the stereotypical image of 'frigid Japanese'.[6] However, when introducing *Junji* to my American friends there were both subtle and not-so-subtle intimations, often delivered in a joking style, of *Junji*'s being physiologically inadequate to fulfill my sexual needs. Similarly, in her ethnographic study of East/West desirability Karen Kelsky describes an encounter with a western man whose remark alludes to his perceived 'phallic preeminence':

> 'You've dated Japanese men, right?' asked Ken, an IBM manager I met in an international dating party. 'Are their dicks really as small as they seem?' (Kelsky, 2001: 424)

I recall that part of my coping strategy when faced with sexist racial stereotyping was to reply with the title of the 1970s Maria Muldaur song, 'It ain't the meat it's the motion'.

A best-selling book based on interviews with western women living in Japan, *'Being A Broad in Japan'* (Pover, 2001) contains an interesting range of perspectives on heterosexual relationships with Japanese men. It appears that many of the women explicitly stated that the 'novelty' factor on both sides spearheaded the initial attraction but that as time passed and the novelty wore off communication problems and cross-cultural expectations made the going rough, especially for the western women. The author assesses the situation and offers some advice:

> Most Western women's criteria for potential partners are not met by Japanese men, and for this we should not 'blame' Japanese men (which is an easy option), but recognize that it is because of our expectations that Japanese men do not seem attractive. At the same time, it is important to remember that even in your home country, potential partners were not everywhere just waiting for you to date them. If you are looking for a guy who is physically bigger than you, will take the initiative in the relationship physically or emotionally, will regard you on an equal level and share the same basic value system then you are in for a tough ride wherever you are. Even more so, it seems, in Japan. (Pover, 2001: 212)

The above represents some, but certainly not all, of my own occasionally ambivalent feelings about my relationship with *Junji*, and while our dating period was generally euphoric the situation changed dramatically after our marriage, described in a later section.

Notwithstanding the racialized profiling of our relationship, *Junji* and I, along with interracial partners worldwide, continue to upset sociocultural mandates concerning who can sleep with whom. Eager to master the Japanese language of lovemaking I also had to learn the pragmatically appropriate usage in different contexts. Just as one usually uses the more proper equivalents of cunt (vagina) or dick (penis) during a physical examination or at formal social functions, I recall making a conscious effort to avoid slips with *manko* (cunt, also used as the verb form of intercourse), as I sometimes confused it with *anko* (sweet red bean paste) that also had to be differentiated from *unko* (shit). The informal *chinchin* (dick) was also to be avoided on occasions that called for more lexical discretion. However, after my son was born, I learned that *chinchin*, or its diminutive form *ochinko*, when referring to a boy's penis could be spoken without fear of impropriety and was a regular lexical item of Japanese motherese, or what Rod Ellis describes as 'caretaker talk' (Ellis, 1994: 248). I also learned that the sexual vernacular usage of *shakuhachi* (bamboo flute) refers to fellatio, and imagine my giddy uneasiness when one of my Japanese friends invited me to her home to meet her father, an accomplished *shakuhachi* player who insisted on performing for the American guest! As the intensity of my intimate relationship with *Junji* increased so did my repertoire of sexually charged phrases. Those items that generally occupy the same semantic space as English were relatively easy to remember, for example, the idiomatic expression for orgasm is *iku* (go) and/or *itta* (went), and the word for an erection in the morning is *asadachi* (morning, stand up). Perhaps my most memorable lexical acquisition was the word for scrotum, *kintama* (literally, golden balls), which for me epitomizes the traditionally dominant status of Japanese men. Nowadays, the Japanese syllabary for foreign words, *katakana*, is popularly used for many sexual terms, thus facilitating acquisition for beginning learners of Japanese involved in a romantic relationship, examples are: *jii supo* (G spot), *shikkusu nain* (sixty-nine), *esu emu* (SM) and *inpo* (impotent).

Gender and language scholars report on how erotic desire is discursively constructed (e.g. Cameron & Kulick, 2003), and of current interest in the field is how L1/L2, cross-racial sexual desire plays a significant role 'in the processes, practices and outcomes of second language learning, as well as language maintenance and shift' (Piller, 2002: 270). Individual sexual preferences and the language used for erotic desire and behavior are now viewed as being imbedded in 'the values, beliefs, and practices circulating in a given social context' (Piller & Takahashi, 2006: 61). Hence, what has been widely documented as Japanese women's *akogare* (desire) for western men is enmeshed in larger ideologies manifested in, for example, media discourses that construct anything and anyone western as more desirable than what can be obtained in Japan (see Piller & Takahashi, 2006). On the other hand, western women's desire for Japanese men has not been as well researched and in my own experience and the experiences of many other western women is viewed as going against cross-cultural norms concerning Japanese man/western woman couplings.[7]

As for *Junji* and me, our 30-year marriage has entered a new phase, and our language of sexual intimacy has been stored away with other memorabilia of our romantic past. The majority of our conversations now center on our son, retirement plans, the neighborhood and health issues.

Marriage

With a steady, substantial income and respectable status as a college EFL instructor, CoPs composed of Japanese and non-Japanese colleagues and friends, and a handsome, intelligent romantic partner, my early years in Japan were dreamlike, and I do not recall during this time of ever having any deep feelings of nostalgia for the United States. In preparation for a possible lifelong residence in Japan and marriage to a Japanese man, I diligently studied Japanese *shuuji* (calligraphy), *sadoo* (tea ceremony), Japanese cooking and *ikebana* (flower arrangement) that together constituted a typical regime of *hanayome shugyoo* (bridal training). These cultural activities were all performed in Japanese-only settings and contributed significantly to my growing L2 proficiency. While my connections to the international English-speaking community in *Nagoya* slowly dwindled my Japanese social interactionist sphere expanded as a result of my participation in various activities with non-English-speaking acquaintances and my ongoing relationship with *Junji* with whom I gradually came to speak more Japanese tinged with a distinct *Nagoya* accent.[8]

During our premarital dating phase, *Junji* and I occasionally considered returning to the United States together to pursue educational and professional careers; however, these plans were abandoned in 1980 due to a change of circumstances in *Junji*'s family. His older brother, who was expected to take care of *okaasan* (mother),[9] suddenly announced that because of his job he and his family were moving to another city – an unexpected event that entailed *Junji*'s becoming the principal caretaker of his aging mother. At the time, although I had reservations about living together with *okaasan*, I decided to marry *Junji* who assured me that everything would be okay. After getting married in 1981, we moved into the *hanare* (detached house for a younger couple next to the main house) (see Figure 4.4), and I began my new life as a suburban homemaker and *yome-san* (bride, also daughter-in-law).

As mentioned previously in Chapter 3, my previous life in the United States was very different from the suburban, somewhat rural setting I found myself in beginning from September 21, 1981, a date for me that marks the start of a new series of life and language altering events. Whereas my sphere of social activity prior to marriage consisted primarily of interactions with work colleagues and friends, Japanese and non-Japanese of a certain age and socioeducational background (20s–30s, college educated, well traveled), I suddenly found myself in a different environment alongside suburban housewives and older Japanese, many of whom still spoke about bitter experiences during World War II. Needless to say, my Japanese abilities at this point in time did not allow smooth entry into a world of vegetable gardening, local gossip, traditional Japanese housewife roles and various neighborhood duties, such as being the *hanchoo* (a leader

Figure 4.4 *Hanare*

of a certain number of households responsible for organizing different neighborhood activities). It was only after a few years had passed that I discovered that even for Japanese wives from a different part of our prefecture, it was difficult in the beginning for them to adapt to the particular customs and speech style of our local community. There are many remnants of old *Nagoyaben* (Nagoya dialect, see Note 2, Chapter 2) in my neighborhood such as the adjective *osogai* (*osoroshii*, terrible) and the phrase 'ようきてちょうだやぁた' (*Yoo kite choodatta*) instead of the standard form 'よう来てくださった' (*Yoo kite kudasatta*) (Nice of you to come or used simply to welcome someone) (see Appendix 3 for a list of old *Nagoyaben* words and phrases made famous by *Nagoya*'s newly elected mayor). This linguistic knowledge, however, did not serve to alleviate my growing insecurities of my ever being able to fit in.

Neighbors

In my suburban neighborhood, the majority of the women, especially those in their 50s and 60s, are high school graduates who, if they work outside the home, hold part-time jobs while their husbands are the main breadwinners. Mothers are usually the principal managers of their children's education, which entails attending PTA functions, transporting children to and from *juku* (cram school) and making sure that they do homework and succeed at school. I managed to carry out these duties and resisted becoming a *kyooiku mama* (education mother)[10] while at the same time wanting *Yuji* to succeed in Japanese society. Although younger wives may have graduated from a junior or four-year college they oftentimes follow the traditional pattern of giving up a work career upon marriage to become full-time housewives. Due to Japan's recent economic slump, however, housewives in many age brackets are trying to get or maintain a foothold in the labor market to supplement the family income.

In my critical ethnographic doctoral study of gender and education issues in Japan (Simon-Maeda, 2002), I wrote the following fieldnote entry:

> 'Where have all the fathers gone?' Besides the intensely serious atmosphere inside the school auditorium where the [PTA] conference was held, what immediately caught my ethnographic attention was that the only people in the audience were mothers of the students. I also noticed this same situation at the regular PTA events throughout the year that I attended as our neighborhood's representative. When I asked my focus group participants afterwards why fathers do not attend some of these events, they replied in unison, '*kaisha* (company)', and why mothers do, '*uchi ni iru, paato toka ne*' (at home or part-time jobs). On one occasion, when my husband returned from a PTA function that I could not attend, he remarked, '*Ore dake, otoko no hito!*' (I was the only male). The fact that the top PTA officials, all male, were at the meeting had not alleviated my husband's uneasiness at being the only father among the attendees. (Simon-Maeda, 2002: 115)

I consider *Junji* to be a progressive thinker and a supportive partner, and I could never have completed my doctoral degree nor pursued my academic and professional career if he had been otherwise. Nevertheless, roles for men and women in my local community are defined in ways that oftentimes make it difficult for me to live beyond the constraints of what is expected of a 'good' Japanese wife and mother.

There is not a single person in my neighborhood who can speak English beyond a simple greeting or a few phrases learned at school, and whenever there is a local event such as a seasonal *matsuri* (festival), *omiya sooji* (cleaning the local shrine grounds) or *funenbutsu* (recycling) I chat with everyone in Japanese. *Junji*'s family's ancestral lines date back to the Edo period (1603–1868); therefore, foreigner status notwithstanding, my symbolic capital (see Bourdieu, 1977a) has supplied me with a bit of social standing in the neighborhood. This state of affairs entails the appropriate performance and language of a respectable member of our *han* (group of households). Despite the fact that I am not on very familiar terms with most of my neighbors I am nevertheless expected to greet and/or talk to everyone with a certain amount of linguistic decorum. However, at the same time, I need to avoid an overuse of honorific forms and be adept at striking the right sociopragmatic balance by infusing my speech with some local dialect and self-deprecatory phrases lest I be perceived as the uppity *gaijin*. This is indeed a linguistically delicate balancing act since on an educational and professional career level I am higher up on the socio-economic hierarchy than the majority of my neighbors, male and female. Senko Maynard describes the intricacies of achieving a zone of comfort in Japanese interactions:

> Japanese people normally try to achieve a comfortable level of interaction by physically and emotionally accommodating other, by giving gifts, by repeatedly expressing gratitude, by making others feel important and appreciated, by humbling and often blaming themselves in order not to upset others.... When Japanese speakers wish to achieve greater intimacy with a person to whom they should show social deference, they avoid overuse of politeness expressions or mix the polite style with other expressions of endearment. (Maynard, 1997: 57)

The above is linguistically challenging even for native speakers of Japanese, and English is not without its own array of positive/negative politeness strategies (see Brown & Levinson, 1987) and stylistic expressions for managing interpersonal communication. For a non-native speaker the pragmatic task becomes especially formidable, yet I continue to fumble along hoping some day to reach an illusory zone of social harmony.

Among housewives, the topics of our chit chat are inconsistent with my professional and academic life and instead revolve around mundane affairs such as cooking, child raising, marital issues, gardening and so on. Whenever I leave Japan to attend international conferences I take care that this information does not leak out to the neighborhood where *ryosai kenbo* (good wife, wise mother)[11] discourses prevail, that is, a 'good' wife and mother would not leave her family for long periods abroad in order to pursue her career. Living in a large metropolitan area where there are more professional women would constitute a different social context and a different set of discourses concerning the roles of women in society. While I enjoy conversations with my neighbors I also appreciate the academic mood when talking with female colleagues at my university workplace.

In a typical countryside arrangement, a young married couple lives in the *hanare* (see Figure 4.4), and the wife will go over to the *honya* (main house) to prepare meals and for bath time, as there is usually no kitchen or bathing area in a traditional rural *hanare*. My interactions with *Junji*'s mother were minimal, as I would leave early in the day to go to my college teaching job in the city and would return in the evening. I cannot recall ever having a lengthy conversation with *okaasan*; however, one memorable exchange involved her wrongly assuming that my American background included familiarity with an American strain of eggplant, *beinasu* (literally, American eggplant, a strain plumper than Japanese eggplant). I politely answered *'iie'* (no) and later had a good laugh with *Junji*. Oddly coincidental, there is a Japanese proverb concerning eggplant and daughters-in-law: *akinasu wa yomesan ni kuwasuna* (literally, don't let the daughter-in-law eat fall eggplant). The underlying meaning of this proverb, that is, a daughter-in-law should not be allowed to enjoy eggplant that is most delicious in the fall, implies a power struggle that typically ensues in most societies between a *shuutome* (mother-in-law) and *yome* (daughter-in-law), especially when they are living together in the same household, although this might not always be the case.

As time passed, the long commute to my college teaching job in the city became difficult and I decided to quit my job after a series of miscarriages due to the physical and psychological strain of trying to juggle professional and homemaker duties. Living with my mother-in-law had become increasingly problematic as I was expected to assume more domestic chores than my work schedule allowed, not to mention the friction generated between two people whose lifestyles were at odds due to issues of race, sociocultural background, age, personality, and so on. After a lengthy stay in a hospital that provided special obstetric care for at-risk pregnancies I gave birth at the age of 35 to *Yuji*, our only child (see Figure 4.5). This happy event marked the beginning of another critical episode in my JSL life.

Family Life and Language at Home

I consider my family as my main CoP wherein I am defined as a wife and mother. The ways in which these two identities evolved, together with the language involved in maintaining these two identities, were significantly influenced by surrounding discourses concerning the role of women. Despite major gains made by Japanese women in different spheres of Japanese society, gendered imbalances remain [see Liddle & Nakajima (2000) for an in-depth, longitudinal account of the historical and modern day context of the gendered and classed positions of Japanese women, also see Fujimura-Fanselow & Kameda (1995) for statistical information concerning the situation of Japanese women in different spheres of Japanese society].

Current scholarship concerning gendered Japanese language behavior generally eschews a neat categorization of feminine/masculine speech styles, as Senko Maynard states:

> [T]he speaker's gender is not the only determinant for choosing masculine or feminine speech. Gender interacts with other variables including (1) psychological factors (e.g. social identification), (2) social and ideological factors (e.g. power associated with masculine speech), (3) situational factors (e.g. framing of the situation), and (4) discourse factors (e.g. topic). The choice of feminine and masculine speech style is a complex process. (Maynard, 1997: 75–76)

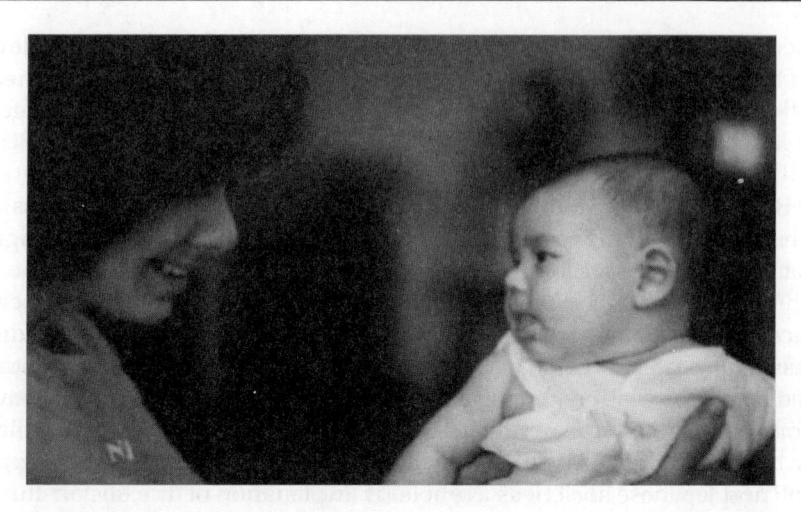

Figure 4.5 *Yuji*

Nevertheless, despite the complexity, Japanese 'masculine and feminine styles differ, and crossing the gender line can result, especially in formal situations, in social disapproval for both male and female speakers' (Maynard, 1997: 78). At the beginning of my life in Japan, flagrant violations of feminine and polite speech forms abounded. Out of a need to be taken seriously, particularly in formal or professional settings, I came to pay more attention to differences in casual and formal speech, male and female styles. Yet, I do not feel completely confident that I now speak proper Japanese in a manner expected of a mature, educated, professional woman. The difficulty that women in western societies face in constructing their professional identities in different contexts has been well documented by feminist discourse analysts (most notably Holmes, 2000, 2007), and the situation for women in Japan has been described as 'more extreme than most' (Coates, 2004: 203). Jennifer Coates, citing Reynolds' (1998) analysis of professional Japanese women's speech behavior, explains that 'there is a conflict in Japan between the contemporary ideology that women and men are equal, and the pressure on women to speak in a way that is *onna-rasiku*' (Coates, 2004: 203). In order to resolve this conflict that stems from the dominant status of Japanese men in the public domain, professional Japanese women are resorting to 'strategies [that] seem to consist predominantly of "defeminising" their language, that is, choosing variants towards the middle of an imaginary masculine–feminine spectrum, and avoiding variants associated with the feminine end of the spectrum' (Coates, 2004: 203). However, Katsue Akiba Reynolds ends her report on a grim note by saying that

> female speech plays a crucial role in keeping Japanese women in traditional roles. Attempts to remove the boundary between the

male/female speech division inevitably end in failure, as a result of self-restraint on the part of female speakers who foresee social punishment. It appears that the way women are supposed to talk has changed little; the norm functions as a conservative force. (Reynolds, 1998: 306)

Because Japanese mothers are considered to be the main caretakers of their children, after *Yuji* was born I felt the need to speak Japanese in a way that conformed to sociolinguistic norms for 'doing Japanese motherhood', which often conflicted with my personal background and career experiences. Nevertheless, despite the ongoing challenges of L2 parenting (discussed in a later section) and the hurdles in constructing my L2 identity as a female professional in a Japanese workplace I have managed to move along and through the periphery of mainstream Japanese society primarily by way of my family CoP, which is a microcosm of my neighborhood CoP and Japanese society as a whole (cf. explanation of 'fractals' in chaos theory wherein complex systems such as a family, school, city and nation are composed of similar recurring features at different levels of scale and complexity).

Special family events such as holiday gatherings, funerals and marriages are times when a newcomer's 'legitimate membership' (Wenger, 1998: 100) is acknowledged through strategic use of the appropriate language and behavior. However, this apprenticeship process becomes problematic when others and I are in a completely unfamiliar relationship. A particularly challenging event in terms of socially acceptable conduct is a Japanese funeral. Knowledge of the ritualized phrase used to address the family members of the deceased (*goshushosama deshita*, literally, grief), the proper way to offer incense before the funeral pyre, and the correct somber attire (all black, simple design, pearls) are the external prerequisites for participating in this solemn event.[12] I recall the time when there was a death in the neighborhood soon after I had become *Junji*'s wife. I dutifully memorized *goshushosama deshita* in preparation for attending the funeral down the street[13] in place of *Junji* who could not attend because of his work schedule. I wore the required all-black formal attire and silently rehearsed the long phrase several times so as not to commit a public faux pas as the *gaijin no yomesan*. When the deceased man's son, who had yet to spot me in the neighborhood, answered the door I said the phrase in the appropriately discreet tone, and he retorted within earshot of everyone, '*Dochira san desu ka?*' (Who are you?), a remark that would not have been forthcoming had I been Japanese and most likely dismissed as a long lost relative. I later tearfully berated *Junji* for sending me to the funeral of someone I had never met at the house of a stranger who caused me a bit of embarrassment. Over the 30 odd years since that incident, I have come to understand through trial and error the sociolinguistic rituals of my community and how I am perceived by others in different situations. Although my neighborhood CoP is still in existence *Junji* and I do not regularly socialize with other families, except for special occasions; hence, my level of participation has decreased over the years. In contrast, my professional CoP has matured as I move up the ranks at my university workplace, described in Chapter 5.

Ultimately, my markedness as a white *gaijin no onna* (foreign woman) in my immediate surroundings is what determines perceptions by other people, especially those with whom I am not in regular contact on a daily basis. In the same vein, the posting below is from a discussion list of the Association of Foreign Wives of Japanese:

> Many foreign women I have spoken to (and of course men, too) comment that over and above everything else (language, different customs etc), the hardest thing about living in Japan is being stared at where ever you go. The more physically different we are from the Japanese norm, the more visible we are. This is something that I personally feel and experience daily as I am tall, 'White' and blond. I think that many of us put a lot of energy into protecting our families (children) from this impersonal gaze. I wonder how some of you experience this visibility and the impact it has on your life and that of your families. (femail posting, April 26, 2006)

The above comment was part of a thread concerning some of the difficulties encountered by foreign women married to Japanese men. I am also a member of this organization, and although many of the postings are about the positive aspects of life in Japan, the majority either explicitly (like the posting above) or implicitly contain negative views of how the 'foreign wife' is depicted in popular discourses, especially Japanese TV media. One program that became the topic of discussion was '*Okusama wa Gaikokujin*' (The Wife is a Foreigner). The majority of the segments focused on how the foreign wives adapted (or not) to the 'unique' Japanese culture or problems assumed to be inherent in international marriages. Figure 4.6 is from a video recording I made (visual documents, June 6, 2007) of a show that depicted a Columbian wife with a disgruntled look on her face serving her Japanese husband a beer. The story was that they had met and dated in Bolivia, and before coming to Japan her husband was more adoring and would always serve beer to his wife. However, after marriage and settling in Japan the husband insisted that she follow the Japanese custom of the wife serving her husband (see Figure 4.6).

Figure 4.7 is from the same program and depicts two foreign wives being instructed in the proper Japanese way of eating *tamagokake gohan* (raw egg on rice) (see Figure 4.7), as if this were the determining factor of a foreigner being familiar with Japanese culture.

Needless to say, for the many foreign wives who have lived in Japan for many years, have professional careers, speak fluent Japanese and have

In the Middle: Love, Marriage, Family 71

Figure 4.6 Serving

Figure 4.7 Eating raw egg

more important concerns than whether or not they can eat a meal or serve their husbands in a 'proper' Japanese style had a problem with the stereotyped images of foreign wives and the *nihonjinron* discourses (see Note 7 in Chapter 3) that prevailed on the show:

> Does anyone have any objections to the program 'Okusama wa gaikokujin?' [The Wife is a Foreigner].... I think it backfires if the aim is to improve 'Kokusai teki' relationships by picking up on minute cultural quirks and blowing them up for all to ogle at ... and by lumping all of us gaikokujin okusan together with the similarities of being simply: female married to a Japanese man and being foreign born. Tokyo TV is actually widening the GAP between us and the 'normal everyday run of the mill' Japanese okusan.... Haven't we passed that point yet? Are all of our men really all that similar just by the fact that they are Japanese??? Are we really all that different as to warrant a whole TV show over???? I think not but let me know if I am waaaaaay off base here. (femail discussion list, June 18, 2007)

The above posting also mentioned that although the three most numerous ethnic groups representing foreign wives in Japan are Korean, Filipina and Korean, they were virtually absent from the program that instead introduced wives predominantly from western countries. I responded as follows:

> I have similar feelings as you about that show. In fact, one of the reasons I joined the foreign wives' group was because after seeing that show I wanted to hear other foreign wives' opinions of what I thought was a very tasteless show. Rather than introducing more foreign wives who, like many of our members, are professional women who have managed to become respected members of their local communities they dwell on women who seem to be forever nothing more than the 'gaijin no okusan'. I had a particular problem with one show about a mother who was very rough with her kids who she was determined to make into fashion models (a stereotypical job for 'haafu' kids). There are many problems revolving around women from third world countries who end up being in very oppressive situations with nasty mother-in-laws in rural areas where they are expected to work from morning to night. Of course this is not true in every situation, but I get the feeling that the show is not interested in portraying the tough conditions for some of these women and instead focuses on ethnic food parties where the wives are valued for their cooking skills above anything else. (femail discussion list, June 20, 2007)

The thread continued with opinions from others who agreed and others who enjoyed the show and did not find it objectionable. At any rate, the show has been discontinued, but an introduction to the show and some of its features can still be found at <http://www.tv-tokyo.co.jp/okusama>.

Paradoxically, although most foreign wives in Japan receive a lot of unsolicited attention, we are made invisible by legalities concerning our legal status, as explained by another list member:

> Despite our day-to-day hyper visibility in Japanese society, the Japanese system often renders us invisible. The clearest example of this is that we are not routinely listed in our family's 'juminhyo' (residence certificate) or the 'toosekihyo' (family registration). As foreigners we can not be included in the most basic unit of Japanese society; the household (setai). As a result, it can look as if our children have no mother and our husbands no wife. I wonder how aware you are of this issue and whether it is one that affects your life. In addition, as foreign women it is very difficult to be listed as head of household. In my own case, since coming to Osaka my daughter (aged 12) had to become the official head of household and only when I really pushed the person-in-charge at the City Hall did they add a small comment that I was the de facto head of household. As a foreigner I was told that I could not be listed as head of household. Has anybody else experienced this? Women and their responsibilities in any society are easily rendered invisible, but for foreign women here in Japan the situation is amplified. Again, I wonder if anybody else has had experiences of being made invisible within the system and, if so, what the impact of this has been on you and your family. (femail posting, April 26, 2006)

The ways in which a foreign wife is positioned by prevalent societal norms and institutions significantly influence our L2 identities and language behavior deployed to either contest or accommodate to gendered inequities that affect all women in Japanese society.

My everyday domestic chores such as shopping, paying bills and so on are not linguistically difficult; however, for more detailed tasks that necessitate the reading and writing of official documents (taxes, insurance, banking) I usually rely on my husband. This situation has ultimately prevented my attaining a higher level of language proficiency needed to become a full participating member of Japanese society. Relying on a partner as a linguistic interpreter to the detriment of one's L2 development has been reported by Marya Teutsch-Dwyer in her study of a male, Polish speaker visiting the United States whose 'social positioning ... nurtured by his American girlfriend and other female linguistic "caretakers" may have slowed down the formal acquisition of the second language to a considerable degree' (Teutsch-Dwyer, 2001: 176). After a 14-month observation period, Teutsch-Dwyer noted that her informant's L2 grammatical development had been hampered by his being doted on by his girlfriend who cared for his social and linguistic needs, much like a mother would care for her child. The author's conclusions emphasized the value of adhering to a poststructuralist interpretation of the dynamic relationship between identity and language, as '[l]earners create their own language and their own communicative strategies based on their perceptions of their positions as male or female in the social reality imposed on them in the new cultural, social, and linguistic environment' (Teutsch-Dwyer, 2001: 178–179). Although I do not expect to ever become totally confident of my JSL abilities and socialization strategies I have nevertheless found a comfortable 'contact zone'[14] (Pratt, 1991: 33) that I am able to move in, around and outside of as my life circumstances change.

As mentioned above, everyday routines in the *Maeda* household are conducted mostly in Japanese. However, as anyone versed in family blowups knows (i.e. anyone with a family) when tempers flares fiery speech patterns emerge from the dark depths of our primeval language repository. In the early years of our married life, *Junji* and I would argue in a codeswitching assemblage of English four-letter words and their Japanese equivalents such as *kuso* (shit), *chikushoo* (damn) and *baka yaroo* (stupid idiot), which are also part of my Japanese road-rage vocabulary. Because our house is adjacent to another house, after our cooling down period *Junji* and I would often joke how our arguing in English or a codeswitching variant was a good thing because the neighbors would not be able understand what we were arguing about. Early-stage marital difficulties, mostly involving in-law issues, have faded away over time and our quibbling is now interspersed with sarcastic jabs oftentimes delivered in a joking style. As professionals with full-time jobs, there is a constant tug-of-war over household duties, and the following exchange (fieldnotes, January 17, 2010) is typical of our quibbling:

***Junji*:** [at the sink washing dishes] *Itsuka watashi wa sara arai shinagara koko de taorete shinu.*
Someday while washing dishes I'll drop dead.
Andy: *Osara zenbu aratte kara ne.*
After you finish washing all the dishes, right?
***Junji*:** [chuckle]

My black humor was preceded by a conversation with *Junji* about one of his close friends who had just been diagnosed with pancreatic cancer and also about the wife of another friend who had died from a heart attack a week prior. The topic of death had thus cropped up several times over this short time frame, and similar to Kyoko Mori's analysis of how she once used humor at a funeral in the United States to lift the spirits of a colleague whose mother had died, a coping strategy the author claims 'is a common Midwestern antidote to sadness' (Mori, 1997: 186), my joke was intended to ameliorate the gloomy scene. *Junji*'s first line was his own therapeutic joke, for as Jyotsna Vaid explains, 'the very distancing that makes it possible for something to be rendered as funny may make it possible to discount or dismiss the depth or intensity of an underlying sentiment' (Vaid, 2006: 154). While I would not joke about death with someone I was not close to, for someone with whom I am on intimate terms the humor performs the perlocutionary function (see Austin, 1962) of relieving that person's sorrow, for a while at least.

Relatedly, the findings of Ingrid Piller's study of bilingual partners 'doing couplehood' attest to how the participants' 'private language is a constitutive factor in the make-up of their relationship ... [and] words and expressions are most characteristic of these hybrid languages' (Piller, 2002: 242). On a conversational level, *Junji's* and my Japanese/English codeswitching style has been fashioned from our 35 years of couplehood constructed from experiences in both the United States and Japan such that conversations, for example, about my family, the Red Sox baseball team or American friends living in *Nagoya* are typically interspersed with English words, for example, 'Wow! Janet [my sister] now has 13 huskies, *shinjirarenai* (unbelievable)', '*Ano damn* Red Sox *kyonen* championship *o torenakatta kara Daisuke ga* spring camp *de ganbaranai to dame*' (Those damn Red Sox didn't win the championship last year so Daisuke [Japanese pitcher] had better do his best in spring camp) or '*Raishuu* John *no* birthday party *ga aru kara ikoo*' (Next week is John's birthday party so let's go).

For both *Junji* and me, as explained in the opening sections of this chapter, the L1 or L2 words or expressions used when codeswitching are semantically latched onto certain persons, places and experiences. Because we live in Japan, the majority of our conversations are in Japanese, but the many instances of our codeswitching attest to the interplay of individual identities, our joint identity as a couple, cultural backgrounds and L2 proficiency that together oftentimes override exclusive allegiance to the use of the dominant societal language (Japanese) and its ideological underpinnings of national affiliation. A close look at stories from bi/multilingual couples about language choices [see collection in Pavlenko (2006) and also see Burck (2005)] reveals how the linguistic varieties of couples' private talk are a continual working out of differences in individual, racial and national origins (e.g. Japanese/Anglo-American) while simultaneously trying to forge an identity as a couple or family unit out of oftentimes contradictory identity affiliations. Ingrid Piller describes the situation thus:

> Identity is crucially about similarity and difference ... When we talk about who we are we talk about the groups we belong to and we negotiate the boundaries between 'us' and 'them', or the Self and the Other.... That means that many different groups in society vie for the right to define who is 'in' and who is 'out' and individuals draw on and align themselves with different discourses at different times. Appealing to diverse discourses produces multiple identities. This multiplicity of identity is compounded in couple talk where two different types of

identity constructions are pursued simultaneously: that of the individual member of the unit, as well as that of the unit. For cross-cultural couples identity talk is quite a challenge: they are part of discourse communities in which national belonging plays a central role in the construction of in- and out-groups. (Piller, 2002: 185)

The challenge of forging our couple identity is ongoing and inflected by the popular assumption that interracial marriages are problematic due primarily to differences in language and culture. However, in Piller's data obtained from English–German bilingual couples the researcher found that her participants 'are not passively at the mercy of the discourses available in their society. Rather, they produce and re-produce them, they bend and challenge them in their own subjective ways' (Piller, 2002: 276). Similarly, in Takigawa's microanalytic study of how a Japanese wife–American husband dinner table conversation turns into an argument over a Japanese language item, the author 'did not find any cases where the source of the argument was specifically due to the couple's cultural differences' (Takigawa, 2008: 39) and, moreover, that misunderstandings are 'nothing unique to intercultural couples' (Takigawa, 2008: 39). The point being made by both researchers is that although cultural backgrounds are an integral part of the identity formation of a cross-cultural couple, individual subjectivities as well play a crucial role in wife–husband relationships. My own ethnographic data compiled from discussions on the Association of Foreign Wives of Japanese (AFWJ) <www.afwj.org>, a national organization that 'aims to provide members with friendship, support and mutual help in adapting to Japanese society' (AFWJ brochure), attest to the multi-layered character of intercultural marriages. While scanning through a large stack of past and current AFWJ journals to add to this book's ethnographic data archives, I noticed that the majority of comments concerning intercultural marriage problems were attributed most often to individual personality dissonance rather than to cross-cultural factors. As part of her research on communication patterns between foreign wives and their Japanese husbands, one AFWJ member distributed an informal questionnaire in 2003 to a small sample that yielded some interesting information concerning perceptions of international marriages. It appears that:

> Most wives felt that they were 'just husband and wife', and that the person was more important than the culture they came from. However, they felt that people outside the home, in Japan, did not always view them as such, and that other people's reactions were greatly influenced by the fact they are an international couple.

In the conclusion to the same study, the researcher states:

> While couples ought to anticipate ethnic and social differences, and realize that the personality is socially influenced, every person is

unique and will not necessarily carry each culturally attributed trait. In fact, some of the women responding to the questionnaire noted that they had difficulty in separating cultural and personal characteristics when it came to their husbands. In addition, while it is clear that here is a potential for miscommunication between partners of different cultures, through the solutions to these problems come tremendous potential for originality and innovation for methods of communicating. (documents, January 10, 2010)

As the research studies and anecdotal data in previous sections illustrate, intercultural relationships are inherently imbedded in but are *not* absolutely constricted by larger sociocultural discourses and belief systems described by Piller (2002) in Bakhtinian terms as a 'polyphony [in which] many voices, from different ideological vantage points, speak in talk and text' (Piller, 2002: 276). Another voice was added to the polyphony in the *Maeda* household when our son, *Yuji*, was born in 1986.

L2 Parenting

With the birth of *Yuji*, Japanese motherese, or what is sometimes referred to as infant-directed speech (IDS), became a part of my JSL repertoire, and similar to bi/multilingual individuals' accounts of child raising my language choices were intertwined with how I positioned myself and wished to be positioned by others as a particular kind of parent.

By listening to mothers with small children in the neighborhood and watching kiddy shows on TV, I gradually became familiar with the particular characteristics of Japanese baby talk. Some examples are: onomatopoeic sounds – *shii* (to pee) *buubuu* (a car) *wanwan* (a dog) *nyanko* (cat), parts of the body *chinchin* or *chinko* (penis), *chichi* (breast milk), *otete* (baby's hands), games *inai inai baa* (peek-a-boo) and actions – *ne ne* (sleep), *tachi tachi* (stand up), *pachi pachi* (clap hands). Repetition, raised voice pitch, vowel elongation and word/gesture coordination are all part of the baby talk package, and I diligently tried to incorporate these features into my interactions with *Yuji*. While putting forth the disclaimer 'that maternal, or parental, behaviour varies extensively within, as well as between cultures' (Richards, 1998: 44), in his review of cross-cultural studies of motherese speech patterns Richards mentions that:

> For Japanese mothers the following descriptions are typical: 'more empathy with the child's needs', 'less talk', 'quicker to comfort the child', closer physical proximity'. Apparently, Japanese mothers were also less demanding in terms of their children's politeness, an interesting contrast with American mothers who seemed to be very insistent on the child using polite forms of speech even to the mother. (Richards, 1998: 43)

I did not attach a microphone to *Yuji* when he was baby, as some early language acquisition researchers are wont to do with their own children; therefore, I am not certain whether our spoken interactions match the above observations of Japanese parenting linguistic styles. However, what I generally recollect is a codeswitching variety of motherese, for example, '*Yu-kun's*[15] gotta go to *hoikuen*, cereal *hayaku tabenasai*' (*Yuji* has to get ready to go to nursery school, hurry up and eat your cereal) that evolved into the particular linguistic manner in which *Yuji* and I now interact.

As many years have passed since my child-rearing days I wanted to get some opinions from others who have recently gone through (or are still in the throes of) L2 parenting. I posted the quote above from Richards (1998) to an online discussion group to which I belong asking members for their reactions that I have combined into a composite passage below:

> Last week I went to one of those hoikuen [nursery school] get togethers where all the mothers sit around and talk about their kids. The teacher was asking the mothers what concerns they had about raising their 3-year-olds. Most people talked about stuff like eating and table manners, bedtime routines, toilet training etc. When the teacher asked me I said that I was in the midst of trying to teach my DS [dear son] to be polite, to say 'the magic word', to greet people correctly etc. and my biggest worry was whether or not DS spoke Japanese as politely as his English. Well everyone looked at me as if I'd just lifted my skirt and danced around, they seemed really confused. Afterwards I wondered if my Japanese had been weird and I'd used a bad word by mistake. After reading your post I realize that they were probably thinking 'What is she talking about?' Thank you all for helping me to understand that. Japanese children run around uncontrolled in supermarkets, clinics, stores, in most public places, while the mothers chat with each other, as if it is totally acceptable. I have seen countless children scream at their mother 'baka' [idiot] and even strike them. I have also heard mothers say to their child 'dai kirai' [I despise you] if the child doesn't do what they want. In my experience, and based on numerous conversations I have had over the past quarter of a century (!) with Japanese university students, Japanese mothers, and my own (half-Japanese, half-American) children, Japanese children are not taught to say thank you to their parents. The parents feel it is unnatural to have their children say please, thank you, gochisoosama deshita [a polite phrase used after a meal], etc. to them for every little thing and so they do not drill it into them at home. How many of us, on the other hand, have said a million times to our children from the time they could speak, 'What's the magic word?' or simply had them parrot the words 'thank you' after we have done something for them, even just handing them a drink. The Japanese parents would of course like their children

to express thanks to those outside the family unit, but if there is no practice at home this is unlikely to happen. (documents, March 5, 2010)

I replied to the postings by saying that cross-cultural comparisons of any social practice (marriage, dating, schooling) abound in stereotypes inevitably based on personal experiences and intuitions oftentimes merging into a general pattern, yet there are always outliers that make life interesting. Local experiences are in fact constituted by a larger conglomeration of national, international and global ideologies, and language choice plays an important role in how we self-identify as participants or nonparticipants in certain social practices.

The Regime of *Obentoo*

Monolingual parenting both reflects and is highly influenced by surrounding societal standards of how to raise a child promulgated through the large volume of parenting magazines (see Shimoda, 2008 for a cross-cultural comparison of English and Japanese language parenting magazines). Likewise, parenting in Japan generally adheres to normative attitudes that place an inordinate amount of child-raising responsibilities on mothers (see Note 10 concerning *kyooiku mama*), as described in Shimoda:

> The women in the Japanese parenting magazines are almost invariably depicted in a full time mother and housewife role, with a husband in full-time employment. In addition, little or no mention is made of the woman's previous work experience, or her future career plans and aspirations. The Japanese parenting magazines perpetuate the notion that women with children are solely mothers and caregivers and that they have no or little inclination or ability to perform other roles. (Shimoda, 2008: downloaded p. 8)

Because I was a first-time mother in a culture different from the one I was familiar with, I religiously followed the example of mothers in my neighborhood and listened to advice from *Junji*'s older sisters who often stopped by to see how I was doing. I was 35 years old when *Yuji* was born and found child-raising to be physically and psychologically demanding such that I decided to give up my full-time job at the college I had been working at for 10 years. I waited until *Yuji* was three years old and attending nursery school before looking for an EFL teaching job at a university closer to my home. Luckily, the university where I am currently employed was hiring EFL teachers at the time, and I reentered the workforce as one of the many wives and mothers in Japan who go against traditional norms by pursuing their professional careers. The shifting back and forth between full-time motherhood and full-time work was fraught with difficulties, and I sometimes wonder how my life would have unfolded if I had done otherwise. *Junji* was a supportive husband throughout, even when I announced that I would be commuting every weekend to *Osaka* as a student in Temple University's TESOL doctoral program.

Parents in Japan, as in most countries, are recruited and expected to assume various duties (*yakuin*) associated with their children's school matters and extracurricular activities, such as patrolling the route to school, organizing festivals and interschool sports and being the neighborhood liaison with the school. Refusing any of these duties is tantamount to being ostracized from the local community. Most of the full-time working mothers dread the *yakuin* duties, as the meeting times often conflict with our work schedule, which does not automatically constitute an excuse for nonparticipation. Because I had already been in Japan for several years and people were aware of my Japanese ability I could not play the *gaijin* card and skip out from the *yakuin* responsibilities that were to last throughout the 15 years *Yuji* was enrolled in Japanese public schools. In retrospect, taking an active part in my son's school life helped me to better understand the Japanese educational system, which I heretofore only had partial knowledge of as a *gaijin no sensei* (foreign teacher). Deference was called for when speaking with *Yuji*'s teachers at parent–teacher conferences, and I dutifully learned the routine that began with the correct opener upon entering the classroom to speak privately with the homeroom teacher 'Itsumo osewa ni natte orimasu' (Thank you for the continuing care of my child) and ended with the very polite closer 'Arigatoo gozaimashita, shiturei itashimasu' (Thank you very much, please excuse me) together with the requisite deferential bowing of the head. As with funerals, the appropriate attire, speech and demeanor are expected at parent–teacher conferences and nonconformity is to be avoided, especially by mothers who are considered to be the primary directors of their children's educational paths.

An important part of Japanese motherhood is preparing her child's lunch box (*obentoo*) for school and school-related activities. Drawing on Louis Althusser's (1971) theories concerning the subtle ideological forces that regulate our lives, Anne Allison describes how an *obentoo* is a symbolic representation of the Japanese 'social order and the role gender plays in sustaining and nourishing that order' (Allison, 2000: 87):

> The *obentō* comes to be filled with the meaning of mother and home in a number of ways. The first is by sheer labor.... Such labor is intended for the child but also the mother: It is a sign of a woman's commitment as a mother and her inspiring her child to being similarly committed as a student. The *obentō* is thus a representation of what the mother is and what the child should become.... The making of the *obentō* is, I would argue, a double-edged sword for women. By relishing its creation ... a woman is ensconcing herself in the ritualization and subjectivity (subjection) of being a mother in Japan. She is alienated in the sense that others dictate, surveil, and manage her work. On the flip

side, however, it is precisely through this work that the woman expresses, identifies, and constitutes herself. (Allison, 2000: 90–96)

Never having been especially adept at cooking before relocating to Japan, preparing *Yuji*'s school *obentoo* every morning before I left for work was a challenge, as the contents needed to be not only nutritious (fresh ingredients cooked from scratch) but also arranged in an aesthetically pleasing style. I keenly felt *seken* (see Note 4) at play during conversations with other mothers for whom *obentoo* preparation was a popular topic. However, I gradually came to realize that working mothers, like myself, often did not conform to the labor-intensive, rigid *obentoo* regime and resorted to time-saving innovations (frozen foods, microwave) at the risk of being labeled *tenuki o suru okaasan* (negligent mother). Fortunately, *Junji* does not adhere to a 'men as domestically incompetent discourse' (see Sunderland, 2004) and often took (takes) charge in the kitchen.

Looking at Figure 4.8 of *Yuji* and me standing in front of the gate of his elementary school on the day of his entrance ceremony 18 years ago (see Figure 4.8), I recall my insecurities over being able to successfully guide *Yuji* through the Japanese school system. Also of serious concern were reports of bullying in Japanese schools and how children of a different racial background were especially easy targets [see discussion in Kamada (2009) concerning bullying of foreign and mixed racial children in Japan, also see Seibert Vaipae (2001)]. At parent–teacher conferences I would inevitably inquire, '*Yuji ga ijimerarete inai desu ka?*' (Is *Yuji* being bullied?), and the teacher would always reply, '*Iie, tottemo akarukute minna to naka yoku asonde imasu*' (No, he's very cheerful and getting along well with others). I am not sure to this day if teachers' observations were accurate or not, but *Yuji* never mentioned anything about his being bullied throughout his early school years, successfully graduated from a reputable Japanese college, and secured a good job as a public official in our local city hall.

Similar to Burck's (2005) summary below of her participants' experiences of parenting in a second language, I also felt that while something went missing due to my non-Japanese background, the effort invested in learning Japanese and becoming accepted in our community ultimately had a positive effect on my relationship with *Yuji*:

> Parents saw themselves as leaving out aspects of themselves in their second language, and of not being able to draw on the richness of their first language and its interconnectedness with their culture, with resultant losses for their children. However, some parents constructed parenting in their second language as supporting their children to be successful in the dominant culture. And what emerged in the analysis was that a second language had enabled some parents to be more like the kind of parents they wanted to be. (Burck, 2005: 148)

Figure 4.8 Entrance ceremony

As explained in Chapter 3, my father remained a dysfluent English speaker throughout his life after immigrating to the United States and this had a negative affect on our relationship – something I did not want to happen between *Yuji* and me. At the same time that I recognized the importance of cultivating *Yuji*'s Japanese fluency I also hoped that he would become a fluent speaker of both Japanese and English. In order to achieve this goal, shared by several of my American friends married to Japanese men, we formed an English play group that met on Saturday afternoons in *Nagoya* to provide informal English-learning activities for our small children enrolled in Japanese schools. For a year or so, *Yuji* and I would drive into the city to participate in the English playgroup; however, *Yuji*'s main social network came to consist mainly of his Japanese schoolmates, and he subsequently lost interest in the playgroup and English as well.

I often initiate talk with *Yuji* in English, and he will respond (if he responds at all depending on his mood) either in English or Japanese, but for the most part Japanese is our dominant home language with occasional codeswitching, mostly imperative forms such as *'Okaasan, moo sugu dekakeru kara* iron this shirt' (Mother, I'm leaving soon so iron this shirt). After *Yuji* was born and continuing throughout his teenage years, I would take him along with me to the United States during my summer vacations. These trips contributed to his bilingual proclivities in that he was given many opportunities to develop his English interactional style with his American relatives. However, because he was schooled in Japan and socialized daily with his Japanese friends his English proficiency gradually weakened, and now his principal means of communication in and outside of our home is Japanese.

At *Yuji*'s workplace, since it is well known that his mother is American, he is occasionally asked to translate official documents intended for the English-speaking foreign population in our city. A recent example is, 江南市の税務課に連絡して下さい (*Konan-shi no zeimuka ni renraku shite kudasai*, Please contact the Konan City tax office). *Yuji* texted me the above in Japanese asking for help, and I sent back the translation in English. Our usual cellphone back-and-forth texts are a combination of English and Japanese concerning daily matters such as:

Andy: What time are you coming home for dinner?
Yuji: 今日外で食べて来る
Today I'll eat dinner out before coming home
Andy: 了解
Understood

Yuji works in the citizens' affairs section in city hall and handles official matters such as residency and family registration, birth certificates and so on. Rather than going in person to city hall and being oggled at I will usually ask *Yuji*, as my legal proxy, to get a copy of *Junji*'s or my residency and family registration papers. Although it was lunch time and *Yuji* was probably in the cafeteria, I decided to text instead of phoning, as the former is more discreet:

Andy: Momの住民ひょのcopy一つお願いできませんか？
Could you get one copy of Mom's residency form?
Yuji: はい、わかりました
Yes, I understand.
Andy: あと、面倒じゃなければJunjiのこうせきとうほんも
Also, if it's not troublesome please get Junji's family registration, too.
Yuji: なにに使うの？
What are you going to use them for?
Andy: あとで説明します
I'll explain later.
Yuji: [*Yuji* phones] You have to say [write] the reason why.
Andy: Okay, *ginkoo no kooza o hiraku tame*.
(In order to open a bank account.)
Yuji: *Wakatta*.
(I understand.)
(email, February 2010)

As I describe further in the next chapter, when things get too complicated for texting in Japanese I will either resort to using the phone or talking in person, as I intended with my 'I'll explain later' in the segment above. In order for *Yuji* to process the documents a reason had to be stated; therefore, to speed matters along *Yuji* phoned me and switched to English rather than laboring through Japanese texting. As mentioned previously, although *Junji* and I codeswitch as part of our couplehood 'languaging' (see Swain, 2006), *Yuji* never codeswitches when texting or speaking with his father. I attribute this state of affairs to *Yuji*'s English L2 experiences that revolve preeminently around our mother–son relationship.

Many of my native English-speaking female friends married to Japanese men have children that are balanced bilinguals, due to their education at international schools in Japan and their parents' strong determination to maintain the English abilities of their children. It is also not uncommon in discussions with other parents of children of mixed backgrounds to hear how the choice was made to enroll their children in international schools abroad due to one or the other parent's job circumstances and/or personal desire to nurture their children's international perspective. However, in my family's case, because our home is not located near any international schools and *Yuji* had already developed a circle of friends in our local community, *Junji* and I decided to enroll him in Japanese public schools. There were times when I regretted this decision as I watched my friends' children go off to colleges in the United States or other countries and realized that *Yuji*'s English ability would never develop beyond a certain level of proficiency, a situation found to exist in many international families residing in Japan, as reported by Goebel Noguchi:

> With their children attending Japanese schools and without a nearby community of fellow native speakers of English to provide linguistic, cultural and social support for bilingualism, many of the native English-speaking parents in mixed marriages in Japan have found that their children do not learn to speak much English, or even, in many cases, to understand it very well. (Noguchi, 2001: 239)

Noguchi examined a variety of variables (parents' L1/L2 skills, birth order, home language use) deemed to be related to a child's bilingualism and concluded that the L2 proficiency (Japanese/English) of a parent did not significantly influence their children's bilingualism. Moreover, 'parents in mixed marriages, rather than regarding themselves as models of a single language (and thus, serving as models of monolingualism), might be better advised to see themselves as models of bilingualism for their children' (Noguchi, 2001: 266).

Hence, while my 35-year journey on the road to being and becoming a speaker of Japanese has been a personal endeavor it is at the same time shaping and being shaped by other people (husband, son, friends) and surrounding contexts. This last point follows a postmodernist interpretation of how L2 identities are built up through 'engagement in the social world' (Wenger, 1998: 15) and will be elaborated on in the concluding chapter in relation to the benefits of adopting an autoethnographic approach to SLA and applied linguistics research. The next chapter will focus on my career as a professional EFL educator and how formal and informal encounters in my work environment have contributed to my JSL literacy development.

Notes

1. Keiko Yamanaka (2000) reports on the difficulties that *nikkeijin* have had in adjusting to life in Japan, even though they are descendants of Japanese immigrants in Brazil: 'Because of Nikkeijin's ancestry and appearance, Japanese managers and coworkers tended to expect them to behave and speak like Japanese. It did not take the Japanese long to realize that most Nikkeijin are not the Japanese they had expected but "foreigners" who neither spoke Japanese nor conformed to Japanese practices and customs. When expectations of their "Japaneseness" were overtly contradicted, the Japanese often verbally abused them, calling them stupid, secondary Japanese and uncivilized people from a backward country. They were regarded as slow and lazy in their work, impolite and rude in personal interactions' (Yamanaka, 2000: 141).
2. A basic tenet of the situated movement holds that human behavior, of which language is a core component, is not solely the product of abstract reasoning processes, but rather is primarily dependent on an individual's contexts and social interactions. Therefore, theoretical interest shifts from 'the individual as the unit of analysis toward the sociocultural setting in which activities are embedded' (Kirshner & Whitson, 1997: 5).
3. In Kelsky's (2001) ethnography of Japanese women's fetishization of white, western men, the author interweaves her own personal story of her interracial marriage. Similar to my own experiences, Kelsky narrates how racial and sexual stereotypes abound in views of the 'exotic' other. For Kelsky, the fact that she was married to a Japanese man 'proved to have a jarring effect on nearly everyone around, disrupting the establishment of a taken-for-granted agreement about the universal desirability of white American men and the universal abjection of Japanese men' (Kelsky, 2001: 422–423).
4. Yoshio Sugimoto describes *seken* as 'an imagined community that has the normative power of approving or disapproving of and sanctioning individual behavior. . . . as an imagined but realistic entity, *seken* presents itself as a web of people who provide the moral yardsticks that favor the status quo and traditional practices' (Sugimoto, 2003: 281).
5. A well-known social activist in Japan, Aruto Davido maintains a web page http://www.debito.org that provides useful information for foreigners, particularly concerning laws (official and unofficial) that discriminate against non-Japanese.
6. As part of the discourse of Orientalism (Said, 1978) Asian males are usually portrayed as desexualized, wishy-washy individuals in comparison with the stereotypically virile western man. The popular western opinion of the phallic inadequacy of Japanese men can be found in the following bit of information for western women living in Japan: 'If your partner is Western, then Japanese

condoms may be a little on the snug side.... in an effort to eliminate the inferiority complexes that Japanese men have about the size of their penises, ALL Japanese condoms are made tiny so that EVERY Japanese man is too big for them' (Pover, 2001: 161).

7. In Japan, white women are prominently featured as sexualized/objectified beings in pornographic images and ads for beauty products. As one example, Kelksy (2001) describes a Japanese TV commercial for *ramen* in which a busty foreign woman clutches a wimpy Japanese male to her breasts, whereupon the man 'struggles wildly, looking back terrifiedly at the camera as she leads him away into the night' (Kelksy, 2001: 194). Kelsky explains that whereas Japanese women's desire for white men is 'powerfully encoded in some of Japanese women's most formative experiences' (Kelksy, 2001: 148), 'potential sexual union with a white woman is, on the rare occasions when it is depicted, represented as a terrifying and potentially castrating encounter' (Kelksy, 2001: 194). Women from Russia and other former Soviet-bloc countries now constitute a new wave of sex workers coming (being trafficked) to Japan since the fall of the Iron Curtain (Douglass, 2000). As a result, there has been increased sexualization of white women, as indicated by titles of the junk mail that appear regularly in my computer's junk mail folder: 'Beautiful Russian women waiting to meet YOU!', 'I sexual Russian blonde, want to see, come closer', 'How about Russian bride?', 'No woman can make a better wife than a Russian lady pick one here' (collected February 2010).

8. One distinctive phonetic feature of *Nagoyaben* (Nagoya dialect) is the substitution of [æ] for [ai] such that, for example, the word [fu·rai] (fried) is pronounced as [fu·ræ]. To amuse Japanese acquaintances, I sometimes deploy my repertoire of typical Nagoyan words and phrases; a sociolinguistic trope designed to flaunt my status as a seasoned Japanese speaker.

9. I learned the word *ato tori* (succession) and all of its serious implications at this crucial stage of my JSL life. The older son (*choonan*) in a traditional Japanese family is usually the successor and inheritor of the family estate and in turn is expected to care for his aging parents. However, because *Junji*'s older brother had left the family home around the time of our marriage, *Junji* took on the responsibility. This situation proved to be particularly difficult for me as I was expected to also assume caretaking duties for a mother-in-law who was not especially keen on living with an American daughter-in-law.

10. Carol Simons (1991) describes a typical *kyooiku mama* thus:

> 'No one doubts that behind every Japanese student who scores high on examinations – and they are among the highest scoring in the world – there stands a mother who is supportive, aggressive and completely involved in her child's education. She studies, she packs lunches, she waits for hours in lines to register her child for exams, and waits again in the hallways for hours while he takes them. She denies herself TV so her child can study in quiet, and she stirs noodles at 11:00 p.m. for the scholar's snack. She shuttles her youngsters from exercise class to rhythm class to calligraphy class to piano lessons. She makes sure they don't miss their swimming and martial arts instruction. Every day she helps with homework, hires tutors, and works part-time to pay for juku' (Simons, 1991: 59). Although in modern-day Japan there are some *'kyooiku papas'* with socioeconomic factors affecting the level of involvement of either parent, it is nevertheless the mother who is usually the main supporter of her child's educational activities.

In the Middle: Love, Marriage, Family 87

11. Liddle and Nakajima trace the historical origins of the *ryosai kenbo* notion as follows:

    '[T]he Japanese state constructed the nation through its exhortation to and regulation of women in a number of different ways. The family was created as the essential building block of the national structure within which women, as good wives and wise mothers, became the public officials of the home. Women were essential to the family-state system in their roles as household managers, educators of children, and economically efficient consumers saving the family's housekeeping money to pay off the national debt – all of which activities were crucial to building the nation and creating national wealth. During times of war, women were constructed as mothers of the nation and encouraged to produce more children for the army, as well as keeping the family going in the absence of men and engaging in voluntary patriotic activities as a form of national service. These activities were central to establishing colonial rule in East Asia and strengthening the country's military forces'. (Liddle & Nakajima, 2000: 57–58)

12. In his analysis of clothing as a display of conformity to prevailing Japanese societal discourses, Brian McVeigh uses the example of the widespread use of school and company uniforms that 'act as socializing instruments because they are used to instill a sense of solidarity ... 'people may think or feel whatever they want, but not providing a good rendition of one's assigned social role – via clothing, grooming and deportment – is not excused' (McVeigh, 2000: 37–38). The author adds the disclaimer that this is not a unique trait of Japanese society; however, the popular view held by Japanese and non-Japanese alike is that the influence of '*seken*' (see Note 4) on self-presentation is very visible in every sector of Japanese society. The same applies to the particular type of clothing required at funerals or other formal events, but younger generations of Japanese are resisting fashion norms through ever-innovative displays of individuality.

13. Although most Japanese funeral ceremonies are now held outside of the home at special funeral halls, at the time of this episode the families in my neighborhood still held the wake at home in traditional style, and everyone in the deceased's *han* was expected to attend.

14. This term was used by Mary Louise Pratt 'to refer to social spaces where cultures meet, clash, and grapple with each other, often in contexts of highly asymmetrical relations of power, such as colonialism, slavery, or their aftermaths as they are lived out in many parts of the world today' (Pratt, 1991: 33).

15. The diminutive – *kun* is usually attached to a small boy's personal name as a form of address.

Chapter 5
Career Discourse(s)

My professional career CoP that will be highlighted in this chapter is a significant part of my constellation of CoPs that are always in a dynamic state of overlapping, expanding or diminishing in size and importance according to circumstances of life. Figure 5.1, (re)adapted from Scollon and Scollon's (2004: viii) 'nexus of practice model' is a visual depiction of my JSL development located at the nexus of my family, career and social interactions surrounded and set in continuous motion by global Japanese societal discourses (especially those concerned with foreigners), local interactions and socialization practices. Although family and career interactions could be considered as subcategories of my social life, I have instead created a separate category for social interactions in order to differentiate casual encounters with, for example, neighbors, shop clerks, gasoline attendants, and so on, from more private exchanges at home and more career-related discourses circulating at my university workplace. Elements in the figure are not conceived as extraneous variables in a series of linear, cause and effect processes. On the contrary, this representation is intended to illustrate how each component of my JSL life 'has a history that leads into that moment and a future that leads away from it in arcs of semiotic change and transformation' (Scollon & Scollon, 2004: 160) and that analyzing each component in isolation would result in a static, unidimensional interpretation of my Japanese language development. As a descriptor for their scheme concerning the interactive nature of social action, discourse(s) and identity formations, Scollon and Scollon (2004: 30) employ the term 'semiotic ecosystem', Charles Goodwin refers to 'semiotic fields' (2000: 1490) in his study of speech behavior, and more recently Leo van Lier conceptualizes his approach to language learning as 'an *ecological-semiotic* one' (van Lier, 2004: 55, italics in original). These perspectives on language learning and use share a particular theoretical viewpoint that encompasses notions such as those delineated by van Lier (2004) who suggests that for language-learning situations:

(1) The language surrounds the learner in all its complexity and variety.
(2) The language is embedded in the physical and social world, and is part of other meaning-making systems.

Career Discourse(s) 89

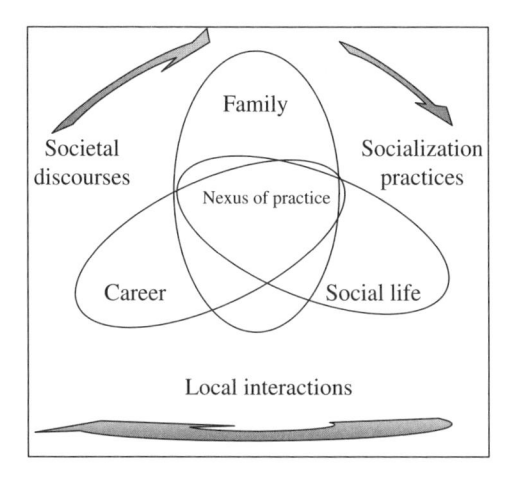

Figure 5.1 Constellation of CoPs

(3) Language learning and language use cannot be clearly distinguished from one another, and both form part of activity and interaction (van Lier, 2004: 55)

The terms 'semiotics' and 'ecological', used separately or conjointly by the theorists mentioned above, are important features in recent SLA and applied linguistics research aimed at providing a more coherent and realistic view of how individuals become proficient (or not) in a second or additional language. This topic and those that were introduced in the opening chapters of this book will be revisited in the concluding chapter where I elaborate on their relevance to my autoethnographic account.

The following sections focus on the significance of global and local discourse(s) surrounding my JSL development that is in a mutually constitutive, ever-evolving relationship with my career identity.

Language at Work

My professional career at a Japanese university has provided me with a viable inroad to Japanese society, especially in higher-education contexts. As I have moved up the ranks from native English instructor to associate professor my Japanese abilities have, out of necessity, progressed accordingly. I am expected to participate in faculty meetings and perform duties that entail a high level of Japanese language proficiency. A working knowledge of *keigo* (polite/honorific forms) is essential when addressing faculty members, students' parents and other individuals who are part of my sphere of professional interactions. Documents concerning departmental business (meeting times and dates, curriculum) or university matters in general (union bulletins, messages from administration) are circulated in

Japanese, and I oftentimes need to send or reply in Japanese to inter- and intradepartment email correspondence.

As mentioned in Chapter 3, I am able to get by when writing in Japanese, thanks to the word processor *henkan* (return) function that changes *hiragana* syllabary into the corresponding *kanji*. For example, in order to copy the sample segment from the novel by Haruki Murakami mentioned in Chapter 3, I first input the *hiragana* for the first word in the first line, とき (*toki*), which I already knew was the pronunciation of this character for 'time'. I then selected the corresponding kanji (時) from the list automatically provided; however, if I had not been sure of the pronunciation I could have scrolled down the list of possible *kanji*, some of which have short explanations to the right, in the hope of making the correct choice (see Figure 5.2).

This task becomes more complicated if I do not know the pronunciation from the start, in which case I count the number of strokes and hunt through a reference book that groups 'the 1,850 characters designated as "standard" for general everyday use in the publishing world' (Sakade, 1989: 8) according to the number of strokes in each character. Needless to say, this search process is time consuming, and it would be an arduous undertaking if it were necessary to handwrite on the spot without resource to a computer something involving complex *kanji*, for example, 驚く (surprise). A Japanese/English dictionary together with a *kanji* reference book are tools I cannot do without when handwriting important messages. At home, I usually use a combination of elementary *kanji*, *hiragana* and English

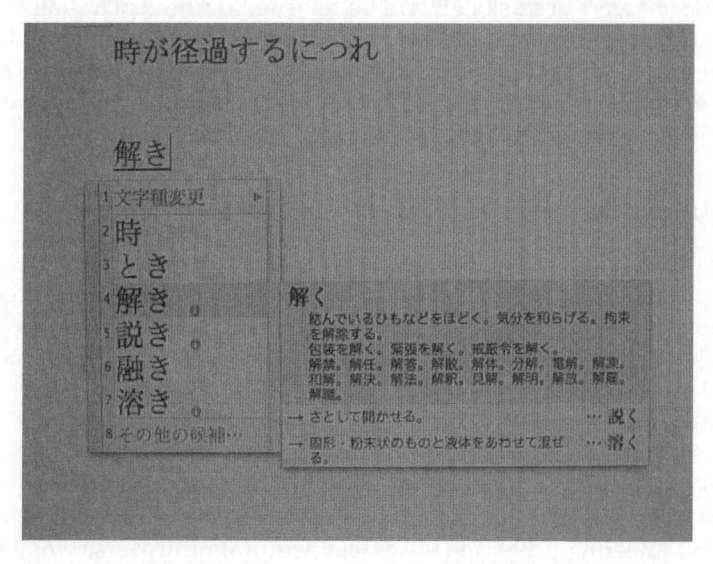

Figure 5.2 *Henkan* funtion

in handwritten notes I leave for *Yuji* for example, れいぞうこの中の curry をあたためて食べてね, Mom (Heat up and eat the curry in the refrigerator), but this style is not acceptable for professional settings. In addition to the challenge of writing in a legible calligraphic style,[1] also difficult is whether a certain sound is elongated or not. For example, I often confuse (八日 *yooka*, the eighth day of the month) with (四日 *yokka*, the fourth day of the month) when speaking and also when inputting *hiragana* to retrieve the corresponding *kanji*.

Xiao Lei (2008) presents a sociocultural view of L2 strategies that I have found instructive in helping me to understand what is involved and what I need to focus on in order to further develop my written JSL literacy. Building on the Vygotskian notion of mediation and Leontiev Activity Theory (1999), Lei defines writing strategies as 'mediated actions which are consciously taken to facilitate writers' practices in communities' (Lei, 2008: 220). A Japanese–English dictionary and kanji reference book are indispensable 'tool-mediated strategies' (Lei, 2008: 224); however, a sociocultural perspective entails recognition and utilization of additional strategies that facilitate writing processes. In particular, 'community-mediated' and 'society-mediated' strategies (Lei, 2008: 227–228) are essentially what I need and depend on most at my current level of written Japanese proficiency. That is to say, in line with current theories of second language acquisition that contest the Cartesian dualism of mind and body (see Atkinson, 2002), my composing a written document in Japanese is not purely a solo cognitive performance but rather is embedded in and enacted through my social network. Relatedly, James Paul Gee (1999) describes the socially mediated properties of language as a meaning-making system in which '[t]he context of an utterance (spoken and written) is everything in the material, mental, personal, interactional, social, institutional, cultural, and historical situation in which the utterance was made' (Gee, 1999: 54). Also, in his expanded view of affordances, van Lier proposes that

> language is part of action, of physical artifacts, of the actions of others. Learners pick up information from all these sources – physical, social, and symbolic – and use them to enrich their activities. In this way, learners are socialized into the social and cultural practices of the language and the people who use if for various purposes. (van Lier, 2004: 53)

Socio-interactionist views promise a more hopeful path to literacy enhancement beyond the drudgery of searching through dictionaries and kanji reference books in order to compose messages or fill out forms in Japanese. I increasingly find myself relying on 'the actions of others' for completing simple writing tasks, for example, when filling out a work-related form for my university, 名古屋経済大学 (*Nagoya Keizai Daigaku*) I suddenly forgot how to write the kanji for 経 (*kei*). When I mentioned this to the secretary who was standing by and watching me filling out the form she explained, '糸偏に又の下に土' (*Ito hen ni mata no shita ni tsuchi*), that is, the compound kanji 経 is composed of the radical (basic) *kanji* for 'thread' (糸) on the left, the radical for 'again' (又) on top and the radical for 'dirt' (土) underneath. In other words, this *kanji* character is composed of three radical elements all of which I am familiar with, and thus my memory was stimulated making it possible for me to successfully write the compound *kanji*. I then got stuck on writing the *katakana* for *so* (ソ) that I often confuse with ン (the n sound) as in the word 'personal computer' (パソコン) that I also needed to write on the form. Again, the friendly secretary first offered, '冬のソナタのソ' (*Fuyu no sonata no so*, the *so* as in Winter Sonata [a popular Korean soap opera]). However, when she noticed my hesitation she then wrote ソ on her left palm with her right index finger, a social action that constituted a 'physical affordance' in helping me write the word (fieldnotes, November 12, 2004). A detailed description of my work environment below further illustrates how I rely on socially mediated affordances to manage my professional college educator identity in a second language.

Workplace Discourse(s)

At my workplace I am regarded as a somewhat atypical *gaijin* – a strange individual who, even to this day, receives curious glances and incredulous remarks from Japanese people in my daily round of social interactions. Students and colleagues at my university, as well as casual acquaintances, often comment on what they perceive to be my Japanese demeanor with the remark, '*Maeda-san, nihonjin da na*' (Ms Maeda, you are indeed a Japanese) or even '*Andy-san nihonjin yori nihonjinrashii*' (Andy, you're even more Japanese-like than the Japanese), despite the obvious differences between my 'identity kit' (Gee, 1996), that is, the way I look, talk and behave compared to a native Japanese. I always laugh at these remarks that sometimes make me feel I am in a never-ending comedy schtick, for example, while riding along in a golf cart with my golf buddies during our monthly golf outings, an acorn fell from a tree and landed on the golf cart. I said, '*Aa donguri da*' (Ah, an acorn) and the person sitting next to me responded with '*Sugoi naa donguri shiteiru da*' (Wow, you know about acorns), which I interpreted to mean that she was not only surprised that I knew what an acorn looked like but that I also knew the Japanese translation. I reminded my friend, as I have done on numerous occasions in the past, that I have been in Japan for many years and that it is only '*atarimae*' (common sense) that I should be able to speak Japanese (fieldnotes, November 17, 2003).

I am constantly bewildered by comments like the above that construct me as being Japanese-like when I display even an elementary knowledge of Japanese or Japanese customs, and wonder what might cause a foreigner in the United States to be thought of as being American-like –

Career Discourse(s) 93

English spoken with a Bronx accent? Raucous language and behavior at sports events? A preference for pizza and doughnuts? Needless to say, stereotypes of one's own and others' cultural and linguistic behavior are entrenched in all of our psyches, and problems arise when these preconceived notions are not in synch with what we are (or what we think we are) and what we might be trying to become [cf. Menard-Warwick's (2009) discussion of the identity constructions of immigrants in the US vis-à-vis majority linguistic and cultural norms, also see Kamada's (2010) study of the hybridized identities of children of mixed racial backgrounds in Japan].

A textual manifestation of how I am discursively and hence socioculturally positioned in my workplace setting and consequently in Japanese society is an episode involving a message on the notice board outside my office. The first message on the left (see Figure 5.3) written on a large manila envelope says, 'Andy *no rusu no toki jisshuusei kobetsuhyoo koko ni irete kudasai*' (When Andy[2] is not here place your individual practice teacher forms inside here [the envelope]). This endeavor entailed approximately 10 minutes of retrieving from a kanji reference book the necessary *kanji* for 留守 (*rusu*, absent) and copying the title from the form itself 実習生個別表 (*jisshusei kobetsuhyoo*, practice teacher individual form). Later that day, a student of mine named *Megumi*, passing by my office on her way to class wrote on the board, 'Andy *kanji jooza da ne* by *Megumi*' (Andy, you're good at *kanji*) with a cute drawing of a popular cartoon figure called *anpan* (sweet red bean paste) *man* (see Figure 5.4).

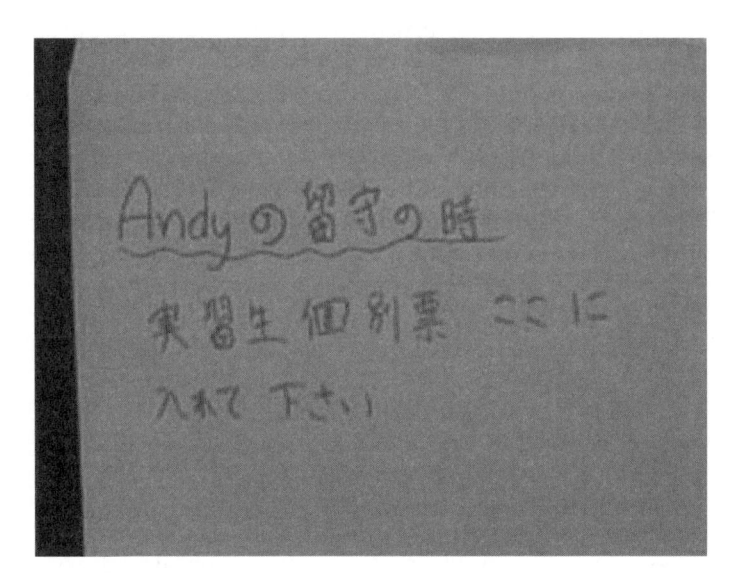

Figure 5.3 Message board

Figure 5.4 Cute drawing

This discursive positioning by others is due in large part to what they (mistakenly) perceive to be my advanced Japanese literacy, disregarding the fact that I have lived in Japan for over 30 years. As mentioned in Chapter 3, my father remained a dysfluent English speaker for the remainder of his 58 years after he emigrated to the United States at the age of 14, and although my L2 literacy level has surpassed my father's, I am ashamed, despite comments by outside observers, that after so many years I cannot function as a balanced bilingual (see Note 6 in Chapter 3) in Japanese society. This is not false modesty on my part but rather an honest assessment also shared by others who, unlike *Megumi* above, have no reservation about criticizing my JSL abilities, as illustrated by a recent exchange (fieldnotes, February 24, 2010) with one of my more outspoken students. In the midst of my explanation about a decision made at a faculty meeting concerning graduation requirements, *Chiho* interrupts:

Chiho: Andy, *senseitachi no kaigi no toki nihongo wakaru?* [said in a teasing tone]
Andy, do you understand the Japanese at teachers' meetings?
Andy: *Un, hotondo wakaru yo.*
Uhm, I understand almost everything.
Chiho: *Tokidoki* Andy *ga watashitachi no kaiwa demo wakaranai toki aru mitai. Ne, nan nen nihon ni iru?* [said with a raised eyebrow]
Sometimes it seems like Andy doesn't understand what we [students] are talking about. How many years have you been in Japan?

Andy: *Sanjyuugo nen, soo da ne, demo daitai wakaru yo.*
Thirty five years, well, but for the most part I understand.
Chiho: *Ato,* Andy *no hatsuon ga okashii toki aru, dakedo saigo made kiku to wakaru.*
Also, Andy's pronunciation is strange sometime, but if we listen to the end we can understand.
Andy: *Arigatoo wakatte kurete.* [said sarcastically]
Thanks for understanding.

Unlike students' comments that are usually made in a teasing manner and that I respond to in a friendly teacher–student bantering style, there are instances of remarks made by other people in my workplace that are a source of irritation. These people consider me to be completely lacking in the reading and writing skills needed to carry out my job duties. Consider the following exchange (fieldnotes, December 10, 2009) between the administrator in charge of collecting new course syllabi that needed to be forwarded to the Ministry of Education (*Monbushoo*) for approval. *Hara-san* (pseudonym), with whom I have had numerous interactions over the course of my 10-year employment at the university, sent me an email message attached with a template for filling in the outline of my new course syllabus. I usually resort to the phone when answering departmental matters, especially when something important needs to be confirmed:

(on the phone)
Andy: *Maeda desu ga, atarashii jyugyoo no ken ...*
Maeda here, about the new course ...
Hara-san: (chuckling noise)
Andy: *Dooshite waratte iru desu ka?* [said annoyingly]
Why are you laughing?
Hara-san: *Wakaranai naa to omotta.*
I thought perhaps you didn't understand [the attachment].
Andy: *Nihongo de kakeru dakedo chotto jikan kakaru.*
I can write it in Japanese but it will take a bit of time.

Hara-san's chuckling interruption before I could finish my first line indicated her perception, much like the clerk's in the bookstore (Chapter 3), that I could not handle a task that necessitated the required level of Japanese proficiency. Her elongated '*naa*' is also an inappropriately casual form that would not be used when speaking with Japanese teachers. After the phone call, I promptly got to work on the form, asked a colleague (who I will introduce below) to make some minor adjustments, and emailed it back to *Hara-san*, who I hoped had grasped the meaning of my annoyed voice on the phone. While for the most part a certain degree of politeness pervades my interactions at work there are times, like the above incident, when I feel that some people feel free to apply a different set of sociopragmatic rules when dealing with me.

Similar to my preference for using the phone instead of written communication, our department head, who speaks fluent German and somewhat fluent English, often phones me and speaks only in Japanese when there is a sticky matter that needs to be straightened out. His most recent phone call (January 30, 2010) was about a sudden curriculum change, and in his typical self-deprecatory style he began with, '*Boku no eigo wa are dakara denwa shita no*' (My English is such that I phoned), and I responded with '*Sono koto wa nai*' (That's not so). When the matter was settled, I closed the conversation with, '*Tsugi no toki nihongo de okutte kudasai, yomeru kara*' (Next time please send it [the message] in Japanese because I can read it). What is involved in this short exchange is not only a negotiation of which language is to be used for communication but, more importantly, it is a negotiation of my identity as a capable member of our faculty. That is, intradepartment messages are circulated in Japanese, and although I am the least interactive member online, I make a point of responding (albeit in simplified Japanese) when a response is called for, or make it clear either in person or on the phone that I have read the message and am aware of what is going on in our department.

Walk the Walk and Talk the Talk

Notwithstanding the various opinions of my Japanese abilities, they are generally considered by most people in my workplace to be adequate enough, and I am increasingly asked to carry out job-related duties that were not expected of me when I began my tertiary-level teaching career in Japan in 1975. For example, due to declining university enrollment figures teachers are required to visit high schools (高校訪問, *kookoo hoomon*) in the area to speak with the 進路の先生 *shinro no sensei* (guidance counselor). We bring along brochures of our university and lay out reasons for why prospective students can receive a solid educational experience and how our department in particular has high job placement figures, since there continues to be a steady demand for kindergarten teachers despite Japan's current economic slump. For this particular task, I have to walk the walk and talk the talk[3] of a salesperson presenting an attractive product to the customer. I pick out sedate clothing for the day, make sure my hair is under control, polish my shoes, get my *meishi* (calling card) (see Figure 5.5) ready and silently (or at times aloud) rehearse the spiel while driving to the designated high school.

My *meishi* is an intertextual[4] artifact of my professional identity crafted from the discursive presentation of the name of my university 名古屋経済大学短期大学部 (*Nagoya Keizai* University, junior college division), academic department 保育科 (Early Childhood Education) and rank 准教授 (Associate Professor). In handing someone my *meishi* I am, in effect, signaling my membership in a higher-education CoP that is part of mainstream

Career Discourse(s) 97

```
名古屋経済大学短期大学部

保育科
准教授
前田 アンドレア

〒484-8504 犬山市内久保61-1
Tel.0568-67-0616(#1415)  Fax.0568-67-0724
E-mail andy@nagoya-ku.ac.jp
```

Figure 5.5 Calling card

Japanese society. However, my first name written in *katakana*, アンドレア, together with my *gaijin* embodiment signify[5] that although I am associated with Japanese society by virtue of my family name 前田 (*Maeda*) and my institutional affiliation, I am simultaneously perceived, that is, positioned as a non-Japanese citizen, a foreigner. Likewise, my faculty profile on our department's homepage http://www.nagoya-ku.ac.jp/faculty/j_college/childcare/professor/maeda_a/ is also an intertextually co-constructed display of my insider and outsider positions fluctuating in significance according to surrounding societal discourses:

前田アンドレア准教授　プロフイール

Maeda Andrea

I have taught EFL in Japan since 1975 and received a Doctorate in Education degree from Temple University in 2002. My doctoral thesis was an ethnographic study of junior college women's attitudes toward gender and education. I have published articles in *TESOL Quarterly*, *Language Teaching*, *International Multilingual Research Journal* and am currently writing a book-length autoethnographic account of my Japanese language-learning experiences.

Similar to self-promotional styles of academics worldwide, a list of affiliations and publications establishes my location not only in our university's hierarchy but also in a global academic community. For publications (see References section) I now attach my US family name (Simon) to my Japanese surname (*Maeda*), even though the latter is not legally recognized in either country. I currently hold permanent resident status, but unless I acquire Japanese citizenship my name and legal domicile, 本籍 (*honseki*), as recorded on official documents such as my license and alien registration card (see Figure 4.2) clearly indicate that I am a foreigner.

The choice to use a hyphenated surname on publications is not due to any nostalgic longing for my American past, nor is it an attempt to project a trendy cosmopolitan image. Instead, I feel that this discursive hybridization is an apt representation of how I straddle two different (yet continually intersecting) worlds of past, present and future events about to unfold. In other words, as Scollon and Scollon would explain (see Figure 5.1), my being and becoming a JSL speaker is continually under construction at the nexus (intersection) of my experiences in the United States before moving to Japan, my everyday interactions and my imagined life in the future.

A manual (see Appendix 5) of the routine for visiting high schools is prepared by our university and handed out to teachers beforehand; nevertheless, my anxiety always reaches level orange when the guidance counselor asks me a question that cannot be handled by simply pointing out that particular section in the brochure, even though there is a suggested response provided in the manual for this type of situation. These responses, along with others, should be delivered in a very formal style that is often beyond my current spoken capabilities. Most of the high schools we visit have shepherded some of their graduates into our department and are already quite familiar with our university. However, in light of our institution's serious need of more applicants for its financial survival I feel a keen responsibility to present myself in a highly professional style with the required language repertoire. At the same time, I find myself shamelessly resorting at times to my *gaijin*-ness as an excuse for a lack of knowledge about academic details or hoping that the hearer, in this case the guidance counselor, will be left with a positive impression, that is, my existence as a tertiary-level educator indicates our university's allegiance to Japan's *kokusaika* (internationalization) ideology.[6] I also occasionally play my *gaijin* trump card for avoiding unsolicited interactions outside of work settings. For example, while writing this section, the doorbell rang and I answered the door to find two women with religious materials in hand asking if I would take some time to read the contents. Various proselytizing groups regularly make the rounds in my neighborhood, and when I cut them off with '*Sumisen, nihongo yomemasen*' (Sorry, I can't read Japanese) they complacently leave without further ado. However, this avoidance tactic will not fly in my workplace, as I describe below.

Meetings

Faculty meetings are crucial sites for the (re)negotiation of my professional identity within our departmental community of practice. Concepts from Wenger's (1998: 100–174) CoP model help to explain how my JSL interactional styles both depend on and influence my different levels of participation as a faculty member. Since I recently transferred to the Early Childhood Education Department from a different department in our university, I am still in an apprenticeship mode. In any type of CoP, 'newcomers must be granted enough legitimacy to be treated as potential members' (Wenger, 1998: 101), and my *inbound trajectory* to full participation in our department will evolve through *mutual engagement* with colleagues. In practical terms, participating in various career-related arenas entails Japanese fluency at a level beyond what is adequate for the other two spheres in my constellation of CoPs (see Figure 5.1). During department meetings, I am the most silent member since (a) I am still unfamiliar with the intricacies of department matters, for example, *Monbushoo* (Education Ministry) course requirements for attaining an early education teacher license, (b) the *tatemae* (outside) and *omote* (inside)[7] of curriculum decisions and hiring practices and (c) my linguistic inability (or self-perception thereof) to make a cogent contribution to the topic under discussion. Despite supportive congenial colleagues who I unhesitatingly interact with on a daily basis (especially at our extracurricular drinking soirées), I nevertheless do not yet feel fully confident of my professional voice during meetings.[8] However, despite my insecurities, there are times like the following example that offer a glimmer of hope. At a recent meeting (fieldnotes, January 15, 2010), *Suzuki-sensei* (pseudonym) introduced the topic of a survey that he had administered to first-year students concerning attitudes toward their academic life. The statistical analysis was passed around the table and we were asked to make comments. *Sato-sensei* (pseudonym) pointed out a design flaw that led to spurious findings, and I added that '*Watashi no zemisei shika shirimasen ga ankeeto no toki ii kagen ni kotaeru kara* reliability *ya* validity *no mondai ga arimasu*' (I only know about my own seminar students, but they do not take care when answering questionnaires; therefore, there is a reliability or validity problem). I often codeswitch with English words at meetings knowing that my highly educated colleagues will be familiar with, for example, the terms 'reliability' and 'validity' for which I do not know the Japanese equivalents. *Sato-sensei* then showed agreement with her, '*Soo da nee, gakuseitachi ga mannaka no tokoro zutto*' [making a long downward gesture with her right hand simulating marking with a pencil] *maruku suru kara*' (Yes, right, because students by and large circle the middle answer). In other words, *Sato-sensei* concurred with my opinion that students overwhelmingly select the middle answer, 'Don't know' or 'No opinion', which may have led to unreliable conclusions. What is important here is that I managed a counterargument to *Suzuki-sensei*'s statistical interpretation and was then supported by *Sato-sensei*'s comment that in effect served to legitimize my membership in the departmental CoP.

At the same meeting, the topic of job hunting came up and concern was expressed that career opportunities were not being actively pursued by many students, and that it was teachers' responsibility to urge them to do so. I mentioned that when I ask those who had not yet decided what they plan to do after graduation I often get, *'Nan toka ni naru'* (Something will come up). *Sato-sensei* followed with *'Maeda sensei ga oshatta tori watashi no zemisei mo soo, "Nan toka ni naru"'* (As Maeda teacher said, my seminar students are the same, 'Something will come up'). Everyone then agreed that this was an unrealistic mindset of students, considering the drastic decrease in jobs in every sector of Japanese society. *Sato-sensei's* uptake and agreement with my opinion together with her use of the polite form of address *'Maeda sensei ga oshatta tori'* legitimized my 'right to speak' (Bourdieu, 1977b: 649), thus adding some punch to my professional identity. I have noticed this collaborative-oriented discourse style among all the members in our department during meetings that provide me with an invaluable site for honing my professional JSL interactional repertoire.

'Don't worry, be happy'

In order to obtain an outside opinion (in addition to the informal opinions I receive almost daily from a variety of people) concerning my Japanese abilities, I asked *Suzuki-sensei* if he would be willing to give me an honest assessment. In the midst of translating a book in his specialized field (clinical psychology) from English to Japanese, *Suzuki-sensei* regularly drops by my office for help. He and I have worked out a deal – I will assist him with the translation, and in return he has promised to bail me out when I need to read or write lengthy documents in Japanese concerning departmental matters, for example, course descriptions or minutes of department meetings. *Suzuki-sensei* has visited my home with his family several times to attend our annual *mochi tsuki* (steamed rice pounding) event (see Chapter 6) and has observed me socializing informally in Japanese with other guests at that particular event, with students on campus, and also with other faculty members at our drinking sessions after school. My ongoing insecurities about my overdependence on native Japanese speakers when I get stuck on tasks that entail a high level of written proficiency surfaced during the course of the short (30 minutes), unstructured, audio-recorded interview. Although the interview was conducted mainly in Japanese, English words occasionally popped up in *Suzuki-sensei's* lines and mine as well, something that was not surprising since he had just returned from a year long sabbatical in the United States and I knew he would understand the English terms I used. I have deleted stretches of dialog that I deemed inconsequential (although interesting from a microanalytical perspective) to the primary purpose of the interview, that is, to have my Japanese abilities appraised by someone who I felt would speak frankly. Several lines of my lead-in questions or comments are omitted. In lieu of the omitted material, I provide a summary in brackets in order to present *Suzuki-sensei*'s insights in a more continuously coherent flow. Dysfluencies in the English translation roughly correspond to those in the original Japanese.

In my university office, January 10, 2010
A = Andy, S = *Suzuki-sensei*

A: First off, about Andy's (see Note 2 in Chapter 5 concerning the way I refer to myself in conversations with Japanese people) Japanese level, the way I speak, the way I live in Japan, anything is okay. Well, for example, at meetings or when I speak to students, the Japanese used in Andy's professional setting, and my Japanese apart from those situations. From *Suzuki-sensei*'s eyes and ears, for example, I can't write Japanese that well so I always indulge in the kindness of *Suzuki-sensei* or *Mizuno-sensei* to help me write things.
S: I think your Japanese level is very high, you can communicate well, and when we Japanese are speaking, of course you understand, and it appears that you can read the material at meetings. As it is, your Japanese proficiency is high. Probably writing is difficult, but you can read most things.
A: At meetings, Andy doesn't speak that much, right? I myself wonder why I don't speak, there are many reasons why I don't, but one reason is that I'm a newcomer, right? But it isn't only because of the way the department works, if Andy speaks weird Japanese she'll be seen as a fool. That's embarrassing, so I hold back. As expected, to a certain extent my formal Japanese is not yet...
S: But there's perhaps no need to be ashamed since you can do that much.
A: So, despite Andy's bad Japanese everybody thinks it's okay?
S: It's okay, because it's not so bad to the extent that it's incomprehensible. When Andy speaks, probably 95% is correct Japanese, so even if you make minor mistakes we understand.

[I mention how the department head, because he's a nice guy and has experienced life abroad as a foreigner, often summarizes what I say in a collaborative style so that everybody understands and I don't feel left out. I also bring up what happened at the previous department meeting when *Suzuki-sensei* introduced the survey statistics and subsequently *Sato-sensei* agreed with my point about the unreliability of the results.]

S: But there's no need to worry about that because everybody understands, almost, around 100% so there's no need to worry.

[I mention that other teachers might think I am resorting to an *amaeru*[9] tactic when I ask for help when, for example, it's my turn to write up of the minutes of departmental meetings.]

S: They don't think it's such a big deal because Andy is checking entrance exams, plus teaching English at the kindergarten, so taking minutes is a trifling matter that maybe you don't have to worry so much about.

[I reiterate that I'm always wondering what the proper balance is between my nagging insecurity about becoming a full participating faculty member due to language deficiencies and relying too much on help from other members.]

S: But worrying a lot about that is perhaps healthy, psychologically healthy. If you don't worry about it then people would say, 'Why is that person' [always relying on others] and if Andy starts saying, 'It's common sense' ... [I'm not a native Japanese speaker so of course I can't do certain jobs] but I think that's a good balance, you're moderately worried, don't worry so much.

[I change the topic and mention how I depend on my husband *Junji* for help with the reading and writing of official documents, and *Suzuki-sensei* says that these documents contain a lot of difficult *kanji* that even Japanese have problems with. He relates that he would have had a lot of difficulty if his American friend in Colorado had not helped him with the paper work necessary to open a bank account. I then respond that when I tell Japanese people I meet that I have been in Japan for over 30 years and still have language difficulties they often say, '*Ma ii ya sonna gurai no nihongo nara.*' ('No big deal, [if you can speak] that much Japanese') but that for immigrants in the United States they are pressured to speak English as quickly and as fluently as possible, to which he replies, '*Kibishikatta Colorado de*' (It was tough [for me] in Colorado). I continue this thread and say that foreign instructors in US colleges need to be highly literate in English.]

S: But compared to English, Japanese syllabary is much more difficult. There's *hiragana, katakana, kanji* so writing Japanese entails much more effort than writing English. If, for example, I were in America for 10 years I would speak English fluently and also be able to write, but even if Americans are in Japan for 10 years I think they may not be able to write Japanese.

[I remind him that I have lived in Japan for over 30 years, yet do not consider myself a proficient writer, and add that Japanese generally do not expect people like me to become fluent Japanese speakers. However, for nonwhite, nonwestern populations here, the story is quite different. I give an example of the Korean instructor in our university who not only lectures in Japanese but also writes notes on the board in Japanese.]

S: However, Chinese and Koreans to a certain extent share the same language [with Japanese], Korean grammar is almost the same as Japanese. For Japanese, the easiest foreign language to learn is Korean, the most difficult is English.

[I then talk about the difficulty I had lecturing in fractured Japanese for a course on gender and language issues last year, and then make a self-mocking joke to finish up the interview.]

A: I guess it's okay [that I'm not so fluent], at my age if I thought of trying to improve from now it would be impossible.

[*Suzuki-sensei* knows I passed the *ikkyu* (top) level of the Japanese proficiency exam and brings this topic up. I downplay my achievement by explaining that my listening score was very high and pulled me through, but that my overall score was just a hair above the cut-off line.]
End of interview

After listening to the interview and spending hours transcribing, I imagined that this was what a psychotherapy session might be like, especially since I knew of *Suzuki-sensei*'s field of expertise. I also should have labeled the interview with the title of Bob Marley's reggae song, 'Don't worry, be happy' because of *Suzuki-sensei*'s numerous exhortations to me to not worry about my Japanese ability. In addition to providing an outsider's opinion of my Japanese proficiency, also of interest was *Suzuki-sensei*'s view of the differences and similarities between languages and language learners. As a highly educated individual who recently spent a year-long sabbatical in the United States and who no doubt encountered many difficulties due to his English inability, I was expecting (sadistically hoping) that he would be more critical of my JSL level, and I deliberately played the devil's advocate by bringing up examples of nonwhite, nonwestern people in Japan and also in the United States who do not have as much sociolinguistic leeway as I do. Instead, his responses were part of the *nihonjinron* discourse (see Note 7, Chapter 3) that depicts Japanese as being a uniquely challenging language to learn, especially for westerners, while Asian racial groups (Koreans and Chinese) have less difficulty. Rather than delving into the actuality of which languages are more or less difficult, since what is involved is a conglomeration of linguistic, sociocultural and individual perspectives, I will quote at length from Takie Sugiyama Lebra's insightful comments concerning the perceived uniqueness of Japanese culture, as I believe they are equally applicable to (mis)conceptions of the Japanese language:

> First of all, there is nothing either inherently unique or universal about Japanese or any other culture. Those who look for things universal are

able to find evidence of such in abundance in Japan, as are those who seek things that are culture-specific. In other words, one and the same observation may be interpreted in either a universalistic or relativistic way, because a cultural boundary is a construct of the observer, not an attribute intrinsic to the object.... Second, rather than reducing the boundary question to a simplistic dichotomy of unique versus universal, as if there is no overlap, it makes more sense to view Japan (or any culture, for that matter) as something in between.... These two extremes – no overlap and complete overlap – though logically possible, are actually unlikely. Somewhere between these two poles however, cultures do find partial overlap, as well as partial disjunction. It is in this area that I try to locate Japanese culture, conceiving of cultural boundary as at best fuzzy and elusive, as many boundaries are. (Lebra, 2004: 256–257)

Lebra's insights speak to the futility of wallowing in dichotomies (linguistic, cultural, racial, etc.) that, while they work in very real ways to bring order to our chaotic lives, can also lead to a humanist illusion that they are absolute, innate structures [see St Pierre (2000) for poststructuralist critiques of humanist thought, also see Note 3 in Chapter 1]. I do not imagine that my own or others' perceptions of me and my Japanese-speaking self will ever reach a plateau of total harmony, due to our natural tendency to construct ourselves in opposition to what we are not (cf. Jacques Derrida's deconstructive theories of *différance*). Ultimately, I should simply trust *Suzuki-sensei*'s assessment, 'Everybody understands, almost, around 100% so there's no need to worry'.

Students as Cultural and Linguistic Informants

Informal exchanges with my students are ongoing opportunities for me to align my JSL identity and literacy development with current sociolinguistic trends. As an example, one of my students is living with her boyfriend who is, as she told me on a previous occasion, *haafu* – Japanese father, Filipino mother. While we were chatting, she received a text message on her cell phone from her boyfriend in Japanese, and when I inquired about his English ability, as I am aware that many Filipinos speak English, she explained that his mother could speak Japanese but was only able to text her son in English. I replied that I also text my son primarily in English but occasionally use *kanji*, which caused the usual surprised reaction. To provoke further reaction, I then mentioned that I can also read newspaper articles and proceeded to read aloud the headline of a newspaper article (see Figure 5.6) that happened to be on my desk – *Keiyaku kigyoo tsunori hoiku muryooka* (seeking business contracts for free childcare).

契約企業募り保育無料化

Figure 5.6 Newspaper headline

Other students who were mingling around produced a joint *'sugoi!'* (Wow!), and when I asked them to supply the pronunciation of the *kanji* 募 that I was not sure of, they said they were not sure either. I then mentioned that I thought it was the same kanji as *bo* as in the word *boshuu*. This word is familiar to me because it is often used with the verb *suru* literally meaning 'to collect', and regularly appears in written and spoken educational contexts as many universities are now struggling to recruit (collect) students.[10] They concurred, and supplied the correct pronunciation, *tsunori*, the noun form of the verb *tsunoru*, which also means to collect (fieldnotes, 1/12/2010).

On another occasion, I asked one of my seminar students, *Masa*, who happened to stop by my office to please read the name, 桐原, of the Japanese publishing firm of a book I was citing in an article. He supplied *sugi* (pine tree, instead of what I discovered later was the correct *kiri* (pawlonia wood) for 桐 and affixed it to the second *kanji* 原 (*hara*), as *Sugihara* is a common family name. However, he then said he wasn't sure about the first *kanji*, and proceeded to look it up using the reference function on his cell phone with no luck. He then added, *'Doko ka de mita koto ga aru ... tomodachi no namae'* ('I've seen this before ... my friend's name') (fieldnotes, 1/15/2010). Notwithstanding the uncommon combination of *kanji* sometimes used for names, there have been many occasions when I have observed how young (18–20-year-old) students at my university can neither read nor write certain *kanji*, thus making me reflect on how literacy development for both L1 and L2 speakers is significantly dependent on one's age, gender and socio-educational background.[11] That is, many of my students do not regularly read newspapers beyond the entertainment or sports sections, nor are they in the habit of watching news or educational programs on TV.

At the beginning of New Year, the traditional greeting is *Akemashite omedetoo gozaimasu, kotoshi moo yoroshiku*. Which combines a celebratory message with something roughly equivalent to asking for someone's continuing cooperation during the New Year. Upon entering my first class period after the winter break, a few students greeted me with, 'Andy, あけおめ ことろ' (fieldnotes, January 12, 2010), which is 'Andy' followed by a shortened version (*akeome kotoro*) of the long greeting noted above. I knew this was the spoken form of their cell phone texting style but jokingly prodded with, *'Sore wa nani go desuka?'* (What language is that?). The reply was, *'Ryakugo, wakamono kotoba'* (an abbreviated word, youth language). On a previous occasion (fieldnotes, January 10, 2010) when students noticed a change in my hairstyle, I recounted that I always confuse the Japanese words, *maegami* (bangs), *mayuge* (eyelashes) and *matsuge* (eyebrows) and had mistakenly told my hairdresser, '*Mayuge kitte kudasai*' (Please cut my eyebrows). This tale naturally caused a round of laughter, and a student proceeded to play a game by saying each of the words and telling me to point to the spot as fast as I could. Thereafter, whenever that student sees me on campus, she initiates the game. Although I sometimes collude in my own othering[12] by playing the role of the foreign buffoon in a comical schtick I feel at the same time that I can develop a pleasant teacher–student relationship that might not always be available to students.

Texting

In his book about the worldwide texting phenomenon, David Crystal notes that there is a great deal of stylistic diversity among texters, and that '[a]ll the popular beliefs about texting are wrong, or at least debatable. Its graphic distinctiveness is not a totally new phenomenon. Nor is its use restricted to the young generation. There is increasing evidence that it helps rather than hinders literacy' (Crystal, 2008: 9). In addition to the speed of relaying messages that abbreviated forms and emoticons provide, Crystal contends that it is the inherent fun or the 'language play' (Crystal, 2008: 71) aspect that compels users to come up with ever-more creative texting techniques. Whereas I need to send work-related emails to colleagues or school officials in standardized Japanese, communicating with students involves familiarity with an abbreviated, informal, emoticon-laden style, as the examples below illustrate. Texting now constitutes teachers' primary way to communicate with students about school matters, and the cell phone (*keitai*) has become one of the many 'mindware upgrades' (Clark, 2001: 4) – a nonbiological device that we use 'to *complement* our basic biological modes of processing' (Clark, 2004: 78, italics in original). As a latecomer to texting, my preferred means of communicating with students is by phone since, as previously explained, my writing abilities are not up to snuff. On the other hand, I have come to appreciate the advantages of texting, that is, the abbreviated genre has freed me from the painstaking task of composing long messages, and I now consider myself a senior member of the *oyayubizoku* (thumb tribe). Consider the following text message (email, January 12, 2010) from a student, *Yumi*, who wanted to use the copy machine in my office:

Yumi: アンディーゼミ室にいる?
Andy, are you in the seminar room?
Andy: まだ、なぜ?
Not yet, why?
Yumi: コピーさせてほしい (´・ω・`)
I'd like to use the copy machine.

Andy: もちょっと待ってね
Wait a bit more okay?
Yumi: はーい＼(ˆˆ)／まだ授業だから終わったら行くネ☺
Okay, I'm still in class and will go after class finishes.
[a few minutes later]
Yumi: やっぱコピーしなくてよくなった(・∀・)ありがとう
I didn't need to make copies after all.

When I asked *Yumi* later what (´・ω・`) meant she replied, *'shonbori'* (despondent) indicating that she was in a fix, since she needed to copy notes from missed classes. The next emoticon ＼(ˆˆ)／ showed glee that I was on my way, and the final (・∀・) is simply a cutesy face commonly used to sign off.

Although I cannot always decipher the emoticons (see Appendix 4 for a list of commonly used Japanese emoticons) and tend not to use them in my replies, I feel they help in establishing a teacher–student bond, and I never discourage students from using them. The following (email, January 11, 2010) is a typical back-and-forth pattern with students reminding them to submit a homework assignment. My students are not English majors, yet they have no problem with the English words I occasionally insert into my messages and will occasionally reply with English words as well:

Andy: みんな新年おめでとう！ 明日か今週中前日のChristmas会についての感想文お願いします。
Minna shinnen omedetoo! Ashita ka konshuu chuu senjitsu no Christmas *kai ni tsuite no kansoo bun onegai shimasu.*
Happy New Year everyone! Tomorrow or this week please [submit] your impressions of the Christmas party.
Emi: 感想って紙に書くかUSBに保存するかどっちにすればいい？
Kansootte kami ni kaku ka USB *ni hoozon suru ka dochira ni sureba ii?*
About the impressions, should I write them on paper or save them on a USB [clip]?
Andy: USBに入れて持ってくね！
USB *ni irete motteku ne!*
Put them on a USB [clip] and bring!

Similar to students' comments about my spoken Japanese (see example above) they also make teasing remarks about my texting errors (fieldnotes, February 24, 2010), for example, 'Andy *kara no meiru itsumo tanoshimi ni shite iru*' (I'm always looking forward to email from Andy). *Chiho* made this remark in reference to an email I had sent the day before to her and a group of students with whom I took a trip to *Okinawa*, 'いよいよ明日しゅぱつだ！必ず７：３０に飛行じょうにつくように' (At last departure is tomorrow!

Be sure to arrive at the airport at 7:30). *Chiho* said the message was understandable but that しゅぱつ (*shupatsu*) was incorrect and should have been written as しゅっぱつ (*shuppatsu*) and also that 空港 (*kuukoo*) is the preferred *kanji* for airport and not 飛行じょう (*hikoojyoo*). *Chiho* often uses the adjective *kawaii* (cute) to describe me and my odd Japanese, but I always feel a bit despondent that at my advanced age (59) my JSL ability is fossilized at the level of a small child. In conversations with other non-Japanese university professors, I have noticed similar feelings of not being able to function at a level of literacy comparable to one's professional status, particularly when there is a sudden need to handwrite work-related documents: '*Watashi wa kakeru kedo shogakusei ga kaita mitai*' (I can write but it looks like something written by an elementary school child) (fieldnotes, February 14, 2010).

Despite the media brouhaha and heated discussions over the adverse effects (linguistic, social, psychological) of texting, I tend to agree with Crystal's (2008) conclusion that 'it is the latest manifestation of the human ability to be linguistically creative and to adapt language to suit the demands of diverse settings. In texting we are seeing, in a small way, language in evolution' (Crystal, 2008: 175).

To counter what critics might deem to be the deleterious effects of texting on my Japanese literacy development, I also receive numerous messages from university office workers, colleagues and others written in a more formal style that I am then able to strategically imitate in my replies. The first example below is from a secretary (name is a pseudonym) in the front office telling me that I paid her too much for a stamp and that she would like to return the money:

前田アンドレア先生
総務企画課　前沢です。
申し訳ありません。今日、切手が不足ですと６５円いただきましたが、郵便局で１５円で良いとのことでした。ご迷惑をお掛けいたしました。６５円お返しいたします。

Maeda Andorea-sensei
Somu kikaku-ka Maezawa desu
Mooshiwake arimasen. Kyoo, kitte ga fusoku desu to 65en itadakimashita ga, yuubinkyooku de 15en de yoi to no koto deshita. Gomeiwaku o okake itashimashita. 65en o watashi itashimasu.

Maeda Andrea teacher [my rank is Associate Professor, yet all teachers regardless of rank are addressed with *sensei* (teacher) attached to our last names. However, department heads and the president are usually addressed with their respective titles, *kachoo* and *gakuenchoo*].
Maezawa [see note 2] of the administrative planning section
I am very sorry. For your letter today I said that an extra 65 yen was needed and I asked you for that amount, but the post office said it [the

amount of postage you had originally affixed] was sufficient. I am sorry that I caused you such trouble. I will return the 65 yen.

Although the above message concerns a trifling matter, unlike *Hara-san*'s rude manner on the phone in a previous example, *Maezawa-san* used the appropriately formal style used to communicate with teachers. Her use of the suffix – *itashimasu*, the polite apologetic form *mooshi wake arimasen* [as opposed to students' *gomen ne* (sorry) with the m(_ _)m emoticon], and the more formal *itadakimashita* instead of the informal *moratta* all served to display *Maezawa-san*'s discursive deference to someone who is a few notches above her in the university hierarchy. Through these daily work-related messages I have come to recognize and use different formal and informal linguistic styles that enhance my participation in my workplace CoP. The following example illustrates how I strategically compose my texting messages modeled on those I receive from other people. *Naitoo-san* (pseudonym) in the Educational Affairs section of the university's administration office emailed to apologize for sending me the wrong course timetable to which I replied telling him to not worry about it and also asking if the office had received the form I sent requesting the use of one of the Information Processing (computer) rooms for my next semester's class (emails, February 22, 2010):

学務部教務課　内藤健次です。
いつもお世話になっております。
先日は間違った時間割表をお送りしてしまいご迷惑をおかけしました。
大変、申し訳ございませんでした。
以上です。　今後ともよろしくお願いいたします。
Gakumu-bu kyoomu-ka Naitoo Kenji desu.
Itsumo osewa ni natte orimasu.
Senjitsu wa machigatta jikan wari hyoo o okurishite shimai gomeiwaku o okake shimashita.
Taihen, mooshi wake gozaimasen deshita.
Ijoo desu. Kongoo moo yoroshiku onegai itashimasu.
Naitoo Kenji of the Educational Affairs department, curriculum section.
I am always indebted to you.
The other day I made a mistake and sent you the wrong course timetable causing you trouble.
I profoundly apologize.
That is all. I ask for your continuing cooperation.
(my reply)
内藤様
気にしないで下さい。
先日私は送りました情報処理室の希望表届きましたか？

宜しくお願いします。
前田
Naitoo-sama
Ki ni shinai de kudasai.
Senjitsu watashi wa okurimashita joohooshori shitsu no kiboo hyoo todokimashita ka?
Yoroshiku onegai shimasu.
Maeda
Mr Naitoo
Please don't worry about it.
Did you receive the request form for the information processing room that I sent the other day?
I ask for your continuing cooperation.
Maeda
(Mr Naitoo's reply)
保育科　前田アンドレア先生
情報処理室の希望届、頂いております。
ありがとうございました。
Houikuka Maeda Andorea sensei
Joohooshori shitsu no kiboo todoki, atsukate orimasu.
Arigatoo gozaimashita.
Early Childhood Education Department *Maeda* Andrea teacher
The request notification for the Information Processing room was received.
Thank you very much.

The email exchange above is a textual exemplification of *wakimae* (discernment), defined by Senko Maynard thus:

> *Wakimae* refers to sets of social norms of appropriate behavior people must observe to be considered polite in society. The manipulation of politeness strategies is a concrete method for meeting the social rules of *wakimae*. While Americans make an effort to diminish social deference, Japanese make an effort to recognize deference and follow the *wakimae* conventions by choosing differentiating expressions. Another aspect associated with *wakimae* is that Japanese society assigns stereotypical speech styles to certain occupations and social status. (italics in original, Maynard, 1997: 55–56)

Mr *Naitoo's* use of the honorific forms (*orimasu, itashimasu, gomeiwaku o okake shimashita*) indicates his lower status in relation to teachers in our university employee pecking order and also displays his humbling stance, especially since he had made a mistake by sending me the wrong form. In response, I wanted to minimize his guilty feeling but, at the same time, needed to uphold the appropriate rules of professional decorum lest I be perceived as being too casual or flippant. Hence, I chose to begin my response with '*Ki ni shinai de kudasai*' (Don't worry about it) as a positive politeness strategy in lieu of the overly polite form (*O ki ni sarenai de kudasai*) that would have unduly inflated the social distance between me and Mr *Naitoo*. This delicate manipulation of polite/casual forms is linguistically challenging even for native Japanese speakers, and through my workplace interactions I am constantly provided with multiple opportunities to become more adept at honorific appropriateness. Hence, from a Bakhtinian perspective, my writing skills will gradually (hopefully) improve through the 'appropriation' of others' texts that I can recycle in my own written messages in order 'to be heard, understood, responded to, and again to respond to the response' (Bahktin, 1986: 127). This last point applies to every aspect of my JSL literacy development and is a major theme that I will reintroduce in the final chapter.

Summary

In Alene Moyer's review of different factors that influence self and other perceptions of second language acquisition, mention is made of how unlike the situation of children who, despite errors, are often praised for their L2 efforts, adults are prone to feelings of frustration (Moyer, 2004: 38). Similarly, when students imitate my spoken Japanese with a *gaijin* accent (Chapter 6) or say that my dysfluent Japanese is 'cute' (see section above) I feel that attaining Japanese nativeness is beyond my reach. At the same time, however, I recognize that 'ultimate attainment' is an illusive goal, and that L2 fluency depends on a cluster of variables of which age is only one factor. My JSL development is a complex, ongoing process involving the interaction of cognitive, psychological and sociocultural phenomena that need to be integrated and finely tuned to fit my life circumstances, as explained by Moyer:

> [A]dult learners may be well-disposed to certain strategies to adjust to cultural gaps, linguistic gaps, and social gaps, attending consciously to their own weaknesses or discomforts in their own ways. As is clear, engaging optimally in this process can lead to exceptional outcomes. (Moyer, 2004: 145)

Thus, despondency or ascribing my L2 deficiencies to insurmountable sociolinguistic differences is a waste of energy that might be better spent on what Moyer advises for late learners, '[T]hey must seek out new social networks, learn new ways of self-expression, and develop new senses of belonging' (Moyer, 2004: 147). Additionally, throughout this chapter and previous chapters as well, I have construed my JSL abilities (or lack thereof) vis-à-vis 'native-speaker' standards embodied in the Japanese people I interact with daily in my various CoPs. However, this unavoidably realistic viewpoint may in the long run be counterproductive if it remains the all-encompassing measure of my L2 achievements. ZhaoHong Han (2004) provides a hopeful way of conceptualizing the acquisition dilemma, particularly its fossilization and interlanguage components:

> First, there is not an absolute critical period in SLA but rather a period of heightened sensitivity to environmental stimuli, within which learning is successful and beyond which learning is *still possible but highly variable and less successful*. This period is biologically founded, hence endogenous in nature, but its function hinges on the interaction between innate neural processes and exogenous stimulation. Second, the critical period applies differentially to certain language domains and subsystems, and hence is modular in nature. Third, CP effects are intricately tied up with cognitive, affective and social factors, not the least of which is L1 transfer. (Han, 2004: 167–168, italics in original)

Seen from this multilayered perspective, a monolithic definition of L2 success/failure is theoretically implausible, and static constructs such as 'native-like' and 'ultimate attainment' begin to lose their relevance to the dynamic, idiosyncratic processes involved in an individual's language-learning trajectory. Clearly, the two conceptions of L2 learning introduced in this summary section entail an investigative approach with a broader lens able to capture the complexities of how an individual acquires a second or additional language. This said, I reiterate the suggestion made in the opening chapter of this book that autoethnography can help to illuminate in ways that statistical analyses alone cannot the intricate interplay of internal and external factors that impact on L2 learning and use.

In the next chapter, I take the reader through two days in a continuous storyline composed from 35 years of engaging with diverse social networks through which I have fashioned my personalized approach to being and becoming a speaker of Japanese.

Notes

1. Japanese children often attend calligraphy (*shuuji*) classes after school, and there are also classes or correspondence courses for adults who want to improve their calligraphic styles as a hobby or for their jobs where neat handwriting is required, for example, secretaries, clerks in public offices and so on. Over the years, however, I have often met self-described sloppy writers, including my husband, relieving some of my guilty feelings about not being able to write in an aesthetically pleasing style. I attended a *shuuji no juku* (a cram school solely for calligraphy) for three years, and this was invaluable training for learning the stroke order and meaning of different *kanji*.
2. 'Andy' is how I am usually addressed by students and friendly colleagues and is also the name I use when I refer to myself, in both spoken and written interactions, except for more formal situations when I introduce myself in person or on the phone with my Japanese surname, *Maeda*. For example, when I call

kindergartens to make an appointment to observe our student teachers I would say, '*Nagoya Keizai Daigaku no hooikuka no Maeda desu*' (Maeda of the Early Education Department of Nagoya Keizai University).
3. James Paul Gee employed the term 'mushfake Discourse' (Gee, 1996: 147) in his description of the ways people (especially those in nonmainstream situations) manage to get by with the (linguistic, material, cultural, etc.) resources on hand. In the same vein, David Block draws on Judith Butler's (1993) 'performativity' theory and states that 'it is easy to see identities and subject positions as performances, that is bodily and linguistic enactments of discourses at particular times and in particular places' (Block, 2007a: 17).
4. Norman Fairclough (2003) explains that intertextuality is 'how texts draw upon, incorporate, recontextualize and dialogue with other texts. It is also partly a matter of the assumptions and presuppositions people make when they speak or write. What is 'said' in a text is always said against the background of what is 'unsaid' – what is made explicit is always grounded in what is left implicit. In a sense, making assumptions is one way of being intertextual – linking this text to an ill-defined penumbra of other texts, what has been said or written or at least thought elsewhere' (Fairclough, 2003: 17).
5. It is far beyond the scope of this book to provide a satisfying explanation of Derrida's (1974/1967) concepts of 'signifier' and 'signified' and their role in deconstructive analyses (see explanation in Denzin & Lincoln, 2000 of deconstruction and its applications in critical theory and feminist research). Instead, I will present St Pierre's (2000) lucid description that is germane both to the discussion above and also to my book's theoretical cornerstone, that is, how realities (being a *gaijin*, expatriate, etc.) are produced through texts (spoken and written) and hence, from a postmodern perspective, are continually subject to innumerable reconfigurations:

> One of the most significant effects of deconstruction is that it foregrounds the idea that language does not simply point to preexisting things and ideas but rather helps to construct them and, by extension, the world as we know it. In other words, we word the world. The 'way it is' is not 'natural'. We have constructed the world as it is through language and cultural practice, and we can also deconstruct and reconstruct it. (St Pierre, 2000: 483)

As an example, both the signified (the concept of being an expatriate) and the signifier (the word 'expatriate') are always contingent on societal discourses concerning the situation of foreigners in Japan, and thus the meaning of the word 'expatriate' is not absolute and is continually open to (re)-interpretation.
6. The ideology of *kokusaika* (internationalization) gained popularity in the 1980s and 'signified the greatly increased weight of the Japanese in the world economy ... [it], however, did not necessarily imply the internal transformation of Japanese society; rather it was accompanied by a continued, perhaps growing Japanese insistence that economic success demonstrated the unique qualities of the Japanese way – a superior, non-Western way' (McCormack, 2001: 275).
7. *Tatemae* and *honne* are described by Sugimoto as being one set in a triad of Japanese ideologies, the other two being *omote/ura* and *soto/uchi*. '*Tatemae* refers to a formally established principle which is not necessarily accepted or practiced by the parties involved. *Honne* designates true feelings and desires which cannot be openly expressed because of the strength of *tatemae*' (Sugimoto, 2003: 28).
8. Janet Holmes has written extensively on the situation of women attempting to construct a professional identity in masculinist dominant workplace settings.

During meetings, the amount of speech is not the sole determinant in establishing an authoritative figure but is rather achieved through a variety of discursive strategies that include, for example, 'making use of both authoritarian, powerful discourse as well as more relationally oriented normative feminine discourse as appropriate' (Holmes, 2007: 4).

9. The term *amaeru* is often described as being a typical Japanese trait of 'presuming on the benevolence of others' (Finkelstein *et al.*, 1991: 219).

10. Sugimoto reports that Japan's declining birthrate 'has inevitably led to a gradual decrease in the student population. Hence, universities and colleges at the bottom end of the hierarchy are finding it increasingly difficult to attract prospective students and to meet their enrollment quotas. Confronting the prospect of losing out in the struggle for survival, these institutions lower the criteria for student selection or accept applicants virtually without entrance examination' (Sugimoto, 2003: 141).

11. For students in our Early Childhood Education department, low literacy levels have become a special concern. As future kindergarten teachers, they will be expected to manage a voluminous amount of correspondence with parents in the form of newsletters and *nikki* (diaries) that are written records of what's going on with the children at home and at school, and unfavorable comments from parents about teachers' writing skills would damage a kindergarten's reputation. Our practice teachers are increasingly receiving negative evaluations of their writing skills from supervisors at kindergartens. Thus, to upgrade the literacy level of students (see Note 10) our department initiated a new course in 2009, *kisooryoku kooza* (basic skill training) aimed at drilling students in reading and writing skills that are needed for their jobs.

12. My tongue-in-cheek use of the term 'othering' is not meant to trivialize a notion that has been problematized, especially by critical race theorists and feminist researchers, as a colonizing practice characteristic of past (white, western, male, privileged) social scientists' studies of 'native' or 'exotic' populations and individuals who are marginalized on the basis of their cultural, racial or gendered backgrounds.

Chapter 6
Where I Am Now: Two Days in the Life of an Expatriate

In this last segment of my autoethnography, I present a composite account constructed from field notes, documents and photos collected over the course of my JSL life before and after the actual research process for this book began in 2004. A typical day in my life includes conversations with family members, colleagues and students at my university, interactions with shop clerks and chit-chat with neighbors, close friends and casual acquaintances.

My mornings usually begin at 6:00 am, and today at the breakfast table with *Junji*, I spot an article in our local Japanese language newspaper, *Chunichi Shimbun*, about a demonstration that occurred at the *Nagoya* city hall concerning voting rights for *zainichi* (Japan-born Koreans). I had read an article on this topic in my English newspaper, *The International Herald Tribune*, a few days earlier about voting rights for non-Japanese permanent residents and knew something was going on. *Junji*'s office is located nearby city hall where the demonstration was being held, and he said that he was tempted to approach one of the demonstrators and ask, '*Boku no yome wa? Zeikin ippai haratte iru no ni tohyoo ken ga konai*' (What about my wife? She's paying a large amount of taxes but her voting ballot doesn't come). As described in earlier chapters, L2 identity formations and sociopolitical contexts are intimately connected, and while my situation is quite different from, in this case *zainichi kankokujin* (Japan-born Koreans), we share a commonality of societal marginalization on the basis of national origin. *Junji* is well aware of the long-standing discriminatory practices against *zainichi* but, at the same time, recognizes on a personal level that I am also excluded from mainstream life due to my foreigner status. Local, national and international news stories printed in English language newspapers in Japan are typically a day or two behind the actual event (what one of my *gaijin* friends likened to reading a history book), and I have developed a habit of reading both the English and Japanese versions of articles that I am interested in. I have noticed this same pattern of reading/listening to both the English and Japanese version of different kinds of media (books, movies) in my son *Yuji* who, for example, will listen to a rental DVD movie in

English and then afterward will select the Japanese language option to listen to the same movie again. I feel that his bilingual proclivities gained through early childhood experiences during short stays in the United States and his daily interactions with me have been retained and will always be available, if he so chooses, for further enhancement.

It is snowing heavily outside, and in order to change the topic I attempt a joke with *Junji*, '*Yuji ga sono* tennis racket *mitai na kutsu o haite shigoto itta hoo ga ii*' (*Yuji* had better wear those shoes that look like tennis rackets to go to work). *Junji* pauses before saying '*Ah, ganjiki* [perfunctory chuckle]' (Oh, traditional Japanese snowshoes) (see Figure 6.1).

My communication strategy of paraphrasing with familiar words gets me through many situations when I am unable to retrieve an unfamiliar or forgotten Japanese lexical item.

After breakfast I feed our dog, Bitz, do the laundry and in between other household duties that need to be taken care of before heading off to work, I watch my favorite morning scoop show on TV, *Tokudane.* Japanese

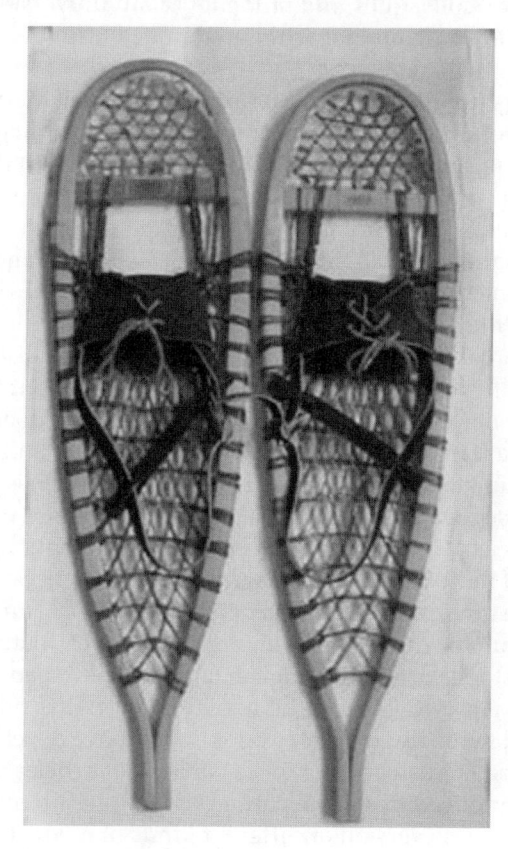

Figure 6.1 Traditional Japanese snowshoes

titles of the scoops always run along the sides of the scenes, and together with the visuals it is not difficult to understand what happened (see Figure 6.2).

In this case, the place where the incident occurred (*Osaka*) is written in the top right corner, the title at the top of the house figure reads *'rikon ni tsuite no hanashiai'* (consultation about divorce), the names and relationship of the people involved in the murder incident are written under the figures, and the text in the bottom right corner briefly explains what happened *'chuukei juu ranshya yonin shiboo rikonbanashi no motsureka'* (broadcast of wild gun fire, four people killed, entanglement over talk of divorce). In other words, a 49-year-old man killed his estranged wife, her mother, an innocent bystander, and then committed suicide. Also on today's show, a well-known American commentator and fluent Japanese speaker, Dave Spector (see Figure 6.3) who usually introduces tabloid material from abroad, is reporting on a very tall western female model visiting Japan for some sort of publicity stunt (see Figure 6.4).

In the screen on the right side of the studio, the tall woman is posing next to another woman, and the title contains a play on the English words 'big' and 'girl' ... 'ビックリ' (*bigguri*, surprise) which is normally pronounced *'bikkuri'*. A life-size placard of the woman is placed next to the female announcer to give viewers a better idea of just how tall she is, 203 cm. Dave Spector is one of the very few Americans who appears

Figure 6.2 Japanese TV show

Figure 6.3 Dave Spector

regularly on Japanese television shows, and he has been described thus: 'Spector's quick mind, and even faster tongue, have forced even his most outspoken critics to concede that his ability to ad lib and crack jokes in rapid-fire, idiomatic Japanese is nothing short of phenomenal' ('Close Up,

Figure 6.4 Tall Western female model

Dave Spector', *The Japan Times Online*, February 2, 2003). One of the questions for this newspaper article was what Spector thought of the common perception that foreigners who appear on Japanese television programs are generally regarded as 'curiosities' rather than being judged on their abilities.

> I wouldn't for a minute pretend that being a foreigner is not why it [TV career] came to be. However, I set a goal early on to be different from other gaijin tarento [foreign TV personalities] by trying to compete with Japanese rather than with other foreigners. I would say that at this point a lot of my appearances are based on my longtime participation in show business here and knowledge of current affairs that do not relate to my being a gaijin per se. (Close Up, Dave Spector, *The Japan Times Online*, February 2, 2003)

I fully understand Spector's desire to not be viewed as a 'curiosity', something that is very difficult considering our white, western visibility and how, as *gaijin*, we are as Laurel Kamada explains, 'positioned as outsiders perpetually unable to ever intrinsically understand the essence of Japanese society, language or customs' (Kamada, 2009: 32). Hence, a *gaijin* who speaks Japanese very fluently is seen as an exotic breed and is often referred to as *'henna gaijin'* (strange foreigner). Notwithstanding the fact that one of Spector's roles on this show is to introduce foreign tabloid material that often serves as fodder for the stereotyping of westerners, his Japanese proficiency is admirable and I do not consider my own JSL ability to be at the same level of fluency. In this way, I find that watching Japanese television has helped me to improve my reading and listening skills and is also a source of up-to-date lexical items and topics. I am reminded of Steven Johnson's (2006) book, *Everything Bad is Good for You*, in which television is described as being one of the many modern, multimodal technologies that have the potential to enhance learning.

After *Yuji* leaves for work on his bicycle, I drive *Junji* to our local train station for his commute into the city. When I start the car, we notice that the GPS screen is displaying a location that *Yuji* drove to last night and I say in a jokingly sneaky voice, *'Aha, kore de yuube Yuji no mokuchi wakaru wake'* (Aha, this is how we can see where *Yuji* went last night). *Junji* corrects my erroneous *'mokuchi'* with *'mokutekichi'* (destination) and I repeat with the corrected form. I recall Ingrid Piller's observation of her German–English bilingual couples' private talk wherein 'unsolicited conversational help' (Piller, 2002: 238) from the more proficient speaker (*Junji*) is sometimes interpreted by the less proficient speaker (Andy) as a face-threatening speech act. However, as the years go by *Junji* often corrects in private my lexical and grammatical errors, and I appreciate the opportunity to fine-tune my JSL fluency. We begin listening to a radio interview with *Konishiki*, a retired *sumo* wrestler originally from Hawai'i. During the course of the interview, *Konishiki* uses the phrase, '*sanpachi gumi*', and at first I think he's talking about a type of fish, *kanpachi* (yellow tail), that we occasionally order at our *sushi* shop. However, after listening a bit more I figure out that *Konishiki* isn't talking at all about fish, and I so ask *Junji* for an explanation, another feature of bilingual couples' private talk, that is, 'calls for help' (Piller, 2002: 234). I am not always in the habit of asking *Junji* for a translation or explanation in Japanese, but on this occasion I am interested in what *Konishiki* is talking about, especially since he and other non-Japanese *sumo* wrestlers are considered to be fluent Japanese speakers and I always feel a bit '*urayamashii*' (jealous) of their advanced Japanese ability. *Junji* explains that *sanpachi* refers to a group (*kumi*) of people known among each other in a certain organization (e.g. *sumo* wrestlers, entertainers, politicians) who were born in the same year, *Showa sanjyuuhachi-nen* (the 38th year of the *Showa* period, 1946) the numeral 3 is *san*, 8 is *hachi*, *kumi* is group and when coarticulated *ha* becomes *pa* and *kumi* becomes *gumi*. Thus, if I could come up with a group of well-known people associated in some way and born in 1951 (my birth year) we could become the *gopachi kumi* (58-year-old group). What is important here is that learning a new vocabulary item involved my past knowledge, present affordances and imagined uses in the future (cf. Eton Churchill's 2008 dynamic systems approach to understanding the microlevel processes involved in vocabulary acquisition).

After dropping *Junji* off with the standard send-off phrase '*ittekimasu*' (what the person leaving says) and '*ittarashai*' (said to the person leaving), I arrive at school around 9:00 am and start to prepare for my first class that begins at 9:30, to catch up on work-related tasks and to talk to students who usually stop by to chat. Today, we have assembled our department's second-year students to announce the winners of a competition involving the best well-designed plan for an imaginary kindergarten field trip. Teachers were asked to write comments on the ballots that were given back to the students during the award ceremony. One of my students, *Masa*, the jokester in my seminar group, reads out the comments I wrote on his ballot with an exaggerated *gaijin* pronunciation. Television personalities often use this mock accent when talking about or with foreigners on their programs, and this is part of the 'othering' of foreigners in Japan [see reference above from Kamada (2009) concerning *gaijin*]. After the ceremony, since it is the last event of the semester, I order pizza for a small group of seminar students who meet every week in my office. When we open the boxes, *Anri* says, '*Oo, kyabetsu*' (cabbage). The topping was actually lettuce, and when I correct with '*retasu*' (lettuce) *Anri* repeats with the exaggerated *gaijin* pronunciation, '*Oo, retasu!*'. I laugh along with the other students while reflecting that, like the example with *Masa* above, the idea of a *gaijin* being a fluent Japanese speaker has yet to enter the Japanese mind-set in a serious way.

As part of my work duties in the Early Education Department, I am required to visit our student teachers who, as part of their practicum requirements, must spend time at social welfare facilities for children who are victims of child abuse, or who for a variety of reasons cannot live at home with their families, or who are having problems adjusting to school. I leave the university around 3:00 pm and head out to a facility that is about a 30-minute drive away from my university. Upon entering the facility, as is usually the case when I also visit kindergartens, I receive curious glances from the children who gather around to get a closer look. One small child asks me the following question, 'フイリぴん人ですか?' (*Fuiripinjin desu ka*, Are you a Filipino?). I was not surprised that out of all the possible nationalities I could be the child asked if I were Filipino, as there are many Filipina women working in bars or factories in the surrounding area. Many of these women are recruited and subsequently exploited by organized Japanese crime organizations, *yakuza* (Douglass, 2000), hence there are ongoing problems with illegal entry issues that create a highly stressful situation at home for Filipina mothers with children who oftentimes have difficulties in regular Japanese schools. I tell the curious child, '*iie amerikajin desu*' (No, I'm an American) and move along to chat with the student teachers. After leaving the facility, I drive down the street and notice the following signboard (see Figure 6.5) on a nearby bar.

I wonder if the child at the facility has also once noticed this sign and how it has influenced his nascent knowledge of the word *gaijin* and his impression of the types of female *gaijin* who work in the bar.

Figure 6.5 Signboard

Before heading home to prepare dinner, I stop at the shop of my close friend, *Mi-chan*, who together with the majority of her regular customers are called either by their first or last names with the personal suffix – *chan* attached to either name. *Chan* is a diminutive 'cutesy' form commonly used for and between girls and young women, close friends of either sex and pets. For example, my husband *Junji* is called *Jun-chan* by old buddies from his high school days, my son *Yuji* is called *Yu-chan*, and one of my female golf buddies sometimes calls me *An-chan*. *Mi-chan*'s shop, a combination boutique and coffee house, is attached to her son's restaurant where housewives frequently gather for afternoon coffee klatches. A common topic of conversation is what we will be preparing for dinner, and when I was asked, 'Andy は?' (What about Andy?), the following exchange ensued:

Andy: *Saa, tabun ... toriniku o miso de, un ... furai pan de ...*
Uhm, maybe, chicken with miso, uhm ... in the fry pan ...
Kato-chan: *Miso nikomi da ne?*
Oh, [something] boiled in *miso*?
Andy: *Chigau, un, miso to sato to mirin o mazete ...*
Wrong, uh, *miso* and sugar and sweet *sake* [making a stirring motion with my hand].
Kato-chan: *Aa, karameru.*
Oh, [add sugar to] thicken and sweeten.
Andy: *So so, karamete.*
Yes, that's right, thicken and sweeten.

The dish I had in mind was chicken sautéed in sweetened *miso*; however, *Kato-chan* had thought I was referring to *miso nikomi udon*, a popular *Nagoya* dish of noodles and vegetables boiled in a thick *miso* broth. This type of conversational scaffolding between native/nonnative speakers has been widely reported in communication strategies (CS) research (e.g. Kasper & Kellerman, 1997), and in line with sociolinguistic perspectives on CS analysis (see Rampton, 1997) I feel that my L2 breakdowns (e.g. delayed lexical retrieval, as in the above data) are usually managed without much psycholinguistic angst when I am among family and friends. This sociointeractional view is elaborated on by Ben Rampton thus:

> Sometimes participants in cross-cultural interactions are seen as the prisoners of their communicative inheritances, it is forgotten that people either enjoy or overcome differences in language or cultural style, and adequate attention is not always given to the way in which participants can accentuate or play down differences according to their immediate situational needs and purposes. (Rampton, 1997: 300)

My stopovers at *Mi-chan*'s shop on the route back from my university to my home are a welcome transition to a more comfortable sociolinguistic setting – a safe and fun place to develop my Japanese abilities. Today, I have brought along a photo album of my high school days to show *Mi-chan*, who enjoys seeing old photos and hearing about my past life in the United States before relocating to Japan. Other customers scramble to get a glimpse, and the usual questioning and commenting begins: 'How old were you at the time?' 'You had a lot of boyfriends, right?' 'Did you ever think you'd end up in Japan married to a Japanese man?' During a pause in the commotion, *Kimi-chan* says, '*Unmei no akai ito da ne*' (The red string of fate). As a display of incomprehension, my 'Huh?' triggered *Kimi-chan*'s next utterance, an explanation involving the image of a ball of yarn with many strings but with only one red string to which *Junji* and I were connected. I am not sure if her explanation is the correct one or not; however, the general meaning was made clear, and an evidently well-known saying in Japan became part of my L2 repertoire. Conversations with 'the girls' at *Mi-chan*'s shop have increased my familiarity with local folk wisdom along with popular Japanese clichés and proverbs that together have enhanced my interactional competence within my social life CoP (see Figure 5.1).

My L2 joking capabilities have also improved as a result of my interactions with women in my age bracket. Similar to reports of L2 minority groups who use humor as a performative strategy 'to express resistance to discourses of social domination' (Vaid, 2006: 162), I have found that the humorous bantering of my middle-aged Japanese female friends is also a way of contesting the norms of a male-dominant society wherein women are expected to act and speak in a 'ladylike' fashion at all times. Sexual activity, or the lack thereof, is a common topic among the women at *Mi-chan*'s shop, and the diverse assortment of mid-life situations (single, widowed, divorced) makes for an interesting array of conversations that range from menopause, sagging breasts and cosmetic surgery to life insurance policies, retirement homes and unruly daughters-in-law. In reply to someone's question of whether I had a boyfriend in high school I reply that due to my flat chest (*Mune ga pechanko deshita*) boys were not attracted to me, and the following exchange unfolded:

Tsuru-chan: *Demo, sore wa kankei nai yoo, ima kono kinpen chikan[1] ga oi kara ki o tsuketa hoo ga ii.*
But that doesn't matter, there have been a lot of sexual perverts around here recently so be careful.
Andy: *Pantsu o oroshitari toka*? [literally, taking down pants]
Like flashing?
Kimi-chan: *Daijoobu. Moshi mikaketara, 'Oo! chichai nee' to ieba ii.*
That's okay. If you happen to see it [penis], just say, 'Oh! so small.' [laughter from everyone]

Mi-chan: *Dakedo, sonna koto ittara, chikan ga okotte koogeki suru kamo shiranai.*
But, if you say that, the pervert might get mad and attack you.
Kimi-chan: *Ja, 'Wow! omigoto nee' to ieba ii.*
Well, then you might say, 'Wow! Admirable.'
[laughter from everyone]

Kimi-chan, who speaks a bit of English because of her overseas business associates, often uses Americanized Japanese (much like my student *Masa* mentioned above) as a joking tactic when I am around and inserts English expletives 'Wow!' and 'Oh!' as in the above segment. In skits about *gaijin* on TV variety shows, Japanese comedians often Americanize their speech in an exaggerated style, thus fueling the marginalization of non-Japanese speakers of Japanese.

Before heading home, I stop at the local shopping plaza to replace the cell battery in my watch. I have forgotten the phrase used when asking for a new battery, and the following exchange is an example of how lexical items that escape me at the moment are subsequently retrieved through a recast from a native Japanese speaker:

Andy: *Tokei no denshi ga kiremashita.*
The battery in my watch has run out.
Clerk: *Aa, denshi kookan desu ne?*
Ah, battery replacement, right?
Andy: *Soo, denshi kookan.*
Right, battery replacement.

Although my use of *'Denshi ga kiremashita'* is neither grammatically nor semantically incorrect, *'Denshi kookan'* is commonly used in this situation and hopefully I will be able to retrieve this phrase next time in order to sound more 'native like'. While paying for the new battery, I notice the following sign (see Figure 6.6) attached to the cash register.

Being a snoopy ethnographer, I ask the clerk why such a sign was posted, and she answers *'Hanzai o fusegu tame'* (to prevent crime) and also to discourage foreigners from asking for change or trying to use foreign currency, things I have never witnessed nor could imagine a foreigner doing. When I ask whether any actual crime data were referred to when deciding which languages to post (English, Russian, Spanish, Portuguese, Chinese, Korean, Arabic) she replies, *'Iie, kan desu'* (No, [it's based on] a hunch). I thank the clerk for the information, and she asks me the question that I am perpetually asked whenever I converse in Japanese with someone I have never met before:

Clerk: *Doko kara desu ka?*
Where are you from?
Andy: *Amerika desu.*
America.

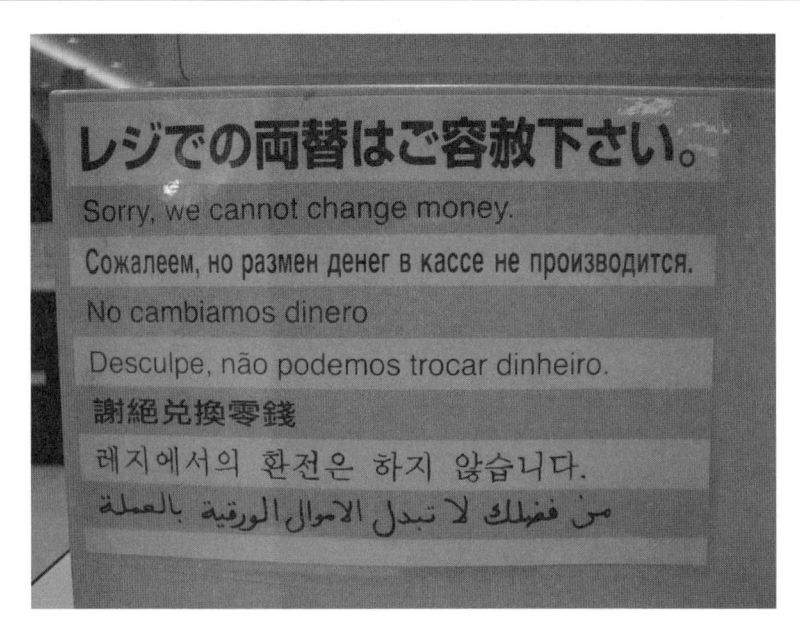

Where I Am Now: Two Days in the Life of an Expatriate 125

Figure 6.6 Cash register sign

Clerk: *Subarashii, ryoohoo dekiru, watashi wa hitotsu shika dekinai, subarashii.* Wonderful, you can do both [speak English and Japanese], I can only do one, wonderful.

Occasionally, when I am asked '*Doko kara desu ka*' (Where are you from?) I will respond with '*Konan-shi*' (Konan city) to throw the listener off balance for a while.

I arrive home around 6:00 pm, and after feeding Bitz (pet dog) and preparing one of *Yuji*'s favorite dishes, *yakisoba* (fried noodles and vegetables) that he can heat up when he gets home from work later, I watch the evening news. Like the morning scoop shows, text envelopes the visuals facilitating comprehension; however, the evening news programs that deal with Japanese politics or the economy need an occasional search in a dictionary or *kanji* reference book, even though I usually understand the general meaning of the report. Today, the top news is about a controversial political figure, *Ichiro Ozawa* (see Figure 6.7), who has been under fire for illegal political funding.

I have no problem reading the text in the top right corner '*Shitsumon wa saki ni ... Ozawa-shi irei kaiken*' (First of all, questions ... Mr *Ozawa*'s unprecedented interview) and also the text on the left side of the screen '*Minshutoo Ozawa Ichiro kanjichoo*' (*Ozawa Ichiro* secretary-general of the Democratic Party). However, a couple of the *kanji* at the bottom of the screen 捜査 (*soosa*, investigation) and 継続 (*keizoku*, continuation) involve some guessing.

Figure 6.7 *Ichiro Ozawa*

Nevertheless, I am able to understand the total meaning of the phrase, especially since I have been following this news topic in my English newspaper concerning the ongoing investigation on Mr *Ozawa*'s illegal political financing.

It is now 7:00 pm and time to leave the house to catch the local train for the trip into the city to attend the birthday party of an American friend who *Junji* and I have known for 35 years. *Junji* is already in the city, and so we meet at *Nagoya* station and change to the subway where I notice the sign that was posted on pillars a few years ago at subway stations across Japan as a measure to protect female passengers from *chikan* on crowded subway cars (see Figure 6.8).

I always interpret this sign to be merely a band aid measure, and that laws in Japan regarding sexual crimes need to be more strictly enforced. We take our seats and listen to the announcements for the next stop given in three different languages in this order: English, Korean, Chinese and Portuguese. English is recognized as an international language, Koreans represent the largest group of non-Japanese residents in Japan, Chinese are the second largest group, and Portuguese-speaking *nikkeijin* from Brazil are the 'new immigrants'. I reflect on why these particular languages came to be selected (as I did above with the sign at the cash register) the order in which they are announced, and how my life in Japan would have played out if English were not considered to be the 'prestige' language. I also think back to the day several years ago when I took the *ikkyuu* (top level) Japanese

Figure 6.8 *Chikan* sign

proficiency exam and was one of the six white westerners out of the 100 or so test takers who were mostly newcomers from mainland China. Because some of the test items contained words written in *katakana* (Japanese syllabary used for foreign words), the Chinese test takers were animatedly chatting during the break about not being able to recognize these loan words since they were not familiar with the original English equivalents, for example, アイドル (idol), ファン (fan), ビル (building) and シンクロナイズドスイミング (synchronized swimming). On the other hand, I had no problem with these items and was able to pass the test while the Chinese group managed to get by on the strength of their *kanji* recognition ability.

After a few stops, we arrive at the station closest to our friend John's (pseudonym) apartment. There is already a large group of people at the party, mainly expatriates like me or folks who have lived in various countries before settling in Japan, or individuals who were originally based in Japan and left for a few years to attend school. Upon entering the party room, a polyphony of English and Japanese codeswitching immediately catches my ethnographic attention, and the small *haafu* (children of mixed racial backgrounds) kids running around the room remind me of my son *Yuji* at that age. I grab a beer and pick out something to eat from the assortment of food and drinks that represent the composition of the party members: *sushi* rolls, fried chicken, potato chips, *chirashi sushi* (vinegared rice with an assortment of vegetables and seafood sprinkled on top), *sake*, oolong *cha* (Chinese tea), brownies and *surume* (dried cuttlefish). I introduce myself to a person I had never met before who proceeds to tell me that he was born in Montana, grew up in Japan, attended the local international high school, left for college in the United States, worked in Europe for a while, returned to Japan, married a Japanese woman and is now the father of a small child with whom he only speaks English so that she will become bilingual. I tell him that I am a longtime resident in Japan to which he replies, 'Oh, but your mind and heart are still American, right?' I answer 'No, not really', and change the topic. A woman sitting next to me explains that she and her Australian husband have been in Japan for several years, and while he is a fluent Japanese speaker she feels that her Japanese has not progressed to a high enough level of proficiency due to her linguistic dependence on her husband. I reply that I consider myself a fairly fluent Japanese speaker yet I still depend on my Japanese husband for many things, especially the reading and writing of complicated documents. I notice several cross-racial (Japanese/Anglo) couples speaking to each other and with other guests in a codeswitching style that *Junji* and I often use when we are in the midst of a mixed racial group. Since it has been a while for me to be immersed in such a large bilingual group I sit back and enjoy the polyphonic moment, open another can of beer, accept a glass of *shochu* (Japanese alcohol distilled from potatoes or barley) from the host, munch on some *senbei* (rice crackers), pose for some photos and invite the host to our house for a vegetable gardening experience. While in this relaxed state, I reflect on how despite the existence of numerous non-Japanese residents who speak various foreign languages in addition to Japanese, Japan is still considered by many to be a strictly monolingual country. Mary Goebel Noguchi and Sandra Fotos' (2001) edited book on bilingualism in Japan in which the authors present compelling evidence that serves to 'explode the myth of Japanese cultural and linguistic homogeneity' (Noguchi & Fotos, 2001: 16) seems ever-more relevant. After saying goodbye to everyone in both English and Japanese, '*Ja ne, mata kondo*' (Okay, next time), 'see ya', 'bye-bye' *Junji* and I leave the party early because we need to prepare for the next day's big neighborhood event held every year in our front yard, *mochitsuki* (steamed rice pounding).

Next Day, December 30

Every year, during the morning hours of December 30, several of our neighbors, Japanese colleagues from my university and American and Japanese friends assemble in our front yard for our annual *mochitsuki* event. Since *Junji's* family is one of the oldest in our neighborhood we have in our possession the *doogu* (implements) handed down from generations of the *Maeda* family that are used only on this special day: *usu* (huge mortar in which the steamed rice is pounded), *kine* (wooden mallets used for pounding) and large *seiro* (steamer); thus we are the designated household for this event. The *mochigome* (glutinous rice) is washed the night before and left to drain overnight. On December 30, neighbors bring their containers of rice and wait their turn to have the rice steamed and then pounded by two people, one to turn over (*tegaeshi*) and knead the blob of steamed rice with a moistened hand while the other person pounds (see Figure 6.9).

Figure 6.9 *Mochitsuki*

Since timing is important lest one's hand gets smashed by the mallet, traditionally a married couple will pound/turn over the steamed rice as a pair while onlookers make snide comments about whether the couple is on good terms or not by noting the (un)coordination of the pounding/kneading. However, our event is gender equal, and men pound/knead as a pair and also take part in shaping the pounded rice into *manjuu* (soft rice cakes eaten on the spot with different toppings) or *kagami mochi* (round, flat, hard New Year decorations), which are the last steps in the process traditionally left to the wives. After everyone helps to clean up the yard, my family and guests join the neighbors for a *boonenkai* (end of the year party) at a local restaurant. As mentioned previously, *Junji* and I do not regularly socialize with neighbors throughout the year; however, the *mochitsuki* event and *boonenkai* are the annual reifications of our established membership in the neighborhood CoP in which the Maeda family is considered as 'old-timers' (Wenger, 1998). Although exhausted from the day's activities, after returning home *Junji* and I grab our *nengajoo* (New Year's cards) (see Figure 6.10) and dash off to the post office so that the cards will be delivered in time for the New Year.

After returning from the post office, I hop into the *ofuro* (Japanese style bath), slip into the *futon* (Japanese bedding), and wonder if someone remembered to feed the dog. Like the *mochitsuki* event, our New Year's cards are also a reification of our *Maeda* family CoP, and the following definition from Wenger will help to explicate the application of the notion of reification to the underlying theme of my JSL story that ends here.

Figure 6.10 New Year's card

[Reification is] the process of giving form to our experience by producing objects that congeal this experience into 'thingness'. In so doing we create points of focus around which the negotiation of meaning becomes organized ... the process of reification so construed is central to every practice. Any community of practice produces abstractions, tools, symbols, stories, terms, and concepts that reify something of that practice in a congealed form ... the products of reification are not simply concrete, material objects. Rather, they are reflections of these practices, tokens of vast expanses of human meanings.... Reification as a constituent of meaning is always incomplete, ongoing, potentially enriching, and potentially misleading. The notion of assigning the status of object to something that really is not an object conveys a sense of mistaken solidity, of projected concreteness. It conveys a sense of useful illusion. The use of the term reification stands both as a tribute to the generative power of the process and as a gentle reminder of its delusory perils. (Wenger, 1998: 57–62)

The above has served as a powerful thinking tool for the interpretive analysis of my JSL experiences as recounted in this book that is in effect a textual reification of my being and becoming a speaker of Japanese. Taking this postmodernist slant on the interpretation of life and language-learning experiences has both theoretical and practical implications for the fields of SLA and applied linguistics – the main topic of the concluding chapter.

Epilogue
Inside out/outside in

While the bulk of my JSL story has focused on my current situation in Japan, I oftentimes become reflexively cognizant of my sociolinguistic existence here paradoxically when I am outside of the country. For example, during a recent summer vacation (fieldnotes, August 2009) in my hometown in Massachusetts I accompanied my friend to a local nail art salon operated by Vietnamese immigrants. While servicing the customers, the staff members were animatedly conversing with each other in Vietnamese interspersed with the necessary work-English phrases directed at the customers, such as 'Please take a seat', 'Put your hands here', 'What color would you like?' As in most countries, foreign workers and immigrants, especially those with only a minimal amount of dominant language fluency, occupy a low rung on the host country's social ladder. At the nail salon, although there is hardly any friendly chit-chat between the staff and customers, I was determined to find out how the person doing my nails had come to be where she is now. After I mentioned that I lived in Japan, Sue (pseudonym) suddenly switched from dysfluent English to fluent Japanese explaining that she had lived in Japan for several years, and after having attended a prestigious high school in *Nagoya* had obtained a nursing certificate. Needless to say, the other staff members, not to mention the customers, were surprised to hear me conversing with Sue in Japanese, one of our two lingua francas (English and Japanese). Some were perhaps also surprised that an Anglo customer would engage in a conversation with an immigrant foreign worker about something other than the color and shape of a nail. During the course of our interaction, my American persona faded away and my Japanese-speaking persona, together with Sue's, conjoined in a 'nexus of practice' (Scollon & Scollon, 2004) that had been originally constructed in Japan and was now being re-deployed for our interactional moment in the nail salon. Despite our disparate backgrounds, Sue and I became connected with a link forged from our shared experiences of being and becoming speakers of Japanese. Whereas I will forever remain the *henna gaijin* (strange foreigner) in Japan, when I step out of the country and meet other Japanese-speaking individuals I invoke my Japanese persona in order to validate my membership in a CoP composed of transplanted individuals who are located both within and beyond Japanese society. Relatedly, David Block comments that 'the development of new language affiliations and expertise later in life is contingent on access to, engagement with, and membership in communities of practice in which the new language mediates communication' (Block, 2006: 36). Thus, although Sue is currently in the process of negotiating entry into her American language community she nevertheless retains a peripheral affiliation with her past Japanese CoP that became animated while communicating with me – another peripheral member of Japanese society.

On a different occasion when I was outside of Japan and came into contact with non-Japanese speakers of Japanese was on the island of Guam (fieldnotes, February 22, 2008). I was there with a group of my Japanese students for their graduation trip, and we happened to be on the beach discussing which activities (banana boat, wind surfing, jet ski) we should do. The marine sports staff working on the beach were local people of various racial/ethnic backgrounds (Filipino, Micronesian, Korean, Chamorro, mixed) who could speak enough Japanese to chat with Japanese customers and explain the rates and conditions of the rentals. When they heard me talking to my students in Japanese they were very surprised (*Nihongo wa sugoi ne*! [Your] Japanese is like wow!) and also curious as to how I had become so fluent. I switched to English and explained that I was married to a Japanese man and lived in Japan. When I asked them where they had learned Japanese the unanimous reply was 'On the job' which reminded me of the experiences of my international student participants in my ethnography of bi/multilingual speakers in Japan who acquired Japanese primarily at their part-time jobs. Sue in the nail salon in Massachusetts, the beach workers in Guam, the international students and I have all managed to acquire a second or additional language, albeit at different levels of proficiency and under various circumstances. However, despite the diversity in our sociocultural backgrounds and present locations, we nevertheless share a commonality that traverses fixed boundaries of national origin, native language, ethnicity, race and skin color. That is to say, through our codeswitching behavior we are linked together in a global community of bi/multilingual speakers whose linguistic repertoire has destabilized outmoded notions of monolingualism wherein a language is categorized as a discreet system and its speakers as inextricably bound to a 'pure' language group and monolithic national identity. As explained in previous chapters concerning the situation of L1 minorities in Japan, sociopolitical differentials restrict opportunities for linguistic and societal interactions, making full participation in mainstream Japanese society an ongoing challenge. At the same time, however, as Blackledge and Creese explain, bi/multilingualism is 'an inventive, creative, sometimes disruptive play of linguistic resources' (Blackledge & Creese, 2010: 56), and that societal boundaries 'are reproduced, contested, challenged, fought over, altered and at times demolished in negotiations which become visible in the fine-grained detail of language interactions' (Blackledge & Creese, 2010: 58). This last point is what my autoethnographic study has attempted to highlight through the story of my own path to bilingualism forged through multiple interactions spanning 35 years of my being and becoming a speaker of Japanese.

Note

1. Many Japanese and non-Japanese women have had unpleasant experiences with *chikan* (gropers on trains, flashers, stalkers), an indication of the pervasiveness of sex-related crimes in Japanese society. I have been groped by *chikan* on the train, in a movie theater, and once caught a man in the act of stealing my underwear (*shitagi doroboo*) from the clothesline outside my home. What is disturbing about crimes committed by *chikan* is that they often go unreported by the victim who feels too embarrassed to report the incident to unsympathetic police whose attitude is that the man has not done anything seriously wrong and that a woman's appearance or walking alone at night are what cause the crimes (Pover, 2001: 27).

Closing Discussion

[1905] Hong Kong. The English-language 'Hong Kong Standard' said in an editorial entitled 'Eccentric Foreigners' that the world is inhabited chiefly by foreigners, who are all eccentric. The paper, which is Chinese-owned and refers to foreigners as anyone not Chinese, criticized the Americans by stating: 'We might point out that the Americans judge others solely on the basis of physical strength. When you meet an American, he does not inquire about your educational attainments or appraise your manners, he simply grips your hand and squeezes it as hard as he can. If you show signs of distress, he will smile contemptuously and thereafter treat you with contumely'. (Our Pages 100, 75 & 50 years ago, *International Herald Tribune* March 16, 2005, p. 2)

After reading and chuckling at the above newspaper story (and looking up the meaning of 'contumely', i.e. contempt) I decided at the time that I would include it somewhere in the book I was planning to write about my JSL life. In the 105-year span since the original piece was written our world has gone through innumerable changes, but ethnocentric stereotypes of people and the diverse languages they use to experience their worlds still exist. One of my aims throughout this book has been to destabilize fixed meanings attached to terms such as 'expatriate', 'foreigner', *'gaijin'*, 'native/nonnative', 'immigrant' that constrict rather than expand our understanding of people 'who engage with the world-in-action, who move in the world in a way that allows the risk of stepping out of one's habitual ways of speaking and attempt to develop different, more relational ways of interacting with the people and phenomena that one encounters in everyday life' (Phipps, 2007: 12).

Writing almost 30 years ago, Clifford Geertz suggested that cultures and the people who inhabit them are anything but self-contained entities:

> The Western conception of the person as a bounded, unique, more or less integrated motivational and cognitive universe, a dynamic center of awareness, emotion, judgment, and action organized into a distinctive whole and set contrastively both against other such wholes and against its social and natural background is, however incorrigible it may seem to us, a rather peculiar idea within the context of the world's cultures. (Geertz, 1983: 59)

Likewise, by calling into question outmoded conceptualizations of language, culture and identity as discrete, homogeneous phenomena current SLA and applied linguistics research has sparked renewed interest in how the interconnectedness of language behavior and identity constructions can be more fully understood in relation to speakers' social contexts. Particularly in critical investigations of bi/multilingual populations, researchers now proceed from a sociopolitically informed view of 'language as a set of resources which circulate in unequal ways in social networks and discursive spaces, and whose meaning and value are socially constructed within the constraints of social organizational processes, under specific historical conditions' (Heller, 2007: 8). Accordingly, our methodologies have followed suit and are steadily moving out of controlled laboratory settings and onto the streets in order to better hear and understand how people actually use language(s) to make sense of the world and their location in it. The 'exotic other' of anthropological lore may now be living next door, within our own home, or even within ourselves, thus changing our idea of what constitutes 'a culture' and consequently the focus of our ethnographic investigations:

> A renewed concept of culture thus refers less to a unified entity ('a culture') than to the mundane practices of everyday life.... Ethnographers look less for homogeneous communities than for the border zones within and between them. Such cultural border zones are always in motion, not frozen for inspection. (Rosaldo, 1989: 217)

My autoethnography has been an inward-looking exploration of my encounters in different 'border zones' and of how the linguistic resources I use on a daily basis are imbedded in, yet not inextricably constrained by, prevalent Japanese societal discourses. In reviewing below the themes of my JSL story I hope to leave readers with new insights on language acquisition and an appreciation of autoethnography's potential to help them imagine their own lives as second and additional language speakers.

Theoretical Starting Point

In the introductory chapters, I presented the central overarching theme of this book, that is, how autoethnography's postmodernist theoretical foundation is well suited to formulating and exploring the complexities of language learning and use. Having said that, however, the point was also made that autoethnography, as one of the many methodologies associated with the qualitative research paradigm, was not being introduced as the best or only way to conduct an investigation of language acquisition. Instead, I emphasized that a positivistic approach alone cannot account for certain aspects of linguistic behavior that are unamenable to controlled experiments and quantification. Specifically, reference was made to how subjective accounts of self/other perceptions of one's language choices, rather than being viewed simply as interesting anecdotal data with no empirical legitimacy, are able to 'broaden the study of language from decontextualized, representational aspects of language to contextualized, performative aspects' (Vaid, 2006: 152). As an example, although my uses of humor with family members and friends in different contexts that I describe in my story are quantifiable (counting the number and types of jokes I produce in Japanese), statistical information alone does not reveal the underlying motives for my jokes, and how, as Vaid explains, bi/multilingual speakers especially those in disadvantaged positions, may 'use humor to play with and through language, to construct shifting identities, to affirm their linguistic and cultural hybridity, and to express resistance to discourses of social domination' (Vaid, 2006: 162). In the same vein, Aneta Pavlenko has proposed that 'introspective data have both relevance and validity and can help us identify sources of bi/multilingual experience that are not directly observable in the study of identify performance' (Pavlenko, 2006: 1).

In short, autoethnography is not to be viewed simply as an 'add-qualitative-data-and-stir' approach used to complement quantitative studies but rather as a stand-alone methodology in its own right capable of bringing to the fore the ways in which speakers resort to a variety of linguistic practices to accomplish certain social goals.

Postmodernism

As outlined in Chapter 1, this book's conceptual framework drew principally on postmodernist interpretations of the inter-relatedness of language, context and identity constructions. The understanding that 'language does not reflect reality but gives it meaning [which is] an effect of language and, as such, always historically and culturally specific' (Weedon, 1999: 102) has important ramifications for how I chose to interpret my JSL experiences. In other words, postmodernism does not adhere to the humanist precept (see Note 3, Chapter 1) that language can unequivocally represent the true essence or meaning of something, but rather that 'the meaning of language shifts depending on social context so that meaning can always be disputed' (St Pierre, 2000: 481). Therefore, as the different episodes in my story illustrate, the meanings of the terms 'expatriate' or 'foreigner' are not fixed and are always contingent on surrounding societal discourses that 'allow certain people to be subjects of statements and others to be objects.... Discourse can never be just linguistic since it organizes a way of thinking into a way of acting in the world' (St Pierre, 2000: 485). This last point was further explicated through reference to James Paul Gee's notion of Discourse, that is, the 'non-language "stuff" [used] to enact specific identities and activities' (Gee, 1999: 7). As an illustration of Gee's

D/discourse concept, in Chapter 5, I described how I manage to 'walk the walk and talk the talk' of an associate professor in a Japanese university. By speaking, writing and behaving at the appropriate level of formality in my workplace interactions I am using language (discourse with a small 'd') to enact my professional identity, to signal my membership in a network of college educators in Japan and to reiterate larger ideologies (Discourse with a big 'D') concerning the value of higher education. What is interesting from a postmodernist perspective is that although I am positioned in a conflicting set of Discourses by virtue of my *gaijin* (foreigner) identity, by deploying my JSL persona on the job different Discourses become 'melded' (Gee, 1999: 21) and, moreover, if

> this sort of thing gets enacted and recognized enough, by enough people, then it will become not multiple strands of multiple Discourses interleaved, but a single Discourse whose hybridity may ultimately be forgotten. The point is not how we 'count' Discourses; the point is the performance, negotiation, and recognition work that goes into creating, sustaining, and transforming them, and the role of language (always with other things) in this process. (Gee, 1999: 21)

In the past, the notion of 'hybridity' has served as a widely used metaphor in academic discussions of multiculturalism and global diaspora. However, in order to avoid 'a hybridist triumphalism as an end in itself' (Spivak, 1999: 403) or 'a history-less fetishization of the metaphor' (Kuortti & Nyman, 2007: 53) this term, along with 'border zones' as used in the Rosaldo quoted earlier, need to be continually reassessed in light of the actualities of people who the terms are intended to describe. Discrimination on the basis of one's ethnic or racial background still exists worldwide, and discussions among intellectuals in privileged positions will not magically alleviate oppressive conditions – an important point addressed in my researcher positionality statement in the Introduction to this book. Hence, Gee's suggestion above that we closely examine the ways we use language to locate ourselves in different Discourses is well taken and entails a methodology capable of highlighting the different strategies that L1 minorities use 'to assert the legitimacy of their racial/ethnic identities within and against dominant language and societal norms' (Simon-Maeda, 2009: 91).

By juxtaposing the situation of language minorities in Japan with my relatively privileged position (Chapter 3) I followed the precept of reflexivity defined in Chapter 1 as being a key component of a postmodernist approach whereby researchers 'use their own experiences in the culture reflexively to bend back on self and look more deeply at self–other interactions' (Ellis & Bochner, 2000: 740). Simply telling the story of my life in Japan without reflecting on the inequitable situations of marginalized individuals with whom I have come into contact (see Simon-Maeda, 2009) would amount to nothing more than a romantic tale of my experiences.

While this might make for interesting reading, it would not contribute much to our understanding of how L2 use is significantly connected to one's location in the host country. As the data segments (Chapter 3) of the Sri Lankan international student in my university reveal, being a fluent Japanese speaker does not automatically guarantee membership in mainstream society. In contrast, my dysfluency has not prevented me from attaining a reputable societal position due to the excessive status and *akogare* (longing) attached to anyone and anything from an English-speaking, western country. Further reflection on this situation, however, resulted in a more complex picture. That is, my gender oftentimes became the determining variable in how I was positioned in Japanese society, not unlike Japanese women who find it difficult to pursue their professional careers due to the constraining remnants of the *ryosai kenbo* (good wife, wise mother) ideology (Chapter 4, Note 11). Aware of the essentializing tendencies of assuming a 'we are all sisters in struggle' (Mohanty, 1988: 65) stance, I nevertheless feel that my experiences and the ways in which my JSL abilities have developed in Japan as a woman are fundamentally different from, although at times overlapping with, those of a man. Moreover, my being a white western woman adds another layer of complexity that other researchers (e.g. Ogulnick, 1998) have commented on and subsequently been criticized for as perpetuating 'fixed images of the Self and Other, confirming that discourses of colonialism are still alive and well' (Kubota, 2005). However, as the narratives in the *TESOL Quarterly* special topic issues on race (Kubota & Lin, 2006) and gender (Davis & Skilton-Sylvester, 2004) effectively illustrate, people self-identify and are identified by others according to different social categories such as race, nationality, gender, ableism, class and so on that are always in a precarious state of flux due to the surrounding societal circumstances. Postmodern feminist theory provides an enlightened way of conceptualizing the discussion here:

> Discourses define what it means to be a woman or man and the available range of gender-appropriate and transgressive behaviour. We learn who we are and how to think and behave through discursive practices. Moreover, subjectivity is embodied, and discursive practices shape our bodies, as well as our minds and emotions, in socially gendered ways. (Weedon, 1999: 104)

Hence, examining identity categories in isolation without acknowledging their inherent interconnectedness results in reductive analyses that do not take into full account what it means to be, for example, a female expatriate in a male-dominated society. Additionally, distinguishing the different types of 'discursive practices' that Weedon mentions above calls for analyses that focus 'less on decontextualized strings of speech or text and more on ways in which certain groups of people and institutions come to regulate and be regulated by multiple discourses (social, political, religious, etc.) that impact our ways of thinking and acting in the world' (Simon-Maeda, 2009: 92). For this purpose, in Chapter 5 I introduced Scollon and Scollon's (2004) 'nexus of practice' concept to explain how my JSL subjectivity has been shaped at the nexus of different communities of practice.

Nexus of practice

Along with the postmodernist interpretation of language and reflexivity, 'how the experience of subjectivity arises out of engagement in the social world' (Wenger, 1998: 15) was presented in the opening chapters of this book as a postmodernist theoretical alternative to positivistic analyses of language learning and use. My JSL speaker subjectivity has been constituted through interactions with a variety of people in diverse spheres of my life in Japanese society; a postmodernist response to humanism's emphasis on the individual as a self-contained entity (note 3 in Chapter 1). Therefore, different subjectivities (wife, mother, foreigner, expatriate, etc.) are better understood as verbs rather than as static, preexisting categories – a notion closely related to Judith Butler's (1993) performativity theory. Chapters 4 through 6 depicted the various performances I enact with family members as a wife and mother, at my workplace as a teacher and colleague and at a friend's party as a bilingual expatriate. The identity work in these different contexts is carried out through an array of spoken and written linguistic strategies (joking, texting, codeswitching, etc.) that facilitate my 'getting by' in different situations.

The arrows in the nexus of practice diagram were intended to illustrate how the different components of my JSL life (societal discourses, socialization practices, local interactions) are continually in a dynamic state that affects the degree of significance and level of my participation in various CoPs (family, social life, career). As an example, in Chapter 4 I described how after the birth of my son my participation and socialization into my local community as a parent was affected by larger ideologies of parenting in Japanese society, particularly those concerning the role that mothers play as the principal managers of their children's educational paths. As a result, my JSL speech behavior needed to be readjusted from that of a professional educator to one that is appropriate among mothers who oftentimes sacrifice their own careers in order to raise their children, a traditionally taken-for-granted norm in Japanese society. Juliet Langman explains the influence of socialization practices on identity construction in this way:

> An individual practices an identity with reference to a wide variety of communities of practice ranging from a school group to a community group, a church group or a family. In such practice, dimensions of identity related to various social categories such as ethnicity, class, and

gender are practiced and negotiated in specific social settings. Yet, and importantly, at various times in an individual's life, a particular community of practice becomes central to that individual's identity practice. (Langman, 2003: 184)

In local interactions with mothers in the neighborhood or teachers at my son's school I made a conscious effort to mould my JSL-speaking persona in a way that would legitimize my membership in my local CoP as a 'good' parent. However, as noted in Chapter 4, as my son is no longer involved with the Japanese educational system and *Junji* and I do not frequently socialize with neighbors, this CoP is not as significant as it once was. Other social CoPs (e.g. afternoon coffee klatches at *Mi-chan*'s, the expatriate community in Nagoya, the foreign wives club) have become more integral socializing components as well as my university career CoP.

To summarize, crafting my autoethnography from a postmodernist conceptual framework has been to engage 'in a constant practice of reflexive attention to the past, present, and future moments of subjectification within complex and contradictory discursive arenas' (Gannon, 2006: 480).

Implications for SLA and Applied Linguistics Research

In Chapter 5, I introduced different theorists' interpretations and applications of semiotics, 'the study of sign-making and sign-using practices' (van Lier, 2004: 57), and I suggested that autoethnography is compatible with alternative research approaches aimed at explicating the role of semiotics in language learning and use. As the primordial sign-making/using practice, spoken language includes the capacity to index (point to, connect to) a particular object (present or nonpresent), phenomenon or concept. Different levels of indexicality were illustrated in the extended data segment in Chapter 3. In line 13 of Excerpt 1, Mahe used his index finger to point in the direction of the nonpresent train timetable, and in line 40 of Excerpt 2 he pointed to the back of his hand while saying 'black, black, black'. Particularly in the second example, Mahe's self-identification as a man of color was manifested through the synchronization of speech and gesticular action that indexed his marginalized status in Japanese society. Indexicality, therefore, is one type of semiotic resource that speakers use to organize and accomplish certain social activities. Additionally, the social function of semiotics can be found in visual and textual material such as photos, signboards, my calling card, alien registration card, newspaper article, New Year's card, homepage biodata and so on that were interspersed throughout the chapters in this book. These visual/textual images index my connection to and participation in different social activities through which my different identities as a wife, foreigner, mother and university instructor have been constructed.

What is important in the above explanation of semiotics is the performative feature of indexicality, explained by Duranti thus:

> To say that words are indexically related to some 'object' or aspect of the world out there means to recognize that words carry with them a power that goes beyond the description and identification of people, objects, properties, and events. It means to work at identifying how language becomes a tool through which our social and cultural world is constantly described evaluated, and reproduced. (Duranti, 1997: 19)

Seen from this perspective, the many examples of codeswitching presented throughout this book are part of the semiotic resource kit that bi/multilingual speakers delve into for indexing their racial/ethnic affiliation. However, van Lier adds that

> sign systems provide the learner with keys to enter into the world, but sometimes the keys are broken, lost or withheld, for a multitude of reasons (including racism and other forms of discrimination, lack of resources, ineffective educational practices, lack of opportunities for participation, excessive psychological distance, and so on). The most important key to becoming a member of a community is the indexing or deictic one, the one that allows for pointing, referring and participating. (van Lier, 2004: 68)

As for SLA and applied linguistics research interests, the crucial word in the above quote is 'participating', because 'to speak a language means to be able to participate in interactions with a world that is always larger than us as individual speakers and even larger than what we can see and touch in any given situation' (Duranti, 1997: 46).

The emphasis on participation in communities of practice is a basic tenet of Wenger's (1998) CoP notion that I delineated in my JSL story as encompassing three broad spheres (social, family, career) that overlap and increase or diminish in importance as my life situation changes. Scollon and Scollon describe these spheres of activity as 'semiotic ecosystems [that] consist of complex interactions among broad sociopolitical forces and deep personal and interpersonal practices' (Scollon & Scollon, 2004: 88) while Charles Goodwin employs the terms 'semiotic field' and 'contextual configuration' (Goodwin, 2000: 1490), the latter of which refers to how different sign systems (speech, gestures) are coordinated (configured) by interactants in specific situations 'to carry out courses of action in concert with each other through talk' (Goodwin, 2000: 1492). Ranging from Goodwin's microanalysis of talk-in-interaction to Wenger's broader sociocultural conceptualization of how language is a social practice through which members in a CoP 'create meaningful statements about the world ... [and] express their forms of membership and their identities as members' (Wenger, 1998: 83) it goes without saying that in current investigations of language use 'the unit of analysis has to be not a component, but a fractal of the larger complex system itself' (Kramsch, 2002: 23). At the same time, Scollon and Scollon (2004) state that 'the broader social issues are ultimately grounded in the micro-actions of social interaction and, conversely, the most mundane of micro-actions are nexus through which the largest cycles of social organization and activity circulate' (Scollon & Scollon, 2004: 8). In line with Scollon and Scollon's important point, throughout my book I inserted spoken and written data segments that represented the working out on a microlevel interactants' meaning-making processes in relation to macrolevel societal ideologies. For example, the exchange with the clerk at the store where I bought the practice materials for the Japanese proficiency test is a microlevel manifestation of the *nihonjinron* ideology (see Note 7, Chapter 3) that excludes foreigners from mainstream Japanese society. An integration of micro- and macro-perspectives resonates with the ecological linguistics (EL) (van Lier, 2004) approach that 'focuses on language as relations between people and the world, and on language learning as ways of relating more effectively to people and the world' (van Lier, 2004: 4). Included in the EL approach are the concepts introduced above (social relations, activity, contexts, participation) with the addition of 'affordances' (van Lier, 2004: 90), two types of which I have presented in Chapter 5 with the example of the Japanese word processor function (tool-mediated) that I rely on when composing documents or email messages and the social (people-mediated) affordances involving spoken and written interactions with colleagues and office workers at my university.

When methodologies matter

In light of the above discussion concerning current SLA/applied linguistics theories that generally 'resist the usual dichotomies, or clear-cut categories of meaning used by traditional approaches' (Kramsch, 2002: 24), how one chooses an appropriate methodology becomes a matter of theoretical concern. That is to say, approaches that eschew dualities of 'individual versus social, representation versus action, not knowing versus knowing, non-native versus native' (Kramsch, 2002: 24) entail the adoption of methodologies that acknowledge the 'fuzzy and unclear social, cultural, historical, political and economic aspects emergent in and around second language learning, rather than sweeping them to the side as "interesting but not relevant"' (Block, 2007b: 90). An emphasis on the theoretical interrelatedness (in lieu of the disconnectedness) of the 'aspects' that David Block lists is a feature not only of qualitative research methodologies but also of alternative approaches that recognize the benefits of interdisciplinary methodological strategies. For example, within my autoethnographic study, I drew on ethnographic, postmodern feminist, discourse analytical, narrative, nexus analysis and CoP theories to explicate the multilayered, interconnected aspects of my JSL life.

My own academic research career that spans a 36-year period beginning in 1974 when Noam Chomsky's transformational generative grammar was in its theoretical heyday up to the present time when one particular theory or methodology does not have a stronghold on the field attests to the growing recognition of the need to use 'a bigger toolkit' (Block, 2007b: 91) to examine language use. This last point holds particular relevance in studies of bi/multilingual, transnational populations where, as illustrated in the current volume, an individual's L2 identity is a complex construction of intra- and interpersonal meaning-making processes.

In sum, ongoing discussions in SLA and applied linguistics circles concerning, for example, the 'multi-competence model' (Cook, 1995: 94) and 'L2 play' (Belz, 2002: 15) along with a surge in bi/multilingual studies (Blackledge & Creese, 2010; Pavlenko, 2006) have collectively served to debunk outdated theories based on a monolingual bias (Firth & Wagner, 1997). My own L2 autoethnography contributes to the discussion by furthering the notion, elaborated on notably by bi/multilingual scholars such as Suresh Canagarajah, that 'language learning and use succeed through performance strategies, situational resources, and social negotiations in fluid communicative contexts' (Canagarajah, 2007: 923). From this perspective, it then follows that traditional assessment criteria (e.g. standardized performance tests) used to judge a speaker's second or additional language proficiency level become problematical.

'Are you fluent?'

At a recent language conference in Japan, after mentioning to a colleague that I was writing a book about how I learned Japanese, her reaction was, 'Are you fluent?' After a slight pause I replied, 'Well, the book is not about whether I'm fluent or not but how I became a speaker of Japanese' (fieldnotes, November 21, 2009). My colleague's query is understandable considering the still prevalent notion among foreign language educators that language learning is fundamentally an individual cognitive endeavor aimed at full attainment of the target language. For myself as well, during the course of writing this book I oftentimes thought, 'Do I really want to let others know about my dysfluency, my illiteracy, my dependence on my husband and son to read/write difficult items in Japanese? This story might be more about how I *didn't* become a speaker of Japanese!' (fieldnotes, January 5, 2010). I do not imagine that my language angst will ever disappear, and I should consider *Suzuki-sensei*'s advice (Chapter 5) to 'not worry' about my Japanese abilities. The literature on lingua franca usage in multilingual communities has helped to alleviate some of my linguistic insecurities. For example, Canagarajah's discussion of lingua franca English (LFE) usage worldwide is also applicable to how best to gauge my JSL abilities:

> In addition to grammatical competence, we have to give equal importance to: language awareness that enables speakers to make instantaneous inferences about the norms and conventions of their multilingual interlocutors; strategic competence to negotiate interpersonal relationships effectively; and pragmatic competence to adopt communicative conventions that are appropriate for the interlocutor, purposes, and situation. (Canagarajah, 2007: 928)

Canagarajah adds that language proficiency 'makes sense only as an intersubjective construction, something achieved by two or more people, based on the strategies they bring to the interaction' (Canagarajah, 2007: 928). Therein lies a more realistic approach to assessing L2 proficiency, conceptualized in Canagarajah's statement as being a process rather than an end product. This concept is also a fundamental principle in Jay Lemke's view of language assessment:

> No test or task that lasts but a few minutes or an hour gauges what we can do with language across the full range of human timescales. Nor can any test or task separate language skills from the social skills and cultural knowledge needed for every task.... Why do we not gauge language development in an L2 ... *longitudinally* over months and years, looking not only at the current 'final state' but at patterns of development: the invariances and changes, the habits won and lost, the emergence of styles and preferences? There is no 'final state' for processes that are always still ongoing in language learning and development. (Lemke, 2002: 84, italics in original)

Seen against the backdrop of my 35-year-long JSL history, my attaining the top level of the Japanese proficiency test is a rather anemic indicator of my Japanese abilities. Proficiency tests are based on artificially constructed 'native-speaker' norms against which a test-taker's interlanguage grammatical domains (e.g. morphology, syntax, lexicon) are located on a fixed scale indicating proximity to or distance from the target language. While this type of measurement produces information on an individual's neurological control of the structural patterns of an L2 at a certain point in time it cannot possibly account for the myriad social factors that determine one's native/nonnativeness. This is an important consideration especially in the case of learners like me who relocate to a foreign country as an adult and continue living there into their senior years.

While every learner's rate of L2 development or decline is unique, maturational factors constitute limits for everyone. However, Han proposes that

> linguistic, cognitive, psychological and social variables may interact to yield differential success/failure across and within learners ... there is a lack of consensus, within the L2 research community, about what 'success' should mean. One question worth asking in this concern is whether success should be researcher-determined or learner-determined. If it is researcher-determined, it will be desirable to achieve, among researchers, some uniformity in determining the degrees and scope of success. If, however, it is learner-determined, then it should be incumbent on researchers to find out what the learner's definition of success is before advancing any claims about success or failure. (Han, 2004: 166–171)

Hence, longitudinal studies that examine a learner's language development over an extended time frame or even a lifespan and that take into serious account the learner's own interpretations of her/his language learning provide a more realistic picture of second language acquisition – the basis of my autoethnographic account.

Writing this book has helped me to reach a better understanding of how language learning does not occur solely as a result of the inner workings of one's cognitive apparatus:

> [I]t is apparent that social and psychological considerations are of primary concern to the learner. Language contact opportunities, perceptions of confidence and satisfaction, and attitudes are all closely connected to one another, as well as to actual fluency. In short, each learner appears to *construct* his or her own experience in the target language as a response to both external and internal factors. Perhaps most interesting of all is the conscious effort, and the amount of self-evaluation and reflection, involved in the process. (Moyer, 2004: 136, italics in original)

Moyer further elaborates on how for learners who reside in the target-language country and who interact everyday, as I do, with native speakers, conscious attention is placed on enhancing their L2 acquisition 'in the interest of attaining certain goals. It therefore makes sense to examine adult SLA considering social and psychological factors *in tandem*, as they operate together, strategically' (Moyer, 2004: 136, italics in original). As the many episodes in my JSL story demonstrate, each of my different communities of practice has involved its own set of goals to which I have expended a certain amount of linguistic effort. A prime example is my workplace CoP where my conscious attention to and subsequent use of different registers of formal/informal, spoken/written Japanese have enabled me to be at least on the right path to reaching my goal of being acknowledged as a competent faculty member in my university.

In closing

Similar to the experiences of individuals who relocate by choice to a new country in adulthood, at the same time that I perceive a loss in parts of my L1 persona my constructed L2 self, despite the constraints, has afforded me with an alternative way of being. Relatedly, Charlotte Burck summarizes her adult research participants' accounts thus: 'New languages were constructed as offering a new and different identity, new ways to express oneself, an ability to take risks and a helpful disruption of assumptions' (Burk, 2005: 99). I have often wondered how my life would have evolved had I not moved to Japan, but while writing this book and reminiscing on my early life experiences it seemed that the foundation had already been laid for how I managed to construct my new JSL persona out of the self I mistakenly thought I had completely left behind in the United States. This reflective observation was sparked by a recent email from a college friend who had been searching for me, and the contents helped me to reaffirm who I was (and who others thought I was) before moving to Japan:

> I tried searching for you on the internet a number of years ago and was certain I'd found you, Andrea Simon, in Japan. There was something about that that seemed to fit. How did you end up in Japan? I'm not surprised however, you were always someone who lived by her own rules, something I admired about you. (email, January 30, 2010)

Needless to say, my 'own rules' needed to be adjusted to meet the realities of my new life in Japan, and the readjustment process has been made possible through ongoing interactions with family members, friends and work colleagues.

My conception of my JSL experiences as being located on a lifelong continuum rather than being a dramatic rupture from my past self coincides with Gupta and Ferguson's comments concerning transnational populations:

> There is a temptation to see displacement as a specific social condition, a form of life that follows from some definitive break with a social life rooted in ancestral places. Yet dislocation is more often a partial and conditional state of affairs, an uncertain predicament that entails neither a clear sense of membership in one's community of origin nor an uncomplicated conviction of having left it behind. (Gupta & Ferguson, 2001: 153)

Likewise, just as individuals are not born with predetermined identities eternally fixed to a singular way of life, language acquisition is a cumulative process that develops over time through a series of social relationships in different communities of practice. This point notwithstanding, there is still a prevalent idea that certain people have a natural language-learning ability; however, '[w]hen ways of being are connoted as 'natural', their construction as such becomes invisible, as does the accomplishment of such constructions ... [located] inside the individual rather than within social processes' (Burck, 2005: 170). As such, an overemphasis on language aptitude needs reassessment by language theorists and practitioners, and a shift to closer examinations of the socially constructed nature of language acquisition is called for.

Although I was someone who 'lived by her own rules' in the United States, after moving to Japan I needed to construct a new set of rules in order to deal with the complexities – something that anyone in any new situation must do to maintain a sense of well-being. While learning and using Japanese has played a major part in my personal (re)construction process, this has been a collective effort distributed among people I have interacted with over the course of 35 years – a sociolinguistic reality that autoethnography has helped me, and hopefully others, to better understand.

Appendix 1
Foreign population

I-13　国籍別在留外国人登録者数
Number of foreign residents registered in Japan

人 *Persons* (%)

国籍 *Nationality*	Year	1980	1990	2000	2006
Asia		734,476 (93.8)	924,560 (86.0)	1,244,629 (73.8)	1,540,764 (73.9)
	S. Korea/N. Korea	664,536 (84.9)	687,940 (64.0)	635,269 (37.7)	598,219 (28.7)
	China	52,896 (6.8)	150,339 (14.0)	335,575 (19.9)	560,741 (26.9)
	ASEAN	13,052 (1.7)	74,909 (7.0)	229,043 (13.6)	311,523 (14.9)
	Brunei Darussalam	–(–)	9 (0.001)	14 (0.001)	35 (0.002)
	Cambodia	164 (0.02)	1171 (0.1)	1761 (0.1)	2353 (0.1)
	Indonesia	1448 (0.2)	3623 (0.3)	19,346 (1.1)	24,858 (1.2)
	Laos	264 (0.03)	959 (0.1)	1677 (0.1)	2478 (0.1)
	Malaysia	744 (0.1)	4683 (0.4)	8386 (0.5)	7902 (0.4)
	Myanmar	186 (0.02)	1221 (0.1)	4851 (0.3)	5914 (0.3)
	Philippines	5547 (0.7)	49,092 (4.6)	144,871 (8.6)	193,488 (9.3)
	Singapore	681 (0.1)	1194 (0.1)	1940 (0.1)	2392 (0.1)
	Thailand	1276 (0.2)	6724 (0.6)	29,289 (1.7)	39,618 (1.9)
	Vietnam	2742 (0.4)	6233 (0.6)	16,908 (1.0)	32,485 (1.6)
Europe		15,897 (2.0)	25,563 (2.4)	47,730 (2.8)	59,995 (2.9)
Africa		795 (0.1)	2140 (0.2)	8214 (0.5)	11,002 (0.5)
North America		24,743 (3.2)	44,643 (4.2)	58,100 (3.4)	67,035 (3.2)
South America		2719 (0.3)	71,495 (6.6)	312,921 (18.6)	388,643 (18.6)
Oceania		1561 (0.2)	5440 (0.5)	12,839 (0.8)	15,763 (0.8)
Unspecified		2719 (0.3)	1476 (0.1)	2011 (0.1)	1,717 (0.1)
Total		782,910 (100.0)	1,075,317 (100.0)	1,686,444 (100.0)	2,084,919 (100.0)

Source: 第20回出入国管理統計年報 昭和56年版（法務省）
　　　　第30回出入国管理統計年報 平成3年版（法務省）
　　　　第40回出入国管理統計年報 平成13年版（法務省）
　　　　第46回出入国管理統計年報 平成19年版（法務省）
　　　Annual Report on Statistics on Legal Migrants Ed. 1981, 1991, 2001 and 2007 (Ministry of Justice, Japan)

Note: 各年末現在
　　　As of end of each year

Appendix 2
Newspaper article

International couple symbolizes conference

By Robert Moorehead
The Chubu Weekly

KONAN CITY — JALT was established to link Japan closer to world and one local couple is living proof its success.

At the upcoming JALT conference (Nov. 2-5), the logo gracing everything from coffee mugs to T-shirts and posters was designed by local graphic designer Junji Maeda, who together with his American wife, Andrea, have formed a unique working relationship in promoting the conference.

Andrea Maeda sees her role coordinating the conference arts committee, as "a liaison" between JALT and her husband.

"He's the artist, I'm the English teacher," said Andrea Maeda, a 20-year JALT member.

In designing the artwork for the conference, Junji Maeda first studied the "Designing Our Future" theme JALT had produced.

"Before we designed anything, we came up with the concept," Junji Maeda explained.

The conference poster depicts people, with their arms wide open, congregating. The poster also features drawings of famous Nagoya tourist spots.

"For one thing, it's in Nagoya. The other thing is a lot of people gather around and think about the future and education," Junji Maeda said.

He described the people as "gathering around in the Nagoya area, looking for the future."

Maeda originally presented five designs, from which JALT chose one. After some debate, JALT decided on a conference logo that would be similar to the conference logo of Teachers of English to Speakers of Other Language (TESOL), its parent organization.

Andrea Maeda explained that, as part of its efforts to expand its membership, JALT also wanted designs that could "appeal not only to foreigners, not only to Japanese, but also to Pacific Rim countries."

Such a design would be "simple, in a way. It can't be culture-specific," she said.

Junji Maeda said his art is meant to inspire people to "think about education in the future."

After graduating from Aichi Educational University in 1970 Junji Maeda worked as a graphic designer, first at an advertising agency, and then at the Chunichi Publishing Company

At Chunichi, Maeda, 48, wore many hats in producing a small newspaper aimed at young Japanese readers. His duties included graphic design, writing and editing articles, drawing illustrations and taking photographs.

He gradually moved on to free-lance work and has been working as a free-lance graphic designer for the past 19 years. Maeda currently has three assistants working under him at his graphic design studio in Nagoya.

Maeda has also produced several local travel guidebooks, including books in Japanese on the Nagoya area, as part of a national series.

While Maeda wrote the articles, his design staff performed the layout. The Maedas are developing an English version of one of the books.

The Maedas with, son Yuji.

Appendix 3
Typical examples of Mayor Kawamura's 'Nagoya dialect'

Nagoya dialect	Standard form	
どえりゃー (*doeryaa*)	ひじょうに (*hijooni*)	very
やっとかめ (*yattokame*)	久しぶり (*hisashiburi*)	Long time no see.
ご無礼します (*goburei shimasu*)	失礼します (*shitsurei shimasu*)	Excuse me.
きんのう (*kinnoo*)	きのう (*kinoo*)	yesterday
ちょこっと (*chocotto*)	ちょっと (*chotto*)	a bit
とろくせゃあ (*torokuseya*)	アホらしい (*ahorashii*)	How stupid.
よーけ (*yooke*)	たくさん (*takusan*)	too much
えりゃー (*eryaa*)	疲れる (*tsukareru*)	tired
どべ (*dobe*)	ビリ (*biri*)	last place
まわし (*mawashi*)	準備 (*jyunbi*)	preparation
まんだ (*manda*)	まだ (*mada*)	not yet
ぬくとい (*nukutoi*)	温かい (*atatakai*)	warm

Downloaded April 3, 2010 http://takashi-kawamura.com

Appendix 4
Examples of Japanese emoticons

Emoticon	Emotion
(ˆ_ˆ) or (ˆ_ˆ)	Laughing
(>_<)>	Troubled
m(_ _)m	Apologizing
(—_—)	Grinning
(￣□￣;)	Surprised
(#^.^#)	Shy
(——;)	Worried
(*^▽^*)	Joyful
(ˆ▽ˆ)	Laughing
(´·ω·`)	Snubbed
(·∀·)	Laughing
(T▽T)	Crying
(*￣m￣)	Dissatisfied
(´∀`)	Laughing
(⌒▽⌒)	Laughing
(ˆvˆ)	Laughing
ヽ(´ー`)┌	Mellow
('-'*)	Laughing
('A`)	Snubbed
(°◇°)	Surprised
(*°∀°)	Infatuation
(·ω·)	Joyful

http://whatjapanthinks.com/2006/08/14/japans-top-thirty-emoticons
downloaded January 16, 2010.

Appendix 5
Manual for high school visits

(Document, Summer, 2009)

- 話し上手、聞き上手になるよう心がけて下さい。一方的に伝える内容を伝えるだけでなく、高校側のお話しも相手の目を見てしっかり聞くようにして下さい。

Be careful to speak well and listen well. Do not just relay information, look straight into the eyes and listen intently to what the guidance counselor says.

- 返答に窮する質問などをされた場合には「申し訳ございませんが、わたしには分かりかねますので、早急に事務局からご連絡させていただきます」とお伝えいただき、すみやかに入学広報部までご連絡下さい。

When you are asked a question that you are unable to answer say 'I am very sorry but I am unable to answer; therefore, let me inquire at the school office' and contact the admissions office as soon as possible.

- ［応接から玄関まで］
「本日はお忙しいところ、お時間をいただきましてありがとうございました。今後ともよろしくお願いいたします」と言い、頭を下げて退出して下さい。

Say, 'Thank you very much for taking time out of your busy schedule, best regards for your continuing cooperation', bow your head, and leave.

References

Allison, A. (2000) *Permitted and Prohibited Desires: Mothers, Comics, and Censorship in Japan*. Berkeley, CA: University of California Press.
Altarriba, J. (2006) Cognitive approaches to the study of emotion-laden and emotion words in monolingual and bilingual memory. In A. Pavlenko (ed.) *Bilingual Minds: Emotional Experience Expression and Representation* (pp. 232–256). Clevedon: Multilingual Matters.
Althusser, L. (1971) Ideology and ideological state apparatuses. In *Notes Toward an Investigation in Lenin and Philosophy and Other Essays* (pp. 111–123). New York: Monthly Review Press.
Annual Report on Statistics on Legal Migrants (1981–2000) Ministry of Justice. Tokyo: Japan.
Anzaldúa, G. (1987) *Borderlands/La Frontera: The New Mestiza*. San Francisco: Lute.
Atkinson, D. (1999) TESOL and culture. *TESOL Quarterly* 33, 625–654.
Atkinson, D. (2002) Toward a sociocognitive approach to second language acquisition. *The Modern Language Journal* 86, 525–545.
Atkinson, D. (2011) *Alternative Approaches to Second Language Acquisition*. London: Routledge
Austin, J.L. (1962) In J.O. Urmson and M. Sbisà (eds) *How to Do Things with Words* (2nd edn) Lecture IX. Cambridge, MA: Harvard University Press.
Bailey, K. (1983) Competitiveness and anxiety in adult second language learning: Looking at and through the diary studies. In H. Seliger and M. Long (eds) *Classroom Oriented Research in Second Language Acquisition* (pp. 67–83). Rowley, MA: Newbury House Publishers.
Baker, C. (1996) *Foundations of Bilingual Education and Bilingualism*. Clevedon: Multilingual Matters.
Bakhtin, M.M. (1981) From the prehistory of Novelistic Discourse. In M. Holquist (ed.) *The Dialogic Imagination: Four Essays* (C. Emerson and M. Holquist, trans.). Austin, TX: University of Texas Press.
Bakhtin, M.M. (1986) The problem of the text. In C. Emerson and M. Holquist (eds) *Speech Genres and Other Late Essays* (V. McGee, trans.) (pp. 104–131). Austin, TX: The University of Texas Press.
Bamberg, M. (2005) Narrative discourse and identities. In J. Christoph Meister, T. Kindt and W. Schernus (eds) *Narratology Beyond Literary Criticism: Mediality, Disciplinarity* (pp. 213–238). Berlin: Walter de Gruyter.
Barthes, R. (1981) *Camera Lucida*. New York: Hill and Wang.
Baxter, J. (2003) *Positioning Gender in Discourse: A Feminist Methodology*. New York: Palgrave Macmillan.
Bayley, R. and Schecter, S.R. (2003) *Language Socialization in Bilingual and Multilingual Societies*. Clevedon: Multilingual Matters.
Belcher, D. and Connor, U. (eds) (2001) *Reflections on Multiliterate Lives*. Clevedon: Multilingual Matters.

Belz, J. (2002) Second language play as a representation of the multicompetent self in foreign language study. *Journal of Language, Identity, and Education* 1, 13–39.
Benwell, B. and Stokoe, E. (2006) *Discourse and Identity*. Edinburgh: Edinburgh University Press Ltd.
Berger, L. (2001) Inside out: Narrative autoethnography as a path toward rapport. *Qualitative Inquiry* 7, 504–518.
Besemeres, M. (2006) Language and emotional experience: The voice of translingual memoir. In A. Pavlenko (ed.) *Bilingual Minds: Emotional Experience, Expression and Representation* (pp. 34–58). Clevedon: Multilingual Matters.
Bhaba, H. (1985) Signs taken for wonders: Questions of ambivalence and authority under a tree outside Delhi, May 1817. *Critical Inquiry* 12, 144–165.
Bhatia, T.K. and Ritchie, W.C. (eds) (2006) *The Handbook of Bilingualism*. Malden, MA: Blackwell Publishing Ltd.
Blackledge, A. and Creese, A. (2010) *Multilingualism*. London: Continuum.
Block, D. (2003) *The Social Turn in Second Language Acquisition*. Washington, DC: Georgetown University Press.
Block, D. (2006) *Multilingual Identities in a Global City*. New York: Palgrave Macmillan.
Block, D. (2007a) *Second Language Identities*. London: Continuum.
Block, D. (2007b) Socializing second language acquisition. In Z. Hua, P. Seedhouse, L. Wei and V. Cook (eds) *Language Learning and Teaching as Social-Interaction* (pp. 89–102). New York: Palgrave Macmillan.
Bochner, A.P. (2001) Narrative's virtues. *Qualitative Inquiry* 7, 131–157.
Bochner, A.P. and Ellis, C. (2000) Autoethnography, personal narrative, reflexivity: Researcher as subject. In N.K. Denzin and Y.S. Lincoln (eds) *Handbook of Qualitative Research* (2nd edn) (pp. 733–768). Thousand Oaks, CA: Sage Publications.
Bourdieu, P. (1977a) *Outline of a Theory of Practice*. Cambridge: Cambridge University Press.
Bourdieu, P. (1977b) The economics of linguistic exchanges. *Social Science Information* 16, 645–668.
Bourdieu, P. (1991) *Language and Symbolic Power*. Cambridge: Polity Press.
Brown, P. and Levinson, S. (1987) *Politeness: Some Universals in Language Usage*. Cambridge: Cambridge University Press.
Bruner, J. (2001) Self-making and world-making. In J. Brockmeier and D. Carbaugh (eds) *Narrative and Identity: Studies in Autobiography, Self and Culture* (pp. 25–38). Amsterdam: John Benjamins Publishing Co.
Bucholtz, M. (1995) From mulatta to mestiza: Passing and the linguistic reshaping of ethnic identity. In K. Hall and M. Bucholtz (eds) *Gender Articulated: Language and the Socially Constructed Self* (pp. 351–374). New York: Routledge.
Burck, C. (2005) *Multilingual Living*. New York: Palgrave Macmillan.
Butler, J. (1993) *Bodies That Matter: On the Discursive Limits of "Sex"*. New York: Routledge.
Cameron, D. and Kulick, D. (2003) *Language and Sexuality*. Cambridge: Cambridge University Press.
Canagarajah, S. (2007) Lingua franca English, multilingual communities, and language acquisition. *The Modern Language Journal* 91, 923–939.
Churchill, E. (2008) A dynamic systems account of learning a word: From ecology to form relations. *Applied Linguistics* 29, 339–358.
Clandinin, D.J. and Connelly, F.M. (2000) *Narrative Inquiry: Experience and Story in Qualitative Research*. San Francisco, CA: Jossey-Bass.
Clark, A. (2001) *Mindware: An Introduction to the Philosophy of Cognitive Science*. Oxford: Oxford University Press.

Clifford, J. (1986) Introduction: Partial truths. In J. Clifford and G.E. Marcus (eds) *Writing Culture: The Poetics and Politics of Ethnography* (pp. 1–26). Berkeley, CA: University of California Press, Ltd.
Close Up, Dave Spector (2003) One-man media airs his view. *The Japan Times Online* February 2, 2003.
Clough, P. (2002) *Narratives and Fictions in Educational Research*. Buckingham: Open University Press.
Coates, J. (2004) *Women, Men and Language: A Sociolinguistic Account of Gender Differences in Language*. London: Pearson Education Limited.
Conrad, J. (1912/1996) *The Collected Letters of Joseph Conrad, Volume 5, 1912–1916*. Cambridge: Cambridge University Press.
Cook, V. (1995) Multi-competence and the learning of many languages. *Language, Culture and Curriculum* 8, 93–96.
Crystal, D. (2008) *Txting: The Gr8 Db8*. Oxford: Oxford University Press.
Davis, K.A. (1995) Qualitative theory and methods in applied linguistics research. *TESOL Quarterly* 29, 427–453.
Davis, K.A. and Skilton-Sylvester, E. (2004) Looking back, taking stock, moving forward: Investigating gender in TESOL. *TESOL Quarterly* 38 (3), 381–404.
Davies, C.A. (2008) *Reflexive Ethnography: A Guide to Researching Selves and Others* (2nd edn). New York: Routledge.
Denzin, N.K. and Lincoln, Y.S. (eds) (1994) *Handbook of Qualitative Research*. Thousand Oaks, CA: Sage Publications.
Denzin, N.K. and Lincoln, Y.S. (eds) (2000) *Handbook of Qualitative Research* (2nd edn). Thousand Oaks, CA: Sage Publications.
Denzin, N.K. and Lincoln, Y.S. (eds) (2005) *The Sage Handbook of Qualitative Research* (3rd edn). Thousand Oaks, CA: Sage Publications.
Derrida, J. (1974/1967) *Of Grammatology* (G.C. Spivak, trans.). Baltimore, MD: John Hopkins University Press (original work published 1967).
Douglass, M. (2000) The singularities of international migration of women to Japan: Past, present and future. In M. Douglass and G.S. Roberts (eds) *Japan and Global Migration: Foreign Workers and the Advent of a Multicultural Society* (pp. 91–122). Honolulu, HI: University of Hawai'i Press.
Duranti, A. (1997) *Linguistic Anthropology*. Cambridge: Cambridge University Press.
Duranti, A. and Goodwin, C. (eds) (1992) *Rethinking Context: Language as an Interactive Phenomenon*. Cambridge: Cambridge University Press.
Ellis, R. (1994) *The Study of Second Language Acquisition*. Oxford: Oxford University Press.
Ellis, C. and Bochner, A.P. (1996) *Composing Ethnography: Alternative Forms of Qualitative Writing*. Walnut Creek, CA: AltaMira Press.
Ellis, C. and Bochner, A.P. (2000) Autoethnography, personal narrative, reflexivity. In N.K. Denzin and Y.S. Lincon (eds) *Handbook of Qualitative Research* (2nd edn). (pp. 733–768). Thousand Oaks, CA: Sage Publications.
Erikson, E.H. (1968) *Identity: Youth and Crisis*. New York: W.W. Norton.
Fairclough, N. (2003) *Analyzing Discourse: Textual Analysis for Social Research*. New York: Routledge.
Fawcett, C. (2001) Archaelogy and Japanese identity. In D. Denoon, M. Hudson, G. McCormack and T. Morris-Suzuki (eds) *Multicultural Japan: Palaeolithic to Postmodern* (pp. 60–80). Cambridge: Cambridge University Press.
Fine, M. (1994) Working the hyphens: Reinventing self and other in qualitative research. In N.K. Denzin and Y.S. Lincoln (eds) *Handbook of Qualitative Research* (pp. 70–82). Thousand Oaks, CA: Sage Publications.

Finkelstein, B., Tobin, J.J. and Imamura, A. (eds) (1991) *Transcending Stereotypes: Discovering Japanese Culture and Education*. Yarmouth, ME: Intercultural Press, Inc.

Finley, S. (2005) Arts-based inquiry: Performing revolutionary pedagogy. In N.K. Denzin and Y.S. Lincoln (eds) *Handbook of Qualitative Research* (3rd edn) (pp. 681–694). Thousand Oaks, CA: Sage Publications.

Firth, A. and Wagner, J. (1997) On discourse, communication, and (some) fundamental concepts in SLA research. *Modern Language Journal* 81, 285–300.

Foucault, M. (1972) *The Archaeology of Knowledge* (A.M. Sheridan, trans.) New York: Pantheon Books.

Foucault, M. (1978) *The History of Sexuality: Vol. 1. An Introduction*. New York: Pantheon Books.

Foucault, M. (1980) Truth and power. In C. Gordon (ed.) *Power/Knowledge: Selected Interviews & Other Writings*. New York: Pantheon Books.

Freeman, M. (2001) From substance to story. In J. Brockmeier and D. Carbaugh (eds) *Narrative and Identity: Studies in Autobiography, Self and Culture* (pp. 283–298). Amsterdam: John Benjamins Publishing Company.

Fujimura-Fanselow, K. and Kameda, C. (1995) *Japanese Women: New Feminist Perspectives on the Past, Present, and Future*. New York: The Feminist Press at The City University of New York.

Fukuoka, Y. (2000) *Lives of Young Koreans in Japan*. Melbourne: Trans Pacific Press.

Gannon, S. (2006) The (im)possibilites of writing the self-writing: French poststructural theory and autoethnography. *Cultural Studies<=>Critical Methodologies* 6, 474–495.

Gee, J.P. (1996) *Social Linguistics and Literacies: Ideology in Discourses* (2nd edn). London: Taylor & Francis.

Gee, J.P. (1999) *An Introduction to Discourse Analysis: Theory and Method*. London: Routledge.

Geertz, C. (1973) Thick description: Toward an interpretive theory of culture. In C. Geertz (ed.) *The Interpretation of Cultures* (pp. 3–30). New York: Basic Books.

Geertz, C. (1983) 'From the native's point of view': On the nature of anthropological understanding. In C. Geertz (ed.) *Local Knowledge: Further Essays in Interpretive Anthropology* (3rd edn) (pp. 55–70). New York: Basic Books.

Gelb, J. (2003) *Gender Policies in Japan and the United States*. New York: Palgrave Macmillan.

Goebel Noguchi, M. (2001) Introduction: The crumbling of a myth. In M. Goebel Noguchi and S. Fotos (eds) *Studies in Japanese Bilingualism* (pp. 1–23). Clevedon: Multilingual Matters.

Goebel Noguchi, M. and Fotos, S. (eds) (2001) *Studies in Japanese Bilingualism*. Clevedon: Multilingual Matters.

Goodwin, C. (2000) Action and embodiment within situated human interaction. *Journal of Pragmatics* 32, 1489–1522.

Gupta, A. and Ferguson, J. (eds) (2001) *Culture, Power, Place: Explorations in Critical Anthropology*. Durham, NC: Duke University Press.

Han, Z.-H. (2004) *Fossilization in Adult Second Language Acquisition*. Clevedon: Multilingual Matters.

Haraway, D. (1988) Situated knowledges: The science question in feminism and the privilege of partial perspective. *Feminist Studies* 14, 575–599.

Harris, C.L., Berko Gleason, J. and Aycicegi, A. (2006) When is a first language more emotional? Psychophysiological evidence from bilingual speakers. In A. Pavlenko (ed.) *Bilingual Minds: Emotional Experience Expression and Representation* (pp. 257–283). Clevedon: Multilingual Matters.

Heller, M. (2007) *Bilingualism: A Social Approach*. New York: Palgrave Macmillan.

Herdina, P. and Jessner, U. (2002) *A Dynamic Model of Multilingualism: Perspectives of Change in Psycholinguistics*. Clevedon: Multilingual Matters.

Hoffman, E. (1989) *Lost in Translation: A Life in a New Language*. New York: Penguin Books.

Holland, D., Lachicotte, W., Skinner, D. and Cain, C. (1998) *Identity and Agency in Cultural Worlds*. Cambridge, MA: Harvard University Press.

Holman Jones, S. (2005) Autoethnography: Making the personal political. In N.K. Denzin and Y.S. Lincoln (eds) *The Sage Handbook of Qualitative Research* (3rd edn) (pp. 763–792). Thousand Oaks, CA: Sage Publications.

Holmes, J. (2000) Women at work: Analyzing women's talk in New Zealand. *Australian Review of Applied Linguistics* 22, 1–17.

Holmes, J. (2007) "Did anyone feel disempowered by that?" Gender, leadership and politeness. *Proceedings of IGALA 4*. Valencia: University of Valencia.

Holt, N.L. (2003) Representation, legitimation, and autoethnography: An autoethnographic writing story. *International Journal of Qualitative Methods*, 2, Article 2. On WWW at http://www.ualberta.ca/~iiqm/backissues/2_1final/html/holt.html. Accessed 7.4.10.

House, J. (2003) English as a lingua franca: A threat to multilingualism? *Journal of Sociolinguistics* 7, 556–578.

International Couple Symbolizes Conference (1995) *The Chubu Weekly*, p. 4.

Japan Almanac (2005) *The Asahi Shimbun Japan Almanac 2005*. Tokyo: The Asahi Shimbun Company.

Johnson, S. (2006) *Everything Bad Is Good For You: How Today's Popular Culture Is Actually Making Us Smarter*. London: Penguin Books Ltd.

Kamada, L. (2010) *Hybrid Identities and Adolescent Girls: Being 'Half' in Japan*. Bristol: Multilingual Matters.

Kanno, Y. (2003) *Negotiating Bilingual and Bicultural Identities: Japanese Returnees Betwixt Two Worlds*. Mahwah, NJ: Lawrence Erlbaum Associates, Inc. Publishers.

Kasper, G. and Kellerman, E. (eds) (1997) *Communication Strategies: Psycholinguistic and Sociolinguistic Perspectives*. New York: Addison Wesley Longman.

Kellman, S. (2000) *The Translingual Imagination*. Lincoln/London: University of Nebraska Press.

Kelsky, K. (2001) Who sleeps with whom, or how (not) to want the West in Japan. *Qualitative Inquiry* 7, 418–435.

Kinginger, C. (2003) Alice doesn't live here anymore: Foreign language learning and identity reconstruction. In A. Pavlenko and A. Blackledge (eds) *Negotiation of Identities in Multilingual Contexts* (pp. 219–242). Clevedon: Multilingual Matters.

Kirshner, D. and Whitson, J. (eds) (1997) *Situated Cognition: Social, Semiotic, and Psychological Perspectives*. Mahwah, NJ: Lawrence Erlbaum Associates, Inc. Publishers.

Kondo, D. (1990) *Crafting Selves: Power, Gender, and Discourses of Identity in a Japanese Workplace*. Chicago: The University of Chicago Press.

Koven, M. (1998) Two languages in the self/the self in two languages: French-Portuguese bilinguals' verbal enactments and experiences of self in narrative discourse. *Ethos* 26, 410–455.

Koven, M. (2001) Comparing bilinguals' quoted performances of self and others in tellings of the same experience in two languages. *Language in Society* 30, 513–558.

Kramsch, C. (1993) *Culture and Context in Language Teaching*. Oxford: Oxford University Press.

Kramsch, C. (2002) *Language Acquisition and Language Socialization: Ecological Perspectives*. London: Continuum.

Kubota, R. (2006) *Review of onna rashiku (Like a woman): The Diary of a Language Learner in Japan*. On WWW at http://edrev.asu.edu/reviews/rev357htm. Accessed April 2006.

Kubota, R. and Lin, A. (2006) Race and TESOL: Introduction to concepts and theories. *TESOL Quarterly* 40 (3), 471–493.

Kuhn, T.S. (1962) *The Structure of Scientific Revolutions*. Chicago: University of Chicago Press.

Kulick, D. (2006) No. In D. Cameron and D. Kulick (eds) *The Language and Sexuality Reader* (pp. 285–293). New York: Routledge.

Kuortti, J. and Nyman, J. (eds) (2007) *Reconstructing Hybridity: Post-colonial Studies in Transition*. Amsterdam: Editions Rodopi BV.

Ladson-Billings, G. (2000) Racialized discourses and ethnic epistemologies. In N.K. Denzin and Y.S. Lincoln (eds) *Handbook of Qualitative Research* (2nd edn) (pp. 257–277). Thousand Oaks, CA: Sage Publications.

Langman, J. (2003) Growing a Bányavirág (rock crystal) on barren soil: Forming a Hungarian identity in eastern Slovakia through joint (inter)action. In R. Bayley & S.R. Schecter (eds) *Language Socialization in Bilingual and Multilingual Societies* (pp. 182–199). Clevedon: Multilingual Matters.

Lantolf, J.P. (ed.) (2000) *Sociocultural Theory and Second Language Learning*. Oxford: Oxford University Press.

Lantolf, J.P. and Pavlenko, A. (2000) Second language learning as participation and the (re)construction of selves. In J.P. Lantolf (ed.) *Sociocultural Theory and Second Language Learning* (pp. 155–177). Oxford: Oxford University Press.

Lantolf, J.P. and Pavlenko, A. (2001) (S)econd (L)anguage (A)ctivity theory: Understanding second language learners as people. In M. Breen (ed.) *Learner Contributions to Language Learning: New Directions in Research* (pp. 141–158). London: Longman.

Lantolf, J.P. and Thorne, S.L. (2006) *Sociocultural Theory and the Genesis of Second Language Development*. Oxford: Oxford University Press.

Lather, P. (1991) *Getting Smart: Feminist Research and Pedagogy With/in the Postmodern*. London: Routledge.

Lather, P. (2006) Paradigm proliferation as a good thing to think with: Teaching research in education as a wild profusion. *International Journal of Qualitative Studies in Education* 19, 35–58.

Lave, J. and Wenger, E. (1991) *Situated Learning: Legitimate Peripheral Participation*. Cambridge: Cambridge University Press.

Lebra, S.T. (2004) *The Japanese Self in Cultural Logic*. Honolulu, HI: University of Hawai'i Press.

Lee, E. and Simon-Maeda, A. (2006) Racialized research identities in ESL/EFL research. *TESOL Quarterly* 40, 573–594.

Lei, X. (2008) Exploring a sociocultural approach to writing strategy research: Mediated actions in writing activities. *Journal of Second Language Writing* 17, 217–236.

Lemke, J. (2002) Language development and identity: Multiple timescales in the social ecology of learning. In C. Kramsch (ed.) *Language Acquisition and Language Socialization: Ecological Perspectives* (pp. 68–87). London: Continuum.

Leontiev, A.N. (1978) *Activity, Consciousness and Personality*. Englewood Cliffs, NJ: Prentice-Hall.

Liddle, J. and Nakajima, S. (2000) *Rising Suns, Rising Daughters: Gender Class and Power in Japan*. London: Zed Books.

Linde, C. (1993) *Life Stories: The Creation of Coherence*. Oxford: Oxford University Press.

Luykx, A. (2003) Weaving languages together: Family language policy and gender socialization in bilingual Aymara households. In R. Bayley and S.R. Schecter (eds) *Language Socialization in Bilingual and Multilingual Societies* (pp. 25–43). Clevedon: Multilingual Matters.

Malinowski, B. (1967) *A Diary in the Strict Sense of the Term*. New York: Harcourt, Brace & World.

Markus, H. and Nurius, P. (1986) Possible selves. *American Psychologist* 41, 954–969.

Maslow, A. (1968/1999) *Toward a Psychology of Being* (3rd edn). New York: John Wiley & Sons.

Maynard, S.K. (1997) *Japanese Communication: Language and Thought in Context*. Honolulu, HI: University of Hawai'i Press.

McCormack, G. (2001) Kokusaika: Impediments in Japan's deep structure. In D. Denoon, M. Hudson, G. McCormack and T. Morris-Suzuki (eds) *Multicultural Japan: Palaeolithic to Postmodern* (pp. 265–286). Cambridge: Cambridge University Press.

McVeigh, B. (2000) *Wearing Ideology: State, Schooling and Self-Presentation in Japan*. Oxford: Berg.

Menard-Warwick, J. (2009) *Gendered Identities and Immigrant Language Learning*. Bristol: Multilingual Matters.

Mills, S. (2004) *Discourse*. New York: Routledge.

Mohanty, C.T. (1988) Under Western eyes: Feminist scholarship and colonial discourses. *Feminist Review* 30, 61–88.

Mori, K. (1997) *Polite Lies: On Being a Woman Caught between Cultures*. New York: Ballentine Books.

Moyer, A. (2004) *Age, Accent and Experience in Second Language Acquisition*. Clevedon: Multilingual Matters.

Murakami, H. (2009) *1Q84, Book 1*. Tokyo: Shinchosha.

Myers-Scotton, C. (1993) *Duelling Languages: Grammatical Structure in Codeswitching*. Oxford: Clarendon Press.

Neumann, M. (1996) Collecting ourselves at the end of the century. In C. Ellis and A.P. Bochner (eds) *Composing Ethnography: Alternative Forms of Qualitative Writing* (pp. 172–200). Walnut Creek, CA: AltaMira Press.

Norton, B. (2000) *Identity and Language Learning: Gender, Ethnicity and Educational Change*. Harlow: Pearson Education Limited.

Norton, B. and Toohey, K. (2001) Changing perspectives on good language learners. *TESOL Quarterly* 35, 307–322.

Ochs, E. (1986) Introduction. In B.B. Schieffelin and E. Ochs (eds) *Language Socialization across Cultures* (pp. 1–13). Cambridge: Cambridge University Press.

Ochs, E. and Schieffelin, B.B. (1995) The impact of language socialization on grammatical development. In P. Fletcher and B. MacWhinney (eds) *The Handbook of Child Language* (pp. 73–94). Oxford: Blackwell.

Ochs, E. and Capps, L. (2001) *Living Narratives: Creating Lives in Everyday Storytelling*. Cambridge, MA: Harvard University Press.

Ogulnick, K. (1998) *Onna Rashiku (Like a Woman): The Diary of a Language Learner in Japan*. Albany, NY: State University of New York.

Ogulnick, K. (2000) *Language Crossings: Negotiating the Self in a Multicultural World*. New York: Teachers College Press.

Oleson, V. (2000) Feminisms and qualitative research at and into the millennium. In N.K. Denzin and Y.S. Lincoln (eds) *Handbook of Qualitative Research* (2nd edn) (pp. 215–256). Thousand Oaks, CA: Sage Publications.

Our Pages 100, 75 & 50 years ago. (2005) *International Herald Tribune* March 16, p. 2.

Pavlenko, A. (2001) "How am I to become a woman in an American vein?": Transformation of gender performance in second language learning. In A. Pavlenko, A. Blackledge, I. Piller and M. Teutsch-Dwyer (eds) *Multilingualism, Second Language Learning, and Gender* (pp. 133–174). Berlin: Mouton de Gruyter.
Pavlenko, A. (ed.) (2006) *Bilingual Minds: Emotional Experience, Expression and Representation*. Clevedon: Multilingual Matters.
Pavlenko, A. (2007) Autobiographical narratives as data in applied linguistics. *Applied Linguistics* 28, 163–188.
Pavlenko, A. and Lantolf, J.P. (2000) Second language learning as participation and the (re)construction of selves. In J. Lantolf (ed.) *Sociocultural Theory and Second Language Learning* (pp. 155–178). Oxford: Oxford University Press.
Pavlenko, A. and Blackledge, A. (2004) *Negotiation of Identities in Multilingual Contexts*. Clevedon: Multilingual Matters.
Pavlenko, A., Blackledge, A., Piller, I. and Teutsch-Dwyer, M. (eds) (2001) *Multilingualism, Second Language Learning, and Gender*. Berlin: Mouton de Gruyter.
Phipps, A. (2007) *Learning the Arts of Linguistic Survival: Languaging, Tourism, Life*. Clevedon: Channel View Publications.
Piller, I. (2002) *Bilingual Couples Talk: The Discursive Construction of Hybridity*. Amsterdam: John Benjamins Publishing Company.
Piller, I. and Takahashi, K. (2006) A passion for English: Desire and the language market. In A. Pavlenko (ed.) *Bilingual Minds: Emotional Experience, Expression and Representation* (pp. 59–83). Clevedon: Multilingual Matters.
Pillow, W. (2003) Confession, catharsis, or cure? Rethinking the uses of reflexivity as methodological power in qualitative research. *International Journal of Qualitative Studies in Education* 2, 157–174.
Polkinghorne, D. (1988) *Narrative Knowing and the Human Sciences*. Albany, NY: State University of New York Press.
Pover, C. (2001) *Being a Broad in Japan*. Tokyo: Alexandra Press.
Pratt, M.L. (1991) Arts of the contact zone. *Profession* (Vol. 91) (pp. 33–40). New York: MLA.
Racist question costs agency/500,000 yen (2003) *Asahi Shimbun* January 16, p. 20.
Red-faced police released a woman (2006) *Mainichi Shimbun* February 28, p. 2.
Rampton, B. (1997) A sociolinguistic perspective on L2 communication strategies. In G. Kasper and E. Kellerman (eds) *Communication Strategies: Psycholinguistic and Sociolinguistic Perspectives* (pp. 279–303). New York: Addison-Wesley Longman.
Reynolds, K.A. (1998) Female speakers of Japanese in transition. In J. Coates (ed.) *Language and Gender: A Reader* (pp. 299–308). Oxford: Blackwell Publishers Ltd.
Richards, B. (1998) Input, interaction and bilingual language development. In A. Yamada-Yamamoto and B. Richards (eds) *Japanese Children Abroad: Cultural, Educational and Language Issues* (pp. 40–44). Clevedon: Multilingual Matters.
Richardson, L. (2000) Writing: A method of inquiry. In N.K. Denzin & Y.S. Lincoln (eds) *Handbook of Qualitative Research* (2nd edn) (pp. 923–948). Thousand Oaks, CA: Sage Publications.
Rogoff, B. and Lave, J. (1999) *Everyday Cognition: Development in Social Context*. Cambridge, MA: Harvard University Press.
Rosaldo, R. (1989) *Culture & Truth: The Remaking of Social Analysis*. Boston, MA: Beacon Press.
Sacks, H., Schegloff, E.A. and Jefferson, G. (1974) A simplest systematics for the organization of turn-taking for conversation. *Language* 50, 696–735.
Said, E. (1978) *Orientalism*. New York: Vintage.
Sakade, F. (1989) *A Guide to Reading & Writing Japanese*. Rutland: Charles E. Tuttle Company.

Schiffrin, D. (1996) Narrative as self-portrait: Sociolinguistic constructions of identity. *Language in Society* 25, 167–203.
Schmidt, R. and Frota, S.N. (1986) Developing basic conversational ability in a second language: A case study of an adult learner of Portuguese. In R. Day (ed.) *Talking to Learn: Conversation in Second Language Acquisition* (pp. 237–253) Cambridge, MA: Newbury House Publishers.
Schrauf, R.W. and Durazo-Arvizu, R. (2006) Bilingual autobiographical memory and emotion: Theory and methods. In A. Pavlenko (ed.) *Bilingual Minds: Emotional Experience, Expression and Representation* (pp. 284–311). Clevedon: Multilingual Matters.
Schumann, F.M. and Schumann, J.H. (1977) Diary of a language learner: An introspective study of second language learning. In H.D. Brown, C.A. Yorio and R.H. Crymes (eds) *On TESOL '77: Teaching and Learning English as a Second Language: Trends in Research and Practice* (pp. 241–249). Washington, DC: TESOL.
Scollon, R. and Scollon, S.W. (2004) *Nexus Analysis: Discourse and the Emerging Internet*. London: Routledge.
Seibert Vaipae, S. (2001) Language minority students in Japanese public schools. In M. Goebel Noguchi and S. Fotos (eds) *Studies in Japanese Bilingualism* (pp. 184–233). Clevedon: Multilingual Matters.
Shimoda, T. (2008) Representations of parenting and gender roles in the *shoshika* era: Comparisons of Japanese and English-language parenting magazines. *Electronic Journal of Contemporary Japanese Studies*. Posted January 14, 2008.
Siegal, M. (1996) The role of learner subjectivity in second language sociolinguistic competency: Western women learning Japanese. *Applied Linguistics* 17, 356–382.
Simon-Maeda, A. (2002) A critical ethnographic investigation of Japanese junior college female learners' attitudes towards gender and education. Unpublished doctoral dissertation, Temple University. UMI number: 3057113.
Simon-Maeda, A. (2004) The complex construction of professional identities: Female EFL educators in Japan speak out. *TESOL Quarterly* 38, 405–436.
Simon-Maeda, A. (2009) Working the hybridization: A case of bi/multilingual speakers in Japan. *International Multilingual Research Journal* 3, 90–109.
Simons, C. (1991) The education mother (*kyoiku mama*). In B. Finklestein, A.E. Imamura and J.J. Tobin (eds) *Transcending Stereotypes: Discovering Japanese Culture and Education* (pp. 58–65). Yarmouth, ME: Intercultural Press, Inc.
Spivak, G.C. (1999) *A Critique of Postcolonial Reason: Toward a History of the Vanishing Present*. Cambridge, MA: Harvard University Press.
St. Pierre, E. (2000) Poststructural feminism in education. *International Journal of Qualitative Studies in Education* 13, 477–515.
Sugimoto, Y. (2003) *An Introduction to Japanese Society* (2nd edn). Cambridge: Cambridge University Press.
Sunderland, J. (2004) *Gendered Discourses*. New York: Palgrave Macmillan.
Swain, M. (2006) Languaging, agency and collaboration in advanced second language proficiency. In H. Byrnes (ed.) *Advanced Language Learning: The Contribution of Halliday and Vygotsky* (pp. 95–108). New York: Continuum.
Takigawa, Y. (2008) Dealing with misunderstanding: An argument between an American husband and a Japanese wife. *Japan Journal of Multilingualism and Multiculturalism* 14, 26–47.
Tama-chan: Japanese resident!? (2003) On WWW at http://www.fuckedgaijin.com/forums/showthread.php?t=2452&page=2. Accessed 23.2.03.
Teutsch-Dwyer, M. (2001) (Re)constructing masculinity in a new linguistic reality. In A. Pavlenko, A. Blackledge, I. Piller and M. Teutsch-Dwyer (eds) *Multilingualism, Second Language Learning, and Gender* (pp. 175–198). Berlin: Mouton de Gruyter.

Thelen, E. and Smith, L.B. (1994) *A Dynamic Systems Approach to the Development of Cognition and Action*. Cambridge, MA: MIT Press.

Thorne, S.L. (2000) Second language acquisition theory and the truth(s) about relativity. In J. Lantolf (ed.) *Sociocultural Theory and Second Language Learning* (pp. 219–244). Oxford: Oxford University Press.

Tsuda, T. (2003) *Strangers in the Ethnic Homeland: Japanese Brazilian Return Migration in Transnational Perspective*. New York: Columbia University Press.

Vaid, J. (2006) Joking across languages: Perspectives on humor, emotion, and bilingualism. In A. Pavlenko (ed.) *Bilingual Minds: Emotional Experience, Expression and Representation* (pp. 152–182). Clevedon: Multilingual Matters.

van Dijk, T.A. (2008) *Discourse and Context: A Sociocognitive Approach*. Cambridge: Cambridge University Press.

van Lier, L. (2004) *The Ecology and Semiotics of Language Learning*. Norwell, MA: Kluwer Academic Publishers.

Weedon, C. (1997) *Feminist Practice and Poststructural Theory* (2nd edn). Oxford: Blackwell Publishers Ltd.

Weedon, C. (1999) *Feminism, Theory and the Politics of Difference*. Oxford: Blackwell Publishers Ltd.

Wenger, E. (1998) *Communities of Practice*. Cambridge: Cambridge University Press.

Wertsch, J.V. (1998) *Mind as Action*. Oxford: Oxford University Press.

Wierzbicka, A. (2004) Preface: Bilingual lives, bilingual experience. *Journal of Multilingual and Multicultural Development* 25, 94–104.

Yamanaka, K. (2000) 'I will go home, but when?' Labor migration and circular diaspora formation by Japanese Brazilians in Japan. In M. Douglass and S.G. Roberts (eds) *Japan and Global Migration: Foreign Workers and the Advent of a Multicultural Society* (pp. 123–152). London: Routledge.

Index

affordances, 40, 91, 142
– socially mediated, 92
AFWJ
– Association of Foreign Wives of Japanese, 76
Allison, A., 80, 81, 153
Altarriba, J., 21, 153
Althusser, L., 80, 153
amaeru
– presuming on the benevolence of others, 114
Anzaldúa, G., 5, 23, 153
Atkinson, D., 7, 51, 91, 153
Austin, J.L., 75, 153
autoethnography
– benefits of, 135, 136
– difference with classic ethnography, 4
– methodology, 16
– researcher, 4

Bailey, K., 6, 153
Baker, C., 52, 153
Bakhtin, M.M., 9, 47, 77, 111, 153
Bamberg, M., 16, 17, 153
Barthes, R., 3, 5, 153
Baxter, J., 19, 153
Bayley, R. and Schecter, S.R., 6, 52, 153
Belcher, D. and Connor, U., 6, 22, 153
Belz, J., 143, 154
Benwell, B. and Stokoe, E., 13, 154
Berger, L., 27, 154
Besemeres, M., 54, 154
Bhaba, H., 23, 154
Bhatia, T.K. and Ritchie, W.C., 6, 154
bilingualism, 84
– definitions of, 52
Blackledge, A. and Creese, A., 133, 143, 154
Block, D., 7, 11, 21, 22, 26, 32, 38, 51, 113, 132, 142, 143, 154
Bochner, A.P., 4, 38, 154
Bochner, A.P. and Ellis, C., 10, 154
border crossings, 5
border zones, 135
Bourdieu, P., 39, 48, 65, 100, 154
Brown, P. and Levinson, S., 66, 154
Bruner, J., 15, 154
Bucholtz, M., 32, 154
Burck, C., 21, 24, 31, 43, 75, 81, 146, 147, 154
Butler, J., 14, 23, 32, 113, 139, 154

Cameron, D. and Kulick, D., 19, 62, 154

Canagarajah, S., 143, 144, 154
Churchill, E., 120, 154
Clandinin, D.J. and Connelly, F.M., 7, 154
Clark, A., 106, 154
Clifford, J., 15, 134, 155
Clough, P., 7, 155
Coates, J., 68, 155
community of practice, 13, 141
Conrad, J., 51, 155
contact zone, 74
Cook, V., 143, 155
critiques
– of reflexive research practices, 15
Crystal, D., 106, 108, 155
culture, 5, 51, 134, 135
– anthropological model, 5
– Japanese, 103

Davies, C.A., 26, 38, 155
Davis, K.A., 8, 155
Davis, K.A. and Skilton-Sylvester, E., 138, 155
deconstruction, 113
Denzin, N.K. and Lincoln, Y.S., 4, 7, 8, 19, 113, 155
Derrida, J., 104, 113, 155
diary studies
– in SLA and Applied linguistics, 6
discourse
– and discourses, 10, 25, 136, 137
– competing, 17, 19
– humanist, 19
– societal, 87, 113
– workplace, 92–96
doubleness, 24, 31
Douglass, M., 86, 121, 155
Duranti, A., 141, 155
Duranti, A. and Goodwin, C., 21, 155

ecological linguistics, 142
ecological validity, 18
Ellis, C. and Bochner, A.P., 7, 38, 137, 155
Ellis, R., 62, 155
emic
– and etic approaches, 11
– and thick description, 38
Erikson, E.H., 19, 24, 155
ethnography
– researcher as self and other, 26

Fairclough, N., 113, 155
Fawcett, C., 53, 155
Fine, M., 11, 15, 16, 155
Finkelstein, B., Tobin, J.J. and Imamura, A., 114, 156
Finley, S., 4, 156
Firth, A. and Wagner, J., 143, 156
foreign wives
– in Japan, 70–73
Foucault, M., 12, 17, 19, 156
Freeman, M., 18, 156
Fujimura-Fanselow, K. and Kameda, C., 13, 67, 156
Fukuoka, Y., 58, 156

gaijin no onna
– foreign woman, 70
gaijin no yomesan
– foreign bride, 60
gaijin roodoosha
– foreign worker, 33
gaikokujin
– a person outside of the country, 7
gaikokujin toorokusho
– alien registration card, 56
Gannon, S., 4, 27, 140, 156
Gee, J.P., 11, 25, 38, 91, 92, 113, 136, 137, 156
Geertz, C., 11, 156
Gelb, J., 13, 156
Goebel Noguchi, M., 84
Goebel Noguchi, M. and Fotos, S., 128, 156
Goodwin, C., 141, 156
Gupta, A. and Ferguson, J., 5, 146, 156

Han, Z.-H., 50, 112, 145, 156
hanayome shugyoo
– bridal training, 63
Haraway, D., 15, 156
Harris, C.L., Berko, J. and Aycicegi, A., 21, 156
Heller, M., 7, 135, 156
henna gaijin
– strange foreigner, 32, 119
Herdina, P. and Jessner, U., 23, 157
Hoffman, E., 51, 54, 157
Holland, D., Lachicotte, W., Skinner, D. and Cain, C., 5, 6, 157
Holman Jones, S., 8, 157
Holmes, J., 68, 113, 157
Holt, N.L., 4, 157
House, J., 9, 157
humanism
– differences with postmodernism, 19
hybridity, 137

identity
– and identities, 11, 75
– postmodern views of, 19
– professional, 89–104
indexicality, 140, 141

interracial
– dating, 55–62
– marriage, 63–67
intersubjectivity, 15
– and language proficiency, 144
intertextuality, 96, 113
introspective
– analyses of language learning, 7, 136

Japanese
– emoticons, 107, 151
– feminine speech, 67–69
– honorifics, 110
– naming practices, 33
Johnson, S., 119, 157
jyuuminhyo
– resident registration, 56

Kamada, L., 81, 93, 119, 157
Kanno, Y., 6, 22, 157
Kasper, G. and Kellerman, E., 122, 157
keigo
– polite Japanese, 89
Kellman, S., 51, 157
Kelsky, K., 61, 85, 86, 157
Kinginger, C., 51, 157
Kirshner, D. and Whitson, J., 21, 85, 157
kokusai kekkon
– international marriage, 55
kokusaika
– internationalization ideology, 98, 113
Kondo, D., 31, 157
koseki toohon
– family register, 56
Koven, M., 23, 51, 157
Kramsch, C., 23, 142, 157
Kubota, R., 8, 138, 158
Kubota, R. and Lin, A., 138, 158
Kuhn, T.S., 17, 158
Kulick, D., 14, 23, 158
Kuortti, J. and Nyman, J., 137, 158
kyooiku mama, 86
– education mother, 64

L2
– and love, 60
– assessment, 144
– codeswitching, 53, 75
– couplehood, 75
– family life, 64–77
– fossilization, 112
– literacy, 91, 104–6
– parenting, 77–85
– pragmatics, 66
– proficiency, 143–46
– scaffolding, 122
– sexual terms, 62
– texting, 106–11
– writing, 90

Index

Ladson-Billings, G., 8, 158
Langman, J., 139, 158
language
– as a social practice, 13
Lantolf, J.P., 21, 23, 40, 158
Lantolf, J.P. and Pavlenko, A., 18, 21, 51, 158
Lantolf, J.P. and Thorne, S.L., 8, 18, 21, 158
Lather, P., 10, 13, 16, 17, 20, 158
Lave, J. and Wenger, E., 21, 158
Lebra, S.T., 103, 104, 158
Lee, E. and Simon-Maeda, A., 11, 16, 158
legitimate membership, 69
Lei, X., 91, 158
Lemke, J., 25, 144, 158
Leontiev, A.N., 21, 91, 158
Liddle, J. and Nakajima, S., 67, 87, 158
Linde, C., 14, 158
Luykx, A., 53, 159

Malinowski, B., 4, 159
Markus, H. and Nurius, P., 24, 159
Maslow, A., 24, 159
Maynard, S.K., 66, 67, 68, 110, 159
McCormack, G., 113, 159
McVeigh, B., 87, 159
Menard-Warwick, J., 7, 22, 33, 49, 93, 159
Mills, S., 12, 159
Mohanty, C.T., 159
Mori, K., 51, 74, 159
Moyer, A., 50, 111, 145, 159
Murakami, H., 39, 40, 90, 159
Myers-Scotton, C., 23, 159

Nagoyaben, 86
– Nagoya dialect, 64, 150
narrative
– inquiry in SLA and Applied Linguistics, 21–22
– truth, 18
Neumann, M., 4, 159
nexus of practice, 89, 139–40
nihonjinron, 103
– popular stereotyping of Japanese society, 53
nikkeijin, 52, 55, 85
– second-generation Japanese, 54
Norton, B., 13, 22, 32, 159
Norton, B. and Toohey, K., 159

objectivism
– methodology, 3
Ochs, E., 52, 159
Ochs, E. and Capps, L., 8, 159
Ochs, E. and Schieffelin, B.B., 52, 159
Ogulnick, K., 6, 7, 51, 159
Oleson, V., 16, 159
Orientalism, 85
othering, 114
– in qualitative research, 11

paradigm shifts, 20
paradigm wars, 17
partial truths
– in postmodernist theory, 15
Pavlenko, A., 5, 6, 7, 23, 27, 32, 50, 54, 75, 136, 143, 160
Pavlenko, A. and Blackledge, A., 6, 160
Pavlenko, A. and Lantolf, J.P., 160
Pavlenko, A., Blackledge, A. and Creese, A., 22, 26
Pavlenko, A., Blackledge, A., Piller, I. and Teutsch-Dwyer., 160
performativity theory, 14, 23, 113, 139
persona, *see* identity
Phipps, A., 39, 134, 160
photographs
– as ethnographic data, 3, 4
Piller, I., 62, 75, 76, 77, 119, 120, 160
Piller, I. and Takahashi, K., 62, 160
Pillow, W., 14, 15, 160
Polkinghorne, D., 18, 160
positioning
– discursive, 93
positivism
– methodology, 4
postmodernism
– and language, 136–38
– and reflexivity, 14–16, 137
– basis of autoethnography, 12–16
– differences with humanism, 14
– interpretation of photographs, 5
– views of SLA and identity, 23–25
poststructuralism
– and postmodern methodologies, 4, 10
Pover, C., 61, 86, 133, 160
Pratt, M.L., 74, 87, 160

racism in Japan, 38, 44, 52, 85
Rampton, B., 122, 160
reflexivity
– and narratives, 14
– in postmodern feminist theories, 15
regime of truth, 17
reification, 130, 131
researcher
– and essentializing research practices, 11
– positionality, 8
– qualitative, 4
Reynolds, K.A., 68, 69, 160
Richards, B., 7, 77, 78, 160
Richardson, L., 160
Rogoff, B. and Lave, J., 21, 160
Rosaldo, R., 135, 137, 160
ryosai kenbo, 87
– good wife, wise mother, 66

Sacks, H., Schegloff, E.A. and Jefferson, G., 34, 160
Said, E., 85, 160

Sakade, F., 90, 160
Schiffrin, D., 6, 161
Schmidt, R. and Frota, S.N., 6, 161
Schrauf, R.W. and Durazo-Arvizu, R., 54, 161
Schumann, F.M. and Schumann, J.H., 6, 161
Scollon, R. and Scollon, S.W., 98, 132, 141, 142, 161
Seibert Vaipae, S., 81, 161
seken, 87
– gaze of society, 85
semiotic
– ecosystems, 141
– field, 141
Shimoda, T., 79, 161
Siegal, M., 6, 51, 161
Simon-Maeda, A., 7, 34, 39, 52, 65, 137, 139, 161
Simons, C., 86, 161
situatedness, 85
social-interactionist
– views of SLA, 21
socialization
– and language learning, 6
sociopolitical
– implications for language learning, 7, 135
Spivak, G.C., 137, 161
St. Pierre, E., 12, 18, 136, 161
subjectivity, *see* identity
Sugimoto, Y., 52, 58, 85, 113, 114, 161
Sunderland, J., 81, 161

Swain, M., 84, 161

Takigawa, Y., 76, 161
temporality
– in narratives, 8
Teutsch-Dwyer, M., 73, 74, 161
Thelen, E. and Smith, L.B., 21, 162
Thorne, S.L., 6, 162
transferability
– in qualitative research, 8
trustworthiness
– in qualitative research, 8
truth
– in narratives, 18
Tsuda, T., 52, 162

Vaid, J., 74, 123, 136, 162
van Dijk, T.A., 26, 51, 162
van Lier, L., 32, 40, 53, 89, 91, 140, 141, 142, 162

Weedon, C., 12, 14, 23, 25, 136, 138, 162
Wenger, E., 13, 69, 85, 99, 130, 131, 139, 142, 162
Wertsch, J.V., 21, 162
Wierzbicka, A., 43, 162

Yamanaka, K., 85, 162

zainichi kankokujin
– second-generation Koreans, 58